MY FAVOURITE
ENGLISH POEMS

MY FAVOURITE ENGLISH POEMS

◇

gathered

with an Introduction by

JOHN MASEFIELD

Granger Index Reprint Series

BOOKS FOR LIBRARIES PRESS

FREEPORT, NEW YORK

Originally published 1950
Reprinted 1969

Introduction by John Masefield included by
arrangement with The Society of Authors on
behalf of the literary estate of John Masefield

.

STANDARD BOOK NUMBER:
8369-6028-9

LIBRARY OF CONGRESS CATALOG CARD NUMBER:
75-76947

MANUFACTURED
BY
HALLMARK LITHOGRAPHERS, INC.
IN THE U.S.A.

Contents

v

CONTENTS

CONTENTS

Introduction

FOR a good many years, when upon the long journeys and voyages once so pleasant, I wished for a book containing all my favourite poems, and in the leisure of travel planned it. On my return, or arrival, there were other things to do, and the book was never begun.

Latterly, having again read through the work that has so long seemed exquisite or masterly, and having again, most deeply, felt gratitude to the writers, I have made the book, as a part of my thanks on leaving, as a mark of my admiration and delight, and in the knowledge (that all writers share) that nothing so spreads the love of poetry as quotations made in thankfulness, by admirers.

This book, then, contains, within limits, my favourite English poems and lines. The limits mentioned are severe; for the book, though by a poetry-lover, has had to be kept within modest bounds.

From the beginning, I decided that the book should contain only the work of poets, accepted generally as Englishmen, and mainly resident here.

I have omitted, therefore, many dearly-loved poems written in the English tongue by the Irish, the Scotch, the Welsh, and by men of the English-speaking nations beyond the sea. To the best of my knowledge the poets here are all English.

Next, I have made a time-limit. I have tried to exclude any poem, or version of a poem, first written after 1849, so that nothing in the book shall be younger than a hundred years.

To this, I have added a second time-limit. To the best of my knowledge, I have put in nothing that I have not loved or admired for fifty years.

All that is in the book has been, for some reason, or want of reason, very dear. I have included all that lives in my memory, that I know, or have known, by heart, and is still kindling there, with the old delight or the ghost of it.

Another limitation has kept the book fairly closely to original work. It omits almost all work declared or seen to be set translation from a foreign tongue. It includes nothing from the famous English translations from Homer, Lucan, Virgil and other foreign poets; some of these omissions I much regret.

Some of our best poets have taken foreign work and recreated it, making it their own, re-coining it, stamping it with the marks of their souls, so that few, or none, can say, "this is not original". Chaucer, Shakespeare and Milton made new things of old or contemporaneous things. The world calls their greater contributions original. Still, even here, in one or two cases, to my very great regret, some things have had to be omitted.

Most of our poets have adapted occasional foreign phrases here and there in the body of their work: this cannot be counted as set translation. I do not know how it can be counted: "convey, the wise it call". Such adapted or translated occasional phrases may be found here.

If the result, the book, be only curious to some and dreary to others, the remedy is at hand. There is plenty of other corn in the old fields for those to gather who have different tastes in grain. This book contains excerpts from less than fifty of the two hundred English poets, known and named, whose work still deservedly pleases.

The hope that nothing should be in the book that has not delighted me for fifty years has kept out much work that once gave pleasure; for the rest, the admiration has generally grown.

The limitation mentioned, that every line or passage

quoted should have delighted me for fifty years, makes it necessary to say something of that distant time, when I first enjoyed all the light that I now seek to focus.

What delighted youth then, now delights a much diminished company. The delight that is this book was a part of the youth and of the taste of the very great Victorian time, when England led the world.

That time, poetically speaking, was in the great Romantic Movement, that became poetry first here through Thomas Gray and his friends, about the time of the birth of William Blake.

That Romantic Movement seems to have begun with the discovery, by highly cultivated minds, that the past, however savage or superstitious, may have been inspired, may have touched truth, in ways long since improved upon, but still a kind of truth, and a real touch. This concession to the past soon became an interest in the past, of an uncritical kind that hardly distinguished Norman work from Tudor. As the interest grew, conscientious critical study by fine brains soon led to exacter knowledge. Men came to know the Middle Ages, and in the excitement of discovery felt that they were all-important. That mood possessed our immediate Masters, but just before my time scholars had perceived that not all in the Middle Ages was inspired; and that modern man is the son of the Revival of Learning, and follows Cervantes, not Don Quixote.

This discovery had begun to influence young men while I was still a boy. The sensitive among them sometimes found themselves startled and charmed by the grace and delicacy of some little London church (shall we say?) by Sir Christopher Wren. They were surprised at such emotion, and felt that it must be the first onset of old age. It was the first sign of a broadening of the mood of a generation that was still much under Masters who had loved the fourteenth century. Rossetti and William Morris were the Masters of the generation; and to both, in some ways, Chaucer had seemed a supreme poet. Ford Madox Brown, a teacher of our teachers, had painted D. G. Rossetti as Chaucer's self, reading to his King. William Morris had made for the world the greatest book of his time, the *Kelmscott Chaucer*. In the hearts of all their followers the fourteenth century seemed the supreme time. It made one third of our delight.

But in the closing twenty years of the nineteenth century, when England led the world, under a great Queen, the sense of our past was very strong, and pride in it intense. Minds, in turning from the Middle Ages, had perceived an ancient England that had led the world under a great Queen; our pride in that past was intense and our knowledge of it growing. This pride and knowledge made up a second third of our delight.

At that time, in that world, this land led, in intelligence, in wealth, in power, and the pride that these things bring.

Whatever faults that time had, and, like all other times of man, it had many, and very frightful ones, it had virtues such as few times have seen, and advantages such as no other time has known. Of its virtues, I will say only that it had a perfect freedom, an honesty not seen elsewhere, an industry skilled and unflagging, and a crimelessness the wonder of the world. Of its advantages, I need only say that it had Peace, a peace that passes understanding now, and an abundance that had only to be worked for.

The abundance of that time is denied by the causers and upholders of the present scarcity, but it was astounding, and in no thing more remarkable than in the supply and the cheapness of books of every kind. It was then easily possible for the very poorest men and women to buy and possess quite large libraries of the very best books of the world.

During the later nineties of the last century, most of the very best of the English poets could be had for one penny a volume. Much of the very best English prose could be had for fourpence half-penny the volume, each volume a critical edition, in a cloth binding. Men said at the time that in less than fifty years the ink of these cheap books would eat through the paper. It is not so: the little fourpenny-halfpenny books have lasted well. For the same price in paper covers you could buy an immense range of fiction. For ninepence, one shilling and at various prices up to eighteenpence, one could buy a great variety of the picked volumes of the world.

At that time, of course, reading was the main evening amusement for many people for many months of each year. The cinema was only beginning in the world, the motor-car was still only a mockery. The safety bicycle had only just begun to help in the emancipation of women. Bridge was a new game. There was no such thing as broadcasting. The omnibus service across the land in every direction did not exist. Probably all these things have proved to be rivals to reading. Wars and revolutionary governments, often manned by illiterates, by men of mean intelligence, or with debased views of life, have done much throughout Europe to check, to poison, or to destroy study. Even here, reading is less easy than it was, less practised, less respected. It is by very much less abundant and more costly.

Fifty odd years ago, one of the dreams of youth was of a reformed theatre no matter how small where the young men fond of poetry might experiment with poetical plays for those who cared for poetry. We reckoned that there were four thousand poetry-lovers in England (real lovers); that three thousand of these lived in London; and that if each of these would come to the theatre twice a month, and this seemed (to the young) not to be asking too much, then the theatre might come to be. Others might come to love poetry, even that seemed possible to youth: and another few might care enough for the theatre to come to see theatrical experiments.

But all this was but a dream about the theatre: and the theatre, then, was by no means the main interest of most young men fond of literature. The theatre, then, was a quiet land-locked bay, in which men and women of very great skill, and deservedly loved by their followers, kept going a gracious regatta unlike anything ever known ashore. On the beach of the bay a few enthusiasts were playing ducks and drakes and causing some ripples with some hard Norwegian pebbles, which they judged to be the only pebbles. A few others, who had some French, Belgian and Italian pebbles, were forbidden to use them.

Outside the bay was the main Victorian sea: and a grand and stirring place it was.

I must try to say something of the very late and very great Victorian time.

Towards the end of the nineteenth century, all literature was seething round us in a fervour of energy undreamed of to-day. There were more pages of skilled comment on new books and thought published each week then than can be seen in a month (or is it a quarter?) now. Our daily papers (there were nine morning and evening papers of the first rank) were then the best, the best-informed, the best-written, the most dignified and the most honest in the world. Each gave an entire page, or two pages, or more, on one day, or on two days, in each week, to comment upon new books. There were more than half a dozen lively weekly papers, mostly concerned with books and, in a less degree, with the (then harmless) game of politics. There were, besides all these, the fortnightly, monthly and quarterly reviews for the weightier, lengthier and more exhaustive critical studies. In addition to these, there were the papers, reviews and journals of the arts and sciences, the learned societies and fellowships, the professions and the crafts. Besides these there were the many and ever-changing publications of the little companies of friends, who gathered together, issued a prospectus, issued a number or two of some little magazine, and then dispersed: but sometimes lived to see the little magazine sought for by book-collectors.

All this enormous wealth and energy of thought and judgment, with its associate arts of illustration, fine printing and precious binding, attended the wealth and energy of the literary creation of the time, that was varied as the life and as full of movement. We had in full fervour the Imperialist movement, the art for art's sake opposition, the Celtic Renascence, studies from over the seas, a French school, a Kail-yard school, a native product of romance and of sport, and a gifted decadence. With all this, there was an enormous, learned, critical delving into the past, that was made luminous and inspiring to us as never before. But to the young writers of verse of sixty years ago some portions of the past lay dead, and brought no message.

Many widenings of the ways of knowledge helped to increase our delight in Elizabethan literature. Historians and historical novelists had written of the reign of Queen Elizabeth as a time of noble religious feeling, and no less noble adventure in the causes of humanity and civility. Charles Lamb, some sixty years before, had shewn what poets were then writing for the theatre. During the later years of Queen Victoria most of those poets were edited and printed; and then reprinted in editions within the means of even the poorest of poor scholars. All readers had thus come to know something of the mental life of the

Elizabethan time, of the range, energy and splendour of its theatre, of the variety and beauty of its song, and of the sense these things gave of the welfare of our land then, before the poisoning of faction, and the yapping of the demagogue.

To the young readers, who were also young writers, these plays and songs shewed a London more worthily a Queen than the London they knew.

Those who were young then were the first to whom all this power of delight had been made accessible since the Closing of the Theatres in the time of the Rebellion: it was granted to them to know it in greater fulness than had been possible to any man since the death of Shakespeare.

The effect of so much Elizabethan reading upon the young Victorian was profound. It shewed him at once that Victorian London, with all its vast virtue and achievement, was blind to one of the triumphs of man. A little London had made this wonder; the great London ignored it: something was wrong. Something is always wrong in any world or nation governed by men: man is always wrong somewhere. The young of any time perceive where. Those who were young then perceived that the theatre of the time was not fulfilling all the functions expected in the capital of the world, nor those due to the capital of the nation.

Fifty or sixty years ago, the Elizabethan playwrights, other than Shakespeare, were seldom performed in London. Several important plays by Shakespeare were seldom performed. When could we count on seeing *All's Well that Ends Well*, *Coriolanus*, *Measure for Measure*, *Richard the Second*, *Timon of Athens*, *Troilus and Cressida*? Those that were performed often, were sometimes so delayed by scene-changing as to be intolerable. I remember a famous Londoner welcoming a deputation from Stratford-on-Avon with the words "You come from a town where Shakespeare was born. I come from a town where Shakespeare is murdered."

The scholarship then at work upon the Elizabethan playwrights gave, for the first time for centuries, much thought to the theatrical fittings and methods by which their work was made known. Few more helpful and more moving things have been done by English actors than was done then by that most lively imaginative pioneer, the late William Poel, who produced some of the startling plays on a stage of the Elizabethan make, and inspired, I will not say the world, but every young reader who saw them.

That work of the late William Poel was one of the glorious things of the Victorian time. It was true piety, true patriotism.

All the young poets who saw these Poel revivals knew that the theatre he shewed, with an apron-stage, and a balcony over an inner room at the back, was the theatre of his inmost dreams, a theatre suited to poetical method, in which every Elizabethan play then delighting us in the reading would come instantly to life before us.

Since that time, a good many fine old plays have been revived, sometimes on the stage of this time, more often by groups of amateurs with no equipment save their zeal, or some makeshift improvised. The results have varied, according to the life in the play and in the producer; but the impulse to perform the plays would hardly have been so lively but for William Poel.

Readers of Elizabethan plays discovered that a play by Ben Jonson (not one of the best) and a play by Massinger (not one of the most attractive) had had a kind of life upon the stage until about 1850. Old men still sometimes talked of these: the young listened with reverence, as though the talkers had known the poets. A legend ran, that Webster's *Duchess of Malfi* had been played at the old Sadler's Wells Theatre within living memory. I had the honour to talk with an aged lady who had seen the performance, of which, unfortunately, she could remember nothing. Still, she had seen it. To us, who longed to see it, this in itself was much.

Perhaps those young readers, who could not see the plays tested and brought to life, sometimes formed romantic notions of them and exaggerated their importance to the Victorian time. Their importance to themselves could not be exaggerated. They were students of the arts of writing, and longed to know the very life of this art that had once so swayed their country. We longed for those plays. We wondered fifty or sixty years ago (as perhaps their far less fortunate successors have ceased to wonder) why the land that produced such variety of poetry has not a permanent poetical theatre, a permanent Elizabethan theatre, or, more than that, a Critical Theatre, playing the world's poetical masterpieces, so that they may be known for what they are, the thought of great men upon the heart of life.

This wonder grows with age. Why have we not such a theatre or theatres? The dusty answer that the soul receives, when asking this, is not flattering to the varying gangs of Parliament, the city councils, or to the race that chooses these.

To all times, the plays of the hour, of the season, and of the decade, must, necessarily, be more delightful than the plays of the past. Present plays have present laughter, and many theatres in which they can be shewn. Is it much to ask of a great nation, that has produced (shall we say) a hundred and fifty poetical plays of some, or great, or overwhelming interest, that it should have always in its capital city a small theatre manned by four full companies, performing these triumphs of our past, and taking them about the nation, and to the lands of our kindred? In the senseless, wasteful folly, bribery, and opportunism of public life, through the centuries, no single politician, so far as I know, has yet urged this; and as between the first urging and the first achievement a century is likely to pass, such a theatre may not soon be here, to move the world with the glory of the English spirit that is now the one thing left to us.

In some cases, performance has killed esteem for poet and play together: then, a later production of the same play has shown that the ruin was due to faulty casting or imperfect sympathy in the producer: the thing has come to the life we had imagined to be in it. In other cases performance has greatly heightened an admiration already high, by lighting up the strangenesses and letting the glory of the poetry speak for itself.

"Beauty itself will of itself persuade." Still, the Critical Theatre does not yet exist nor is likely to be in my day. I cannot now expect to see certain plays of Beaumont and Fletcher, of Chapman, and of Ben Jonson (to mention a few) that have given me joy in the reading. I am sorry that in this collection I cannot always quote what I have loved in the work of these men. So often, dramatic work does not detach readily for quotation, or when detached comes without its preparation of suspense.

I have said that one third of youth's delight was given then to the study of the Middle Ages, and a second third to the study of work done here between 1580 and 1620. What remained of our delight was given to the work of our own school, that had some touch of the Middle Age and of the time of Shakespeare, but no kinship whatsoever with the men of the century between the Closing of the Theatres and the poems of Thomas Gray.

Schools of thought and art are often exclusive and intolerant. The reactions of mind that bring the changes are often symptoms of violence of change in human affairs. The kinds of poetry we loved were thrust out of favour by puritanic fanaticism, they were brought back into favour by extravagance of revolution, and have since then been blasted from earth by war.

In the last century, the blasting had not happened. Europe was still in the Romantic Movement.

We, who loved the Elizabethans, the men of power, had no feeling for the freaks and cranks of those who followed the men of power with change. Perverse and critical intellect in its joyless gambol is for the select, the sad and the solitary. We, then, were all for an art that drew strength from the deep joy of the universal heart. We were in revolt against whatever it was that killed the Elizabethan theatre. We were in revolt against what remained of puritanism. Plenty remained in those days, enough to poison childhood, blight boyhood, and to make the London Sunday a curse to man. We, who had just come to know the glad madness of our great poets, still knew something of the sour madness of the fanatics, who closed the theatres, and in the name or pretence of this or that great principle, destroyed all consecrated things, blackened every parish with murder, and stifled every liberty. The evil is still rampant among us, using other catch-words, with equal falsehood and malignancy, and now without protest.

With the growth of puritanism three hundred years ago, the poetry for which we cared endured an eclipse here. War strikes fatally at poetry, and war and grinding tyranny held England in irons for nearly twenty years. The poetry of our nation changed. There began here that school of poetry so wisely and wittily judged by Dr. Johnson in the last years of its power.

The scholars who had made us familiar with the great writers of the time of Elizabeth had provided admirable editions of some of the transitional poets of the time of the Puritanic Rebellion. These we read with interest, as we

read nearly all early poetry, liking Herrick much the best.
The others seemed stumpy undergrowth overshadowed by
Milton.

In myself, a dislike of eighteenth century poetry shewed
at the age of eight. I was then extremely fond of the early
poems of Milton, *L'Allegro*, *Il Penseroso*, and those parts of
Comus telling the lovely tale of Sabrina.

Coming across a copy of *The Hind and the Panther*, I
thought that it would be some beautiful animal story such
as that of Chaucer's *Cock & Fox*, but to my horror I
found it something very different. I well remember my
disgust. This way of writing I felt was horrible: just the
kind of thing a grown-up *would* like. At about the same
time, an improving elder read to me, as a model of English
poetry, a passage from Cowper. I decided from these
specimens that that kind of writing, that I now call the
heroic or closed couplet, was detestable. This opinion was
shared by most of the young men of my time. For Milton
we had a tempered admiration. We all loved the early
poems. We all admired the great first two books of
Paradise Lost with their grand imagined scene of desolation
and of fallen spirits; fallen but still sublime. We had deep
delight in the admirable poetical skill with which Milton
tells of the temptation of Eve, and for the last book we had
nothing but the profoundest reverence and respect.

For Dryden and Pope we had no admiration. We liked
the one scene in Dryden's *All for Love*. We liked some of
the passages in *The Rape of the Lock* and we admired the
skill of some of the couplets elsewhere, but fifty years ago
[there can be no doubt] the eighteenth century was out
of favour. Its books lay neglected in great numbers in the
second-hand book shops.

Of the eighteenth century poets who did matter to us
Thomas Gray seemed the greatest. To us he was the
beginner of the Romantic Movement. We were very

grateful also to Bishop Percy, whose *Reliques of Ancient Poetry* helped on that movement.

We were unjust to many brilliant men. The wheel has turned since those days and the eighteenth century is in favour. Perhaps no writer who has once held the popular heart will ever be quite extinguished. He may return into favour unexpectedly, even centuries after his death.

Robert Browning, in one of his less known books, brought into notice Christopher Smart. He was one whom we all read and admired in that century of our dislike.

The great change in thought came late in the century with the French Revolution, and as a part of the revolutionary movement. Wordsworth emerged from the Lake Country with a power that made him the great poet of the time and the fourth of all the poets of England. His judgments on the eighteenth century were our gospels. It is difficult to tell Wordsworth's greatness. When I was young, many were praising him for matters which were (to the Greeks) foolishness, but of his wonder, who can doubt? When thinking of the world of mystery and beauty he opened to us, I have wondered sometimes two things: how much he owed to his lovely sister Dorothy: and how, if by some miracle he might come round that bend in the road, that man who had changed the world to us, his admirers could meet him. Would they not all fall upon their knees?

I have not mentioned William Blake, for he was then very little known. D. G. Rossetti had proclaimed him in the famous two-volume *Life* that he completed after William Gilchrist's sudden death. This generous book had stirred the ever generous Swinburne to an early attempt to find a meaning in the prophetical books, but fifty odd years ago those books were very little known; we knew only the Songs.

For Coleridge we had much admiration, mixed with the

feeling that he was a poet of only three poems, one of them unfinished, one of them due to a drug, and the third, perhaps, mainly due to the presence of Dorothy and William Wordsworth.

For some famous poets of the first twenty years of the nineteenth century we had little liking: we liked George Crabbe; not for the bulk of his work, but for the wild wonder of his outcry in *Sir Eustace Grey*. This wildness and wonder seem due to the use of opium, which Crabbe took occasionally against the malarial fever then common in East Anglia.

Next to Wordsworth, Keats and Shelley seemed to us the great poets of the eighteen-twenties. Shelley converted most of us for a time to vegetarianism; our admiration for Keats was beyond all telling. But of the poets nearer to us, still alive when we were young, two held the world: Tennyson, with an exquisite skill and a mind given to romantic moods in which nothing was left unseen or unwrought, and Browning, holding the keys of life and the knowledge of old Italy. It is hard for this generation to know what those men were to the Victorians.

By the end of the eighteen-eighties most young writers were in rebellion against the mature and later work of Tennyson. The early work was still admired. All writers well understood his superb mastery in many ways of writing, but all young people had suffered in childhood and boyhood from those insistences upon other merits to which elders were ever too prone. The elders, as in the case of Wordsworth, liked work that was (to the Greeks) foolishness. Such work, and such elders, turned all the young to the very different work of his great rival.

In this book there are poems by Tennyson that gave, and give, me great delight. They have precious qualities of feeling, of verse, of language, that no poet with any sense of the art can deny.

The influence of Browning, from the first, was of a very different nature. The qualities of verse and of language are seldom in him, and never for long when they are. The life that we perceived through him was a part of the very life of my time. Now that that life is almost over, I can give thanks for it.

Do readers care for Browning now? Booksellers tell me "Not very much." In the nature of life, it is not possible that they should care for him as we cared. We were lucky beyond most mortals. We were born into a time of peace, plenty and prosperity. The world had not been shaken by savageries and slaughters, the suppression of law and freedom, the weekly rupture of treaty, the daily murder, the hourly falsehood. We believed that Man was progressing, that the world was getting better.

We were born into the great late Victorian peace, at the moment when Ruskin had turned all sensitive minds to the study and admiration of Italy; when travel to any part of Italy was easy; and when the acquired elegance and sweetness of the poetry of the time had made minds long for something rougher and tarter. To all who longed for the curter method, and the knowledge of mediæval and renaissance Italy, the work of the mature Browning was the very gift of Heaven.

No poet of whom I have any knowledge has held a comparable sway upon his readers. For twenty years or more the Victorian world was divided into the elect, who read and knew Browning, and the rest, who perhaps lived, and might possibly, in time, learn, but until then did not matter. The elect, who read and knew him, had most of the shorter poems by heart: they could quote them: they lived by them. These enthusiasts knew the longer poems. Some of the fiercer enthusiasts were known to have read him all through, and to have quarried the quartz even in the depths. I went as far as most of his admirers. Often, I wonder what life would have been to us without Browning. One long unrelieved late Tennyson, with no door into the power and zest and greed for life of the men of the revival of learning.

Many Browning lovers hold that most of his very best work was written after 1849, the time-limitation of this book. Still, some of his best work is here. Those who were young fifty or sixty years ago will remember with what quaking rapture they came to these passages from *Sordello*, and how the glow of illumination told them that this was to be the poem of the time, and that from that point onwards all was to be revelation of Sordello, Dante's Sordello, and of the early thirteenth century. Perhaps, few were granted quite such complete joy, in reading-on, yet these were miracle-working pages, then. *The Bishop orders his Tomb at St. Praxed's Church* has all the weight of the poet's maturity. The passage from *Pauline* is one of the wonders of his boyhood.

To those who were young at the end of the last century Browning was all-important. Lines and stanzas from him are ingrown into our very minds, and if we regard them less than formerly it is because they are now parts of us. How little we regard things vital to us, like pulse or breathing.

The most luminous mind among the younger artists stirred by the early work of Browning and Tennyson was that of Dante Gabriel Rossetti, the son of an Italian Dante scholar living in London, in exile for his opinions.

Dante Gabriel Rossetti was said (in the traditions current among us) to have known all literature and other knowledge by infallible and fiery instinct. Delight and inspiration of all romantic kinds spread from him in every exquisite quality as a kind of communicable fire. A hundred years ago, when he founded the Pre-Raphaelite Brotherhood, he caused the publication of one of the first lively perceptions of the beauty of the poetry of Matthew Arnold. A few years later his personal magic enchanted three impressionable young men at Oxford, William Morris, Edward Burne-Jones and Algernon Charles Swinburne.

Rossetti, Arnold, Morris and Swinburne, in their so different ways, were all to sway young writers profoundly, to their great benefit. In 1849, when this book closes, two of them, Morris and Swinburne, were boys. Thomas Hardy was a boy: George Meredith a youth: Arnold, a maturer mind, still a beginner in the art, and not convinced, as Rossetti ever was, by the ever-glowing flame within him, that the arts are Man's eternal means of "conversing with Paradise." I end this book with poems by Rossetti. What thanks Man can render to the dead I offer here to him.

It has been said that conquerors, politicians and bureaucrats cannot kill the spirit of poetry. They can, and do, kill poets; they can, and do, make the making of poetry, which is the over-flowing joy of the mind, impossible to most, and hard to all, by killing all joy of the mind. How far they will succeed in killing the spirit of poetry in Europe, hitherto the main source of the art, may presently appear. My own dread is that, in the Dark Age threatening the world, its extinction may pass unnoticed, and, by the new savagery, un-mourned.

These poems, lines and fragments are my favourite English poetry.

Most of them must be dear to most lovers of our verse: many may be in other anthologies. I put them into mine. There are no fewer than two hundred known quotable English poets, with an immense range of theme. Below these are hundreds of others who uttered and passed on, and some others whose work, memorable for this or that, and still charming, has outlived their names.

The mind of anyone who has cared for poetry for many years together (assuming for the moment, what is so often denied, that such a thing can be called a mind) is and must be a compost of the poetries that once pleased and later failed to please. Down below are the nursery rhymes, the jingles, the simple tales, the songs that were heard, and the lessons that had to be learned. Above these are the popular poems, the works read by everybody, that have no doubt much commonness, but also some humanity that touches the universal heart. Above these are the utterances of the nation's mind, the marks of transfiguring instants, when a few rare spirits almost mad, as the world thinks (having almost made them so), perceive what all thenceforward will a little perceive through them.

To some of these spirits, after fifty years of joy, I offer this book in thanks. To seven among them, thanks is but a feeble term, for from those seven all that has been glad to me has come.

JOHN MASEFIELD

William Langland

PIERS PLOWMAN

C. Passus I. 163

The sergeants-at-law, who plead at the bar.

Thou might bet mete the myst on Malvern Hills,
Than get a mom of hure mouth till money be hem shewed.

(You might more readily measure the mist on Malvern Hills
than get a mumble (of law) from them till you have shewn them
money.)

C. Passus IX. 305

"I have no penny," quoth Piers, "pullets to buy,
Neither geese ne grys, but two green cheeses,
And a few curds and cream, and a therf cake,
And a loaf of beans and bran, baked for my children.
And I say, by my soul, I have no salt bacon,
Nor no cockneys, by Christ, collops to make
But I have porrets and parsley and many colplontes
And eke a cow and a calf; and a cart-mare
To draw afield my dung while the drought lasteth.
By this livelihood I must live till Lammas time;
By that, I hope for to have harvest in my croft
Then may I dight thy dinner as thee dear liketh.

---

grys: pigs.
green cheeses: fresh cheese, of a kind unlikely to keep.
therf: unleavened.
cockneys: cooks' assistants.
collops: strips or cuts of meat.
porrets: onions.
colplontes: cabbage.
Lammas: the first day (or week) in August when the Loaf-
mass, or first harvest-offering, was made.

I   B

Geoffrey Chaucer

THE PARLIAMENT OF FOWLS

The Proem

The lyf so short, the craft so long to lerne,
Th'assay so sharp, so hard the conquering,
The dredful joye, that alway slit so yerne,
Al this mene I by love, that my feling
Astonyeth with his wonderful worching
So sore y-wis, that whan I on him thinke,
Nat wot I wel whether I float or sink.

For al be that I knowe not Love in dede,
Ne wot how that he quyteth folk hir hire,
Yet happeth me ful oft in bokes rede
Of his miracles, and his cruel ire;
Ther rede I wel, he wol be lord and sire,
I dar not seyn, his strokes been so sore,
But God save swich a lord! I say no more.

Of usage, what for luste, what for lore,
On bokes rede I oft, as I yow told.
But wherfor that I speke al this? Not yore
Agon, hit happed me for to behold
Upon a boke, was writ with lettres old;
And ther-upon, a certeyn thing to lerne,
The longe day ful faste I radde and yerne.

For out of olde feldes, as men say,
Comth al this newe corn, fro yeer to yere;
And out of olde bokes, in good fay,
Comth al this newe science that men lere.
But now to purpos as of this matere—

To rede forth hit gan me so delyte,
That al that day me thoughte but a lyte.

This book of which I make mencioun,
Entitled was right thus, as I shal tell,
'Tullius, of the Dreme of Scipioun';
Chapitres seven hit hadde, of Hevene and Hell,
And Erthe, and soulës that therinnë dwell,
Of which, as shortly as I can hit trete,
Of his sentence I will you seyn the grete.

First telleth hit, whan Scipioun was come
In Afrik, how he meeteth Massinisse,
That him, for joye, in armes hath y-nome.
Than telleth hit hir speche and al the blisse
That was betwix hem, til the day gan misse;
And how his auncestre, African so dere,
Gan in his slepe that night to him appere.

Than telleth hit that, fro a sterry place,
How African hath him Cartagë shewed,
And warnèd him before of al his grace,
And seydë, what man, lered other lewed,*
That loveth comun profit, wel y-thewed,
He should into a blisful place wende,
Ther as the joye is without any ende.

Than askèd he, if folk that now be dede
Have lyf and dwelling in another place;
And African seyde, 'Yea, withoute drede,'
And that our present worlde's lyve's space
Nis but a maner deth, what wey we trace,
And rightful folk shal go, after they dye,
To Heven; and shewed him the Galaxye.

Than shewed he him the litel Earth, that heer is,
To regard of the Hevenes quantite;

* Learned or ignorant.

And after shewed he him the nynë sperës,
And after that the melodye herde he
That cometh of thilke sperës thryës three,
That well is of musyke and melodye
In this world heer, and cause of armonye.

Than bade he him, sin Erthe was so lyte,
Deceivable and full of harde grace,
That he ne shulde him in this world delyte.
Than tolde he him, in certeyn yeres space,
That every sterre shulde come into his place
Ther hit was first; and al shulde out of minde
That in this worlde is don of al mankinde.

Than prayde him Scipioun, to telle him al
The wey to come into that Hevene blisse;
And he seyde, "First, know thy-self immortal,
And loke ay besily thou werke and wisse
To comun profit, and thou shalt nat misse
To comen swiftly to that place dere,
That ful of blisse is and of soules clere.

But brekers of the lawe, soth to seyne,
And lecherous folk, after that they be dede,
Shul whirl about th'erthe alway in peyne,
Til many a world be passed, out of drede,
And than, for-yeven alle hir wikked dede,
Than shul they come into that blisful place,
To which to comen God thee sende His Grace!"—

The day gan failen, and the derke night,
That reveth bestes from hir busyness,
Berafte me my book for lakke of light,
And to my bed I gan me for to dress,
Fulfild of thought and besy heviness;
For bothe, I hadde thingë that I nolde,
And eek I ne hadde thinge that I wolde.

But fynally my spirit, at the last,
For-wery of my labour all the day,
Took rest, that made me to slepe faste,
And in my slepe I mette,* as I lay,
How African, right in that selfe aray
That Scipioun him saw, before that tyde,
Was come, and stood right at my beddes syde.

The wery hunter, slepinge in his bed,
To wood ayein his minde goth anoon;
The judge dremeth how his pleas be sped;
The carter dremeth how his cart is goon;
The riche, of gold; the knight, fights with his foon,
The sicke mette he drinketh of the tun:
The lover mette he hath his lady won.

Can I nat seyn if that the cause were
For I had red of African beforn,
That made me to mete that he stood there;
But thus seyde he "Thou hast thee so wel born
In loking of myn olde book all to-torn,
Of which Macrobie roghte nat a lyte,
That somdel of thy labour wolde I quyte!"—

Prayer

Citherea! thou blisful lady swete,
That with thy fyr-brand dauntest whom thee lest,
And madest me this sweven for to mete,
Be thou my help in this, for thou mayst best;
As wisly as I saw thee north-north-west,
When I began my sweven for to wryte,
So yif me might to ryme and to endyte!

* Mette: dreamed.

The Story

This forseid African me hente anoon,
And forthwith him unto a gate me broghte
Right of a parke, walled with grene stoon;
And over the gate, with lettres large y-wroghte,
Ther weren vers y-writen, as me thoghte,
On eyther side, of ful gret difference,
Of which I shal now sey the pleyn sentence.

"Thorgh me, men goon in-to the blisful place
Of hertes hele and dedly woundes cure;
Thorgh me men goon unto the welle of Grace,
Ther grene and lusty May shal ever endure;
This is the wey to all good aventure;
Be glad, thou reder, and thy sorwe off-cast,
All open am I; passe in, and speed thee fast!"

"Thorgh me men goon," (than spak that other syde)
"Unto the mortal strokes of the spere,
Of which Disdayn and Daunger is the gyde,
Where never tree shal fruit ne leves bere.
This stream you ledeth to the sorwful were,
Ther as the fish in prison is al drye;
Th-eschewing is the only remedye."

Thise vers of gold and black y-written were
The whiche I gan astonied to beholde,
For with that oon encresed ay my fere,
And with that other gan myn herte bolde;
That oon me hette, that other did me colde,
No wit had I, for errour, for to choose
To entre or flee, or me to save or lose.

Right as, betwixen adamauntes two
Of even might, a pece of iren set,
Ne hath no might to movë to ne fro—

For what that on may hale, that other let—
Fared I, that niste whether me was best,
To entre or leve, til African my gyde
Me hente, and shoof in at the gates wyde,

And seyde, "Hit stondeth writen in thy face,
Thyn errour, though thou telle it not to me;
But dred thee nat to come in-to this place,
For this wryting is no-thing ment by thee,
Ne by noon, but he Loves servant be;
For thou of Love hast lost thy tast, I gesse,
As sick man hath of swete and bitternesse.

But natheles, al-though that thou be dulle,
Yit that thou canst not do, yit mayst thou see;
For many a man that may not stonde a pulle,
Yit lyketh at the wrastling for to be,
And demeth yit, wher he do bet or he;
And there, if thou hadst cunning for t'endyte,
I shal thee shewen mater of to wryte."

With that my hond he took in his anoon,
Of which I comfort caughte, and wente in faste;
But Lord! so I was glad and wel begoon!
For over-al, wher I myn eyen caste,
Were treës clad with leves that ay shal laste,
Eche in his kinde, of colour fresh and grene
As emeraude, that joye was to sene.

The bilder oak, and eek the hardy asshe;
The pillar elm, the coffer unto careyne;*
The boxtree piper; holm to whippes lasshe;
The sayling fir; the cipres, deth to pleyne;
The shooter yew, the asp, for shaftes pleyne;
The olyve of pees, and eek the drunken vyne,
The victor palm, the laurel too devyne.

* Coffer unto careyne: coffin.

A garden saw I, ful of blossomy bough-es,
Upon a river, in a grene mede,
Ther as that swetness evermore y-now is,
With floures whyte, blewe, yelowe, and rede;
And colde welle-stremes, no-thing dede,
That swommen ful of smale fisshes lighte,
With finnes rede, and scalës silver-brighte.

On every bough the birdes herde I singe,
With voys of aungel in hir armonye,
Som besyed hem hir birdes forth to bringe;
The litel conyes to hir pley gunne hye,
And further al aboute I gan espye
The dredful roe, the buck, the hert and hinde,
Squirrels, and bestes smale of gentil kinde.

Of instruments of strenges in acord
Herde I so pleye a ravisshing swetnesse,
That God, that Maker is of al, and Lord,
Ne herde never better, as I gesse;
Therwith a wind, unnethe hit might be lesse,
Made in the leves grene a noise softe
Acordant to the birdis songe aloft.

The air of that place so attempre was
That never was grevaunce of hoot ne cold;
Ther wex eek every holsom spyce and gras,
No man may waxë therë seek ne old;
Yet was ther joye more a thousand fold
Then man can telle; ne never wolde it nighte,
But ay cleer day to any mannes sighte.

Under a tree, besyde a welle, I say
Cupid, our lord his arwes forge and fyle;
And at his fete his bowe al redy lay,
And wel his doghter tempred al the whyle
The hedes in the welle, and with hir wyle
She couched hem after as they shulde serve,
Som for to slay, and som to wounde and kerve.

Tho was I war of Plesaunce anon-right,
And of Aray, and Lust, and Curtesye;
And of the Craft that can and hath the might
To doon by force a wight to do folye—
Disfigurate was she, I nil not lye;
And by him-self, under an oke, I gesse,
Sawe I Delyt, that stood with Gentilnesse.

I saw Beautee, withouten any atyr,
And Youthe, ful of game and Iolyte,
Fool-hardinesse, Flatery, and Desyr,
Messagerye, and Mede,* and other three—
Hir names shul not here be told for me—
And upon pilers grete of jasper longe
I saw a temple of bras y-founded stronge.

About the temple daunceden alway
Wommen y-nowe, of whiche some ther were
Faire of hem-self, and some of hem were gay;
In kirtels, all disshevele, went they there—
That was hir office alway, year by year—
And on the temple, of doves whyte and faire
Saw I sittinge many an hundred paire . . .

TRUTH

Sometimes called *A Ballad of Good Counsel*

Flee from the prees, and dwell with sothfastness,
Suffyce thine owen thing, though hit be small;
For hord hath hate, and climbing tikelness,
Prees hath envye, and wele blent overall:
Savour no more than thee bihove shall:

---

* Messagerye: an interchanging of letters and messages, as in happy
  youth.
  Mede: reward, whether as pay for service, or as bribery for
  incitement.

Rule wel thy-self, that other folk canst rede;
And Trouthe shal deliver, hit is no drede.

Tempest thee not all croked to redress,
In trust of Her that turneth as a ball.
Much wele stant in litel busyness;
Beware, therefore, to sporne ageyn an awl.
Stryve not, as doth the crokke with the wall:
Daunte thy-self, that dauntest others' dede;
And Trouthe shal deliver, hit is no drede.

That thee is sent, receyve in buxumness,
The wrastling for the world axeth a fall.
Her nis non hoom, her nis but wilderness:
Forth, pilgrim, forth! Forth, beast, out of thy stall.
Know thy contree, look up, thank God of all:
Hold the high way, and lat thy ghost thee lede:
And Trouthe shal deliver, hit is no drede.

The Envoi

Therefore, thou vache, leve thyn old wrecchedness.
Unto the worlde, leve now to be thrall.*
Crye Him mercy, that of His hy goodness
Made thee of naught, and in especial
Draw unto Him, and pray in general
For thee, and eek for other, Heavenly mede;
And Trouthe shal deliver, hit is no drede.

TROILUS AND CRISEYDE

The End

Go, litel book, go litel my Tragedie,
Ther God thy maker yet, er that he dye,
So sende might to make in som comedie!

* Give up, now, being a slave to the world.

But litel book, no making thou n'envye,
But subgit be to alle Poesye;
And kiss the steps, wher-as thou seest pace
Virgile, Ovyde, Omer, Lucan, and Stace.

And for ther is so greet diversitee
In English, and in wryting of our tonge,
So preye I God that noon miswryte thee,
Ne thee mismetre for defaute of tonge.
And read wher-so thou be, or elles songe,
That thou be understonde, I God beseche!
But yet to purpos of my rather speche.—

The wrath, as I began you for to seye,
Of Troilus, the Grekes boughten dere;
For thousandes his hondes maden deye,
As he that was with-outen any pere,
Save Hector, in his time, as I can here.
But weylaway, save only Goddes wille,
Dispitously him slew the fierce Achille.

And when that he was slain in this manere,
His lighte ghost full blissfully is went
Up to the holowness of the seventh sphere,
In converse letting every element;
And there he saw, with full avysement,
The erratic starres, herkening harmony
With sownes full of hevenish melodye.

And down from thennes faste he gan avyse
This litel spot of Earth, that with the sea
Enbracèd is, and fully gan despyse
This wretched world, and held all vanitee
To respect of the pleyn felicitee
That is in Heaven above; and at the last,
There he was slain, his loking doun he cast.

And in himself he laught right at the woe
Of them that wepten for his death so fast;
And dampned all our work that folweth so
The blinde lust, the which that may not last,
And sholden all our heart on Heaven cast.
And forth he wente, shortly for to tell,
There as Mercurie sorted him to dwell.—

Such fyn hath, lo, this Troilus for love,
Such fyn hath all his grete worthiness;
Such fyn hath his estate real above,
Such fyn his lust, such fyn hath his nobless;
Such fyn hath false worldes brotelness.
And thus bigan his loving of Criseyde,
As I have told, and in this wyse he deyde.

O yonge fresshe folkes, he or she,
In which that Love up groweth with your age,
Repeyreth hoom from worldly vanitee,
And of your heart up-casteth the visage
To thilke God that after His image
You made, and thinketh al nis but a Fair
This world, that passeth soon as flowers fair.

And loveth Him, the which that right for Love
Upon a Cross, our soules for to beye,
First starf, and rose, and sit in Heaven above;
For He nil falsen no wight, dar I seye,
That wol his herte al hoolly on Him leye.
And sin He best to love is, and most meek,
What nedeth feyned loves for to seek?

Lo here, of Pagans' corsed olde rites,
Lo here, what all hir goddes may avail;
Lo here, these wrecched worldes appetites;
Lo here, the fyn and guerdon for travail,
Of Jove, Apollo, of Mars, of such rascaile!
Lo here, the forme of olde clerkes speche
In poetrye, if ye hir bokes seche.—

O moral Gower, this book I directe
To thee, and to the philosophical Strode,
To vouchen sauf, ther nede is, to corecte,
Of your benignitees and zeles gode.
And to that sothfast Crist, that starf on rode,
With al myn herte of mercy ever I preye;
And to the Lord right thus I speke and seye:

Thou Oon, and Two, and Three, eterne on-lyve,
That regnest ay in Three and Two and Oon,
Uncircumscript, and al mayst circumscryve,
Us from visible and invisible foon
Defende; and to Thy mercy, everychoon,
So make us, Jesus, for Thy Grace, digne,
For love of Mayde and Moder Thyn Benigne! Amen

THE CANTERBURY TALES

From THE PARDONER'S TALE

Thise ryotoures three, of which I tell,
Long erst er Pryme* rong of any bell,
Were set hem in a tavern for to drink;
And as they sat, they herd a belle clink
Biforn a corpse, was caried to his grave;
That oon of hem gan calle to his knave,
'Go bet,' quod he, 'and axe redily,
What corpse is this that passeth heer forby;
And look that thou report his name wel.'
  'Sir,' quod this boy, 'it nedeth never-a-del.
It was me told, er ye cam heer, two houres;
He was, pardee, an old felaw of youres;
And sodeynly he was y-slayn to-night,
For-dronke, as he sat on his bench upright;
Ther cam a privee theef, men clepen Death,
That in this contree al the peple sleeth,

---

* Prime: the first of the Day-Hours of the Western Church, some-
times taken as 6 a.m., sometimes as sun-rise.

And with his spere he smote his herte a-two,
And wente his wey with-outen wordes mo.
He hath a thousand sleyn this pestilence:
And, maister, er ye come in his presence,
Me thinketh that it were full necessarie
For to beware of such an adversarie:
Beth redy for to mete him evermore.
Thus taughte me my dame, I sey no more.'
'By Seinte Marie,' said this taverner,
'The child seith sooth, for he hath slayn this yeer,
Hence over a myle, with-in a greet village,
Both man and womman, child and hind, and page,
I trowe his habitacioun be there;
To been avysed greet wisdom it were,
Er that he dide a man a dishonour.'
'Ye, Godde's armes,' quod this ryotour.
'Is it such peril with him for to mete?
I shal him seke by stile and eek by strete,
I make avow to Godde's digne bones!
Herkneth, felawes, we three been al ones;
Let ech of us holde up his hond to other,
And ech of us bicomen otheres brother,
And we wol sleen this false traytour Death;
He shal be slayn, he that so many sleeth,
By Godde's dignitee, er it be night.'
    Togidres han thise three her trouthes plight,
To live and dyen ech of hem for other,
As though he were his owenë boren brother.
And up they sterte al dronken, in this rage,
And forth they goon towardës that village,
Of which the taverner had spoke biforn,
And many a grisly oath than have they sworn,
And Criste's blessed body they to-rent;
'Death shal be dead, if that we may him hente.'
    Whan they han goon nat fully half a myle,
Right as they wold han troden over a stile,
An old man and a poorë with hem met.
This olde man ful mekely hem grette,

And seyde, thus, 'Now, lordes, God yow see!'
  The proudest of thise ryotoures three
Answerd agayn, 'What? cherl, with sory grace,
Why artow al forwrappèd save thy face?
Why livestow so long in so great age?'
  This olde man gan loke in his visage,
And seyde thus, 'For I ne can nat finde
A man, though that I walked in-to Inde,
Neither in citee, ne in no village,
That wolde chaunge his youthe for myn age;
And therfore must I han myn age still,
As longe time as it is Godde's wille.
  Ne death, allas! ne wol nat han my lyf;
Thus walke I, lyk a restelees caityf,
And on the ground, which is my modres gate,
I knockè with my staf, erly and late,
And sey to her, "Leve Moder, let me in!
Low, how I vanish, flesh, and blood, and skin!
Allas! whan shul my bonès been at rest?
Moder, with yow wolde I chaunge my cheste,
That in my chambre longe tyme hath be,
Ye! for an hairë clout to wrappe me!"
But yet to me she wol nat do that grace,
For which ful pale and welked is my face.
  But, sirs, to yow it is no curteisye
To speke unto an old man vileinye,
But he trespasse in worde, or elles in dede.
In Holy Writ ye may yourselven rede,
"Agayns an old man, hoar upon his heed,
Ye sholde aryse;" wherfor I yeve yow reed,
Ne dooth un-to an old man noon harm now,
Na-more than that ye wold men dide to yow
In age, if that ye so long abyde;
And God be with yow, wher ye go or ryde.
I moot go thider as I have to go.'
  'Nay, olde cherl, by God, thou shalt nat so,'
Seyde this other hasardour anon;
'Thou partest nat so lightly, by Seint John!

Thou spak right now of thilke traitour Death,
That in this contree alle our frendes sleeth,
Have heer my trouthe, as thou art his aspye,
Tel wher he is, or thou shalt it abye,
By God, and by the Holy Sacrament!
For soothly thou art oon of his assent,
To slay us yongë folk, thou falsë theef!'

   'Now, sirs,' quod he, 'if that yow be so leef
To finde Death, turne up this croked way,
For in that grove I lafte him, by my fay,
Under a tree, and ther he wol abyde;
Nor for your boost he wol him no-thing hyde.
See ye that oak? right ther ye shul him finde.
God save yow, that boghte agayn mankinde,
And yow amende!'—thus seyde this olde man.
And everich of thise ryotoures ran,
Til they cam to the tree, and ther they founde
Of Florins fyne of golde y-coyned rounde
Wel ny an eightë busshels, as hem thought.
No lenger thannë after Death they sought,
But ech of hem so glad was of that sight,
For that the florins been so faire and brighte,
That doun they sette hem by this precious hord.
The worste of hem he spake the firste word.

   'Brethren,' quod he, 'tak kepe what I shall seye;
My wit is greet, though that I bourde and pleye.
This tresor hath Fortune un-to us yiven,
In mirthe and jolitee our lyf to liven,
And lightly as it comth, so wol we spend.
Ey! Godde's precious dignitee! who wende
To-day, that we sholde han so fair a grace?
But mighte this gold be caried fro this place
Hoom to myn hous, or elles un-to youres—
For wel ye woot that al this gold is oures—
Than were we in heigh felicitee.
But trewely, by daye it may nat be;
Men wolde seyn that we were theves stronge,
And for our owen tresor doon us honge.

This tresor moste y-caried be by night
As wysly and as slyly as it might.
Wherfore I rede, that cut among us all
We drawe, and lat see wher the cut wol falle;
And he that hath the cut, with herte blythe
Shal rennen to the toune, and that ful swythe,
And bringe us bread and wyn ful prively.
And two of us shul kepen subtilly
This tresor wel; and, if he wol nat tarie,
Whan it is night, we wol this tresor carie
By oon assent, wher-as us thinketh best.'
That oon of hem the cut broughte in his fest,
And bad hem drawe, and loke wher it wol fall;
And it fel on the yongeste of hem all;
And forth toward the toun he wente anon.
And al-so sone as that he was ygon,
That oon of hem spak thus un-to that other,
'Thou knowest wel thou art my sworne brother,
Thy profit wel I tellë thee anon.
Thou woost wel that our felawe is agon;
And heer is gold, and that ful greet plentee,
That shal departed been among us three.
But natheles, if I can shape it so,
That it departed were among us two,
Had I not doon a freendes torn to thee?'
    That other answerde, 'I noot how that may be;
He woot how that the gold is with us tweye,
What shal we doon? what shal we to him seye?'
    'Shal it be conseil?' seyde the firste shrewe;
'And I shal tellen thee, in wordes fewe,
What we shal doon, and bringe it wel aboute.'
    'I graunte,' quod that other, 'out of doute,
That, by my trouthe, I wol thee nat biwreye.'
    'Now,' quod the firste, 'thou woost wel we be tweye,
And two of us shul strenger be than oon.
Look whan that he is set, thou right anoon
Arys, as though thou woldest with him pleye;
And I shal ryve him thurgh the sydes tweye,

Whyl that thou strogelest with him as in game,
And with thy dagger look thou do the same;
And then shal al this gold departed be,
My dere freend, bitwixen thee and me;
Than may we bothe our lustes al fulfille,
And pleye at dice right at our owene wille.'
And thus acorded been thise shrewes tweye,
To sleen the thridde, as ye han herd me seye.

This yongest, which that wentë to the toun,
Ful ofte in herte he rolleth up and doun
The beautee of thise florins newe and bright.
'O Lord!' quod he, 'if so were that I might
Have al this tresor to my-self allone,
Ther n'is no man that liveth under the Throne
Of God, that sholde live so mery as I!'
And atte laste the Feend, our enemy,
Putte in his thought that he shold poyson beye,
With which he mighte sleen his felawes tweye;
For-why, the Feend fond him in swich lyvinge,
That he had leve to sorwe him to bringe,
For this was outrely his fulle entent
To sleen hem bothe, and never to repent.
And forth he gooth, no lenger wolde he tarie,
Into the toun, un-to a Pothecarie,
And preyed him, that he him wolde sell
Som poyson, that he mighte his rattes quell;
And eek ther was a polcat in his hawe,
That, as he seyde, his capouns hadde y-slawe,
And fayn he wolde him wreken, if he might,
On vermin, that destroyed him by night.

The Pothecarie answerde, 'Thou shalt have
A thing that, al-so God my soule save,
In al this world ther nis no creature,
That ete or dronke hath of this confiture
Noght but the mountance of a corn of whete,
That he ne shal his lyf anon forlete;
Ye, sterve he shal, and that in lesse while
Than thou wolt goon a-pace nat but a mile;

This poyson is so strong and violent.'
   This cursed man hath in his hond y-hent
This poyson in a box, and sith he ran
In-to the nexte strete, un-to a man,
And borwed of him large botels three;
And in the two his poyson poured he;
The thridde he kepte clene for his drinke.
For all the night he shoop him for to swinke
In caryinge of the gold out of that place.
And whan this ryotour, with sory grace,
Had filled with wyn his grete botels three,
To his felawes agayn repaireth he.

   What nedeth it thereof to sermone more?
For right as they had cast his death bifore,
Right so they han him slayn, and that anon.
And whan that this was doon, thus spak that oon,
'Now lat us sit and drinke, and make us merie,
And afterward we wol his body berie.'
And with that word it happed him, par cas,
To take the botel, ther the poyson was,
And drank, and yaf his felawe drinke also,
For which anon they storven bothe two.

   But, certes, I suppose that Avicen
Wroot never in no canon, ne in no fen,
Mo wonder signes of empoisoning
Than hadde thise wrecches two, er hir ending.
Thus ended been thise homicydes two,
And eek the false empoysoner also.

MURDER WILL OUT

A Tale from within *The Nun's Priest's Tale*

   Oon of the greatest authors that men rede
Seith thus, that whylom two felawes went
On pilgrimage, in a ful good entent;
And happed so, thay came into a toun,

Wher-as ther was such congregacioun
Of peple, and eek so streit of herbergage
That they ne founde as muche as a cotage
In which they bothe might y-lodged be.
Wherfor thay mosten, of necessitee,
As for that night, departen compaignye;
And ech of hem goth to his hostelrye,
And took his lodging as it wolde fall.
That oon of hem was lodged in a stall,
Far in a yerd, with oxen of the plough;
That other man was lodged wel y-nough,
As was his aventure, or his fortune,
That us governeth all, as in commune.

And so bifel, that, long er it were day,
This man mette in his bed, ther-as he lay,
How that his felawe gan up-on him call,
And seyde, "Allas! for in an oxes stall
This night shal I be mordred ther I lye.
Now help me, dere brother, er I dye;
In alle haste com to me," he sayde.
This man out of his sleep for fere abrayde;
But whan that he was wakned of his sleep,
He turned him, and took of this no keep;
Him thoughte his dreem nas but a vanitee.
Thus twyës in his sleping dremed he.
And atte thridde tyme yet his felawe
Cam, as him thoughte, and seide, "I now am slawe;
Bihold my blody woundes, depe and wyde!
Arys up erly in the morwe-tyde,
And at the west gate of the toun," quod he,
"A carte ful of dong ther shaltow see,
In which my body is hid prively;
Do thilke carte aresten boldely.
My gold caused my mordre, sooth to sayn;"
And tolde him every poynt how he was slayn,
With a ful pitous face, pale of hewe.
And truste wel, his dreem he fond ful trewe;
For on the morwe, as sone as it was day,

To his felawes inn he took his way;
And whan that he cam to this oxes stalle,
After his felawe he bigan to calle.

　The hostiler answered him anon,
And seyde, "Sire, your felawe is agon,
As sone as day he wente out of the toun."
This man gan fallen in suspecioun,
Remembring on his dremes that he mette,
And forth he goth, no lenger wolde he lette,
Unto the West Gate of the toun, and fond
A dong-carte, as it went to donge lond,
That was arrayed in the same wyse
As ye han herd the dede man devyse;
And with an hardy herte he gan to crye
"Vengeaunce and justice of this felonye:—
My felawe mordred is this same night,
And in this carte he lyth, gapinge upright.
I crye out on the ministres," quod he,
"That sholden kepe and reulen this citee;
Harrow! allas! heer lyth my felawe slayn!"
What sholde I more un-to this tale seyn?
The peple out-sterte, and caste the cart to grounde,
And in the middel of the dong they founde
The dede man, that mordred was al newe.

　O blisful God, that art so just and trewe!
Lo, how that Thou biwreyest mordre alway!
Mordre wol out, that see we day by day.
Mordre is so wlatsom and abhominable
To God, that is so just and resonable,
That he ne wol nat suffre it heled be;
Though it abyde a yeer, or two, or three,
Mordre wol out, is my conclusion.
And right anoon, the ministres of that toun
Han hent the carter, and so sore him pyned,
And eek the hostiler so sore engyned,
That thay biknewe hir wikkednesse anoon,
And were an-hanged by the nekke-boon.

From *THE MONK'S TALE*

Crœsus

The riche Crœsus, whylom king of Lyde,
Of whiche Crœsus Cyrus sore him dradde,
Yit was he caught amiddes al his pryde,
And to be brent men to the fyr him ladde.
But such a reyn doun fro the welkin shadde
That slow the fyr, and made him to escape;
But to be war no grace yet he hadde,
Til Fortune on the galwes made him gape.

Whan he escaped was, he can nat stente
For to beginne a newe werre agayn.
He wende wel, for that Fortune him sente
Such hap, that he escaped thurgh the rayn,
That of his foos he mighte nat be slayn;
And eek a sweven up-on a night he mette,
Of which he was so proud and eek so fayn,
That in vengeaunce he al his herte sette.

Up-on a tree he was, as that him thoughte,
Ther Juppiter him wesh, bothe bak and syde,
And Phebus eek a fair towaille him broughte
To drye him with, and ther-for wex his pryde;
And to his doghter, that stood him bisyde,
Which that he knew in heigh science habounde,
He bad hir telle him what it signifyde,
And she his dreem bigan right thus expounde.

'The tree,' (quod she) 'the galwes is to mene,
And Jupiter bitokneth snow and reyn,
And Phebus, with his towaille cler and clene,
Tho ben the sunnes' stremes sooth to seyn;
Thou shalt anhanged be, fader, certeyn;
Reyn shal thee wasshe, and sonne shal thee drye;'

Thus warned she him ful plat and ful pleyn,
His doghter, which that called was Phanye.

Anhanged was Crœsus, the proude king,
His royal trone mighte him nat availle.—
Tragedie is noon other maner thing,
Ne can in singing crye ne biwaille,
But for that Fortune alwey wol assaille
With unwar strook the regnes that ben proude;
For when men trusteth hir, than wol she faille,
And covere hir brighte face with a cloude.

The Tale of Hugelin, Count of Pisa

Of the erl Hugelyn of Pyse the langour
Ther may no tonge telle for pitee;
But litel out of Pyse stant a tour,
In whiche tour in prisoun put was he,
And with him ben his litel children three.
The eldest scarsly five yeer was of age.
Allas, Fortune! it was greet crueltee
Such briddes for to putte in such a cage!

Dampned was he to deye in that prisoun,
For Roger, which that Bishop was of Pyse,
Had on him made a false suggestioun,
Thurgh which the peple gan upon him ryse,
And putten him in prisoun in such wyse
As ye han herd, and mete and drink he had
So smal, that wel unnethe it may suffyse,
And therwith-al it was ful povre and bad.

And on a day bifil that, in that hour,
Whan that his mete wont was to be broght,
The gayler shette the dores of the tour:
He herde it wel,—but he spak right noght,
And in his herte anon ther fil a thoght,

That they for hunger wolde doon him dyen.
'Allas!' quod he, 'allas! that I was wroght!'
Therwith the teres fellen from his yën.

His yonge sone, that three yeer was of age,
Un-to him seyde, 'Fader, why do ye wepe?
Whan wol the gayler bringen our potage,
Is ther no morsel bread that ye do kepe?
I am so hungry, that I may nat slepe.
Now wolde God that I mighte slepen ever!
Than sholde nat hunger in my wombe crepe;
Ther is no thing, save bread, that me were lever.'

Thus day by day this child bigan to crye.
Til in his fadres barme adoun it lay,
And seyde, 'Far-wel, fader, I moot dye.'
And kiste his fader, and deyde the same day
And whan the woful fader dead it sey,
For wo his armes two he gan to byte,
And seyde, 'allas, Fortune! and weylaway!
Thy false wheel my wo al may I wyte!'

His children wende that it for hunger was
That he his armes gnow, and nat for wo,
And seyde, "Fader, do nat so, allas!
But rather eet the flesh upon us two;
Our flesh thou yaf us, tak our flesh us fro
And eet y-nough": right thus they to him seyde.
And after that, with-in a day or two,
They leyde hem in his lappe adoun, and deyde.

Him-self, despeired, eek for hunger starf;
Thus ended is this mighty Erl of Pyse;
From heigh estaat Fortune awey him carf.
Of this Tragedie it oghte y-nough suffyse
Who-so wol here it in a longer wyse,
Redeth the grete poete of Itaille,
That highte Dant, for he can it devyse
Fro point to point, nat o word wol he faille.

Occasional Lines

THE PARLIAMENT OF FOWLS

The cock that horloge is of thorpes lite.

THE CANTERBURY TALES

THE PRIORESS
And all was conscience and tender heart.

THE MONK
A lusty man, to ben an abbot able.

THE CLERK OF OXFORD
A Clerk there was of Oxenford also,
That unto Logic hadde long y-go
. . . .
For him was liever have at his bed's head
Twenty bookes clad in black or red
Of Aristotle and his philosophy
Than robes rich, or fiddle or gay psaltry.

And gladly wolde he learne and gladly teach.

THE FRANKLIN
It snowèd in his house of meat and drink.

THE PARSON
But Christë's lore, and His apostles twelve
He taught, but first he followed it himselve.

THE SUMMONER
Of his visage, children were sore afeared.

THE MILLER'S TALE

THE CARPENTER'S WIFE
Full brighter was the shining of her hue
Than in the Tower the noble y-forged new.

THE PARISH CLERK
In twenty manner could he trip and dance
(After the school of Oxenfordë tho)
And with his leggës casten to and fro.

MORNING
A litel after the cockës had y-crow.

THE PROMISED VOYAGE IN THE KNEADING TUB
Then shal thou swim as merry, I undertake,
As doth the whitë duck after her drake.

EARLY MORNING
Till that the bell of Laudës gan to ring
And friars in the chancel gan to sing.

[Lauds, with Prime, made up Matins, or early
Morning Service, beginning properly at sunrise.]

THE POOR WIDOW'S COCK.

(From *The Nun's Priest's Tale*)

She had a cock hight Chaunteclere,
In all the land of crowing n'as his peer.
His voice was merrier than the merry orgon
On Massë days that in the churches gon;
Well surer was his crowing in his loge,
Than is a clock or any abbey orloge.

TROILUS AND CRISEYDE

BOOK I.   218

As proude Bayard ginneth for to skip
Out of the way, so pricketh him his corn,
Till he a lash have of the longe whip,
Then thinketh he "Though I praunce all beforn
First in the trace, full fat and newe shorn,
Yet am I but an horse and horses' law
I must endure and with my fellows draw."

BOOK II.   111

Do wey your book, rise up, and let us daunce
And let us do to May some observaunce.

BOOK II.   918

A nightingale upon a cedar green
Upon the chamber-wall there as she lay,
Full loude sang against the moone sheen.

BOOK III.   690
[*Bed time in Troy*]
There was no more to speken nor to traunce*
But bidden go to bedde with mischaunce,
(If any wight were stirring anywhere)
And let them sleepë that abedde were.

BOOK III.   1060

Of a full misty morrow
Folwen ful ofte a merry summer's day.
And after winter followeth grene May.

* Traunce means here to move about.

Book v. 553
    And farewell, shrine, of whom the Saint is out.

THE KNIGHT'S TALE

Emily's Prayer to Diana

Chaste Goddesse, wel wostow that I
Desire to been a maiden all my life,
Ne never wol I be no love ne wife.
I am, thou wost, yet of thy company,
A maid, and love hunting and venery,
And for to walken in the woodes wild,
And not to be a wife and be with child.

Stephen Hawes

THE PASTIME OF PLEASURE

O mortal folk, you may behold and see
How I lie here, sometime a mighty knight:
The end of joy and all prosperity
Is Death at lastë through his course and might;
After the day there cometh the dark night;
For though the dayë be never so long,
At last the belles ringeth to evensong.

Stephen Hawes, in his Excusation, prays that God may save his book:—

"From mis-metring by wrong impression."

His metre perplexes a modern reader, who cannot help wondering how the author meant it to be spoken.
In the above, without the accented e final in lines 4 and 6, how were the lines saved from lapse? In the last famous, beautiful line, did he speak it

At last the bells ringeth to evensong,
　　or
At last the bellës ringth to evensong?

Christopher Marlowe

TAMBURLAINE THE GREAT

Part I, Act II

Scene v

TAMB.:

"And ride in triumph through Persepolis!"
Is it not brave to be a king, Techelles?
Usumcasane and Theridamas,
Is it not passing brave to be a king,
"And ride in triumph through Persepolis?"

Scene vii

TAMB.:

Nature that framed us of four elements,
Warring within our breasts for regiment,
Doth teach us all to have aspiring minds:
Our souls, whose faculties can comprehend
The wondrous architecture of the world,
And measure every wandering planet's course,
Still climbing after knowledge infinite,
And always moving as the restless spheres,
Will us to wear ourselves, and never rest,
Until we reach the ripest fruit of all,
That perfect bliss and sole felicity,
The sweet fruition of an earthly crown.

Act V

SCENE I

TAMB.:

Virgins, in vain you labour to prevent
That which mine honour swears shall be performed.
Behold my sword! what see you at the point?

1ST VIRG.:

Nothing but fear, and fatal steel, my lord.

TAMB.:

Your fearful minds are thick and misty then;
For there sits Death; there sits imperious Death
Keeping his circuit by the slicing edge.
But I am pleased you shall not see him there;
He now is seated on my horsemen's spears,
And on their points his fleshless body feeds.
Techelles, straight go charge a few of them
To charge these dames, and show my servant, Death,
Sitting in scarlet on their armèd spears.

NOTE ON THE ABOVE

This scene cannot well be by Marlowe. Might it not be by the young Shakespeare?

May not the actors have urged Marlowe to give them a rest from the man-killings of the earlier acts? May they not have begged him to let them kill a few women for a change? May he not have replied, that he was sick of the very thought of writing any more of the work, having the second part still to finish; but that they could write-in a softer scene, if they wished?

Act V

SCENE II

TAMB.:

What is beauty, saith my sufferings, then?
If all the pens that ever poets held
Had fed the feeling of their masters' thoughts,
And every sweetness that inspired their hearts,
Their minds, and muses on admirèd themes:
If all the heavenly quintessence they still
From their immortal flowers of poesy,
Wherein, as in a mirror, we perceive
The highest reaches of a human wit;
If these had made one poem's period,
And all combined in beauty's worthiness,
Yet should there hover in their restless heads
One thought, one grace, one wonder, at the least,
Which into words no virtue can digest.

DOCTOR FAUSTUS

Act I

Faustus and Mephistophelis

FAUST.:

But, leaving these vain trifles of men's souls,
Tell me what is that Lucifer thy lord?

MEPH.:

Arch-regent and commander of all spirits.

FAUST.:

Was not that Lucifer an angel once?

MEPH.:

Yes, Faustus, and most dearly loved of God.

FAUST.:

How comes it then that he is Prince of devils?

Meph.:

O, by aspiring pride and insolence;
For which God threw him from the face of Heaven.

Faust.:

And what are you that live with Lucifer?

Meph.:

Unhappy spirits that fell with Lucifer,
Conspired against our God with Lucifer,
And are for ever damned with Lucifer.

Faust.:

Where are you damned?

Meph.:

In hell.

Faust.:

How comes it then that thou art out of hell?

Meph.:

Why this is hell, nor am I out of it:
Think'st thou that I who saw the face of God,
And tasted the eternal joys of Heaven,
Am not tormented with ten thousand hells,
In being deprived of everlasting bliss?
O Faustus! leave these frivolous demands,
Which strike a terror to my fainting soul.

Faust.:

What, is great Mephistophilis so passionate
For being deprivèd of the joys of Heaven?
Learn thou of Faustus manly fortitude,
And scorn those joys thou never shalt possess.

Scene xvi

Faust.:

> Ah, Faustus,
> Now hast thou but one bare hour to live,
> And then thou must be damned perpetually!
> Stand still, you ever-moving spheres of Heaven,
> That time may cease, and midnight never come;
> Fair Nature's eye, rise, rise again and make
> Perpetual day; or let this hour be but
> A year, a month, a week, a natural day,
> That Faustus may repent and save his soul!
> O lente, lente currite, noctis equi!
> The stars move still, time runs, the clock will strike,
> The Devil will come, and Faustus must be damned.
> O, I'll leap up to my God! Who pulls me down?
> See, see where Christ's blood streams in the firmament!
> One drop would save my soul—half a drop: ah, my Christ!
> Ah, rend not my heart for naming of my Christ!
> Yet will I call on him: O spare me, Lucifer!—
> Where is it now? 'tis gone; and see where God
> Stretcheth out his arm, and bends his ireful brows!
> Mountain and hills come, come and fall on me,
> And hide me from the heavy wrath of God!
> No! no!
> Then will I headlong run into the earth;
> Earth gape! O no, it will not harbour me!
> You stars that reigned at my nativity,
> Whose influence hath allotted death and hell,
> Now draw up Faustus like a foggy mist
> Into the entrails of yon labouring clouds,
> That when they vomit forth into the air,
> My limbs may issue from their smoky mouths,
> So that my soul may but ascend to Heaven.
>
> *(The clock strikes the half hour.*
> Ah, half the hour is past! 'twill all be past anon!
> O God!

If thou wilt not have mercy on my soul,
Yet for Christ's sake, whose blood hath ransomed me,
Impose some end to my incessant pain;
Let Faustus live in hell a thousand years—
A hundred thousand, and—at last—be saved!
O, no end is limited to damnèd souls!
Why wert thou not a creature wanting soul?
Or why is this immortal that thou hast?
Ah, Pythagoras' metempsychosis! were that true,
This soul should fly from me, and I be changed
Unto some brutish beast! all beasts are happy,
For, when they die,
Their souls are soon dissolved in elements;
But mine must live, still to be plagued in hell.
Curst be the parents that engendered me!
No, Faustus: curse thyself: curse Lucifer
That hath deprived thee of the joys of Heaven.
                    (*The clock strikes twelve.*
O, it strikes, it strikes! Now, body, turn to air,
Or Lucifer will bear thee quick to hell.
                    (*Thunder and lightning.*
O soul, be changed into little water-drops,
And fall into the ocean—ne'er be found. (*Enter Devils.*
My God! my God! look not so fierce on me!
Adders and serpents, let me breathe awhile!
Ugly hell, gape not! come not, Lucifer!
I'll burn my books!—Ah Mephistophilis!
                    (*Exeunt Devils with Faustus.*

                Enter CHORUS.

CHO.:

Cut is the branch that might have grown full straight,
And burnèd is Apollo's laurel bough.

EDWARD THE SECOND

Act V

SCENE v

K. EDW.:
    They give me bread and water, being a king.

Edmund Spenser

THE SHEPHEARDS CALENDER
(October)

But, ah! Mæcenas is yclad in clay,
And great Augustus long ygo is dead,
And all the worthies liggen wrapt in lead,
That matter made for poets on to play.

THE FAERIE QUEENE

BOOK I. Canto IV. 33

WRATH:

And him beside rides fierce revenging Wrath
Upon a lion, loath for to be led;
And in his hand a burning brond he hath,
The which he brandisheth about his head:
His eyes did hurl forth sparkles fiery-red,
And starèd stern on all that him beheld;
As ashes, pale of hue, and seeming dead;
And on his dagger still his hand he held,
Trembling through hasty rage when choler in him swelled.

His ruffian raiment all was stained with blood
Which he had spilt, and all to rags y-rent;
Through unadvisèd rashness woxen wood,
For of his hands he had no government,
Ne cared for blood in his avengëment:
But when the furious fit was over-past,
His cruel facts he often would repent;
Yet (wilful man) he never would forecast
How many mischieves should ensue his heedless haste.

37

Full many mischiefs follow cruel Wrath:—
Abhorrèd Bloodshed, and tumultuous Strife,
Unmanly Murder, and unthrifty Scathe,
Bitter Despite, with Rancour's rusty knife,
And fretting Grief, the enemy of Life;
All these, and many evils moe, haunt ire;
The swelling Spleen, and Frenzy raging rife,
The shaking Palsy and St. Francis' Fire;
Such one was Wrath, the last of this ungodly tire.

And, after all, upon the waggon-beam
Rode Satan, with a smarting whip in hand.

BOOK I.   Canto IX.   40

DESPAIR speaks:
     "He there does now enjoy eternal rest
     And happy ease, which thou dost want and crave,
     And further from it daily wanderest:
     What if some little pain the passage have,
     That makes frail flesh to fear the bitter wave?
     Is not short pain well borne that brings long ease,
     And lays the soul to sleep in quiet grave?
     Sleep after toil, port after stormy seas,
     Ease after war, death after life, does greatly please."

    . . .   .

UNA speaks:
     Come, come away, frail, feeble, fleshly wight,
     Ne let vain words bewitch thy manly heart,
     Ne devilish thoughts dismay thy constant sprite . . .
     In heavenly mercies hast thou not a part?

BOOK I.   Canto XII.   42

       Now strike your sails, ye jolly mariners
       For we be come unto a quiet road.

Mammon's House

Book ii.   Canto vii.   29

Both roof, and floor, and walls were all of gold,
But overgrown with dust and old decay,
And hid in darkness, that none could behold
The hue thereof: for view of cheerful day
Did never, in that house, itself display,
But a faint shadow of uncertain light,
Such as a lamp whose life does fade away,
Or as the moon, clothe'd with cloudy night,
Does shew to him that walks in fear and sad affright.

In all that room was nothing to be seen
But huge great iron chests and coffers strong,
All barred with double bends, that none could ween
Them to efforce by violence or wrong;
On every side they placèd were along,
But all the ground with skulls was scatterèd
And dead men's bones, which round about were flong,
Whose lives, it seemèd, whilom there were shed,
And their vile carcasses now left unburièd.

vi.   31

Old Genius the porter of them was.

vi.   42

There is continual Spring, and Harvest there
Continual, both meeting at one time.

Book ii.   Canto xii.   23

    Spring-headed Hydræs and sea-shouldring Whales.

    [A line said to have delighted John Keats.]

Book ii.   Canto xii.   47

AGDISTES

        . . . . That celestial power, to whom the care
Of life, and generat-i-on of all
That lives, pertains, in charge particulare.
Who wondrous things concerning our welfare,
And strange phantòmes doth let us oft foresee,
And oft of secret ill bids us beware:
That is our Self, whom though we do not see,
Yet each doth in himself it well perceive to be.

The Music at the Bower of Bliss

Book ii.   Canto xii.   71

    The joyous birds shrouded in cheerful shade,
Their notes unto the voice attempered sweet;
Th' angelical soft trembling voices made
To th' instruments divine respondence meet:
The silver-sounding instruments did meet
With the base murmur of the water's fall:
The water's fall with difference discreet,
Now soft, now loud, unto the wind did call:
The gentle warbling wind low answerèd to all.

The Song

Book II.   Canto XII.   75

So passeth, in the passing of a day
Of mortal life, the leaf, the bud, the flower,
Ne more doth flourish after first decay,
That erst was sought to deck both bed and bower
Of many a lady and many a paramour:
Gather therefore the Rose, whilst yet is prime,
For soon comes Age that will her pride deflower:
Gather the rose of love whilst yet is time,
Whilst loving thou mayst lovèd be with equall crime.

Book III.   Canto XI.   28

Like a discoloured snake, whose hidden snares
Through the green grass his long bright burnisht back declares.

Be Bold

Book III.   Canto XI.   50

And as she backward cast her busy eye,
To search each secret of that goodly stead,
Over the door, thus written she did spy
BE BOLD: she oft and oft it over-read,
Yet could not find what sense it figurèd:
But whatso were therein, or writ or meant,
She was no whit thereby discouragèd
From prosecuting of her first intent,
But forward, with bold steps, into the next room went.

Much fairer than the former was that room,
And richlier by many parts arrayed:
For not with arras made in painful loom,
But with pure gold it all was overlaid,
Wrought with wild Anticks, which their follies played,
In the rich metal, as they living were:
A thousand monstrous forms therein were made,
Such as False Love doth oft upon him wear,
For love in thousand monstrous forms doth oft appear.

And all about, the glistering walls were hong
Withwar like spoils, and with victorious preys
Of mighty Conquerors and Captains strong,
Which were, whilome, captivèd in their days
To cruel Love, and wrought their own decays:
Their swords and spears were broke and hawberks rent,
And their proud garlands of triumphant bays
Trodden in dust with fury insolent,
To shew the victors' might and merciless intent.

The warlike Maid, beholding earnestly
The goodly ordinance of this rich place,
Did greatly wonder, ne could satisfy
Her greedy eyes with gazing a long space;
But more she marvelled that no footing's trace
Nor wight appeared, but wasteful emptiness,
And solemn silence over all that place:
Strange thing, it seemed, that none was to possess
So rich purveyance, ne them keep with carefulness.

And, as she lookt about, she did behold,
How, over that same door, was likewise writ,
BE BOLD: BE BOLD: and everywhere, BE BOLD,
That much she mused, yet could not construe it
By any riddling skill or common wit.
At last, she spied, at that room's upper end,
Another iron door, on which was writ,
BE NOT TOO BOLD: whereto, though she did bend
Her earnest mind, yet wist not what it might intend.

Thus she there waited until eventide,
Yet living creature none she saw appear:
And now sad shadows gan the world to hide,
From mortal view, and wrap in darkness drear:
Yet nould she doff her weary arms, for fear
Of secret danger, ne let sleep oppress
Her heavy eyes with Nature's burden dear,
But drew herself aside in sikkerness
And her well-pointed weapons did about her dress.

Sir Philip Sidney

SONNET XXXI

With how sad steps, O Moon, thou climb'st the skies!
How silently! and with how wan a face!

SONNET XXXIX

Come Sleep! O Sleep! the certain knot of peace!
The baiting place of wit! the balm of woe!
The poor man's wealth! the prisoner's release!
Th'indifferent judge between the high and low!
  With shield of proof, shield me from out the prease
Of those fierce darts, DESPAIR at me doth throw!
O make in me those civil wars to cease!
I will good tribute pay if thou do so.
  Take thou of me, smooth pillows, sweetest bed,
A chamber deaf to noise and blind to light,
A rosy garland, and a weary head:
  And if these things as being thine by right,
Move not thy heavy Grace, thou shalt in me
Livelier than elsewhere, STELLA'S image see.

SONNET LXXIII

Love still a boy, and oft a wanton is;
Schooled only by his mother's tender eye.
What wonder then, if he his lesson miss;
When for so soft a rod, dear play he try?
  And yet my Star, because a sugared kiss
In sport I suckt, while she asleep did lie:

Doth lower; nay, chide; nay, threat for only this!
   "Sweet! It was saucy LOVE, not humble I."
   But no 'scuse serves: she makes her wrath appear
In Beauty's throne. See now! who dares come near
Those scarlet judges, threat'ning bloody pain?
   O heavenly fool! Thy most kiss-worthy face,
Anger invests with such a lovely grace;
That ANGER'S self! I needs must kiss again!

From *SONNET LXXIV*

I never drank of Aganippe's well;
Nor never did in shade of Tempe sit:

William Shakespeare

LOVE'S LABOUR'S LOST

Act V

Scene II

ARMADO:

  This side is Hiems, Winter, this Ver, the Spring: the one maintained by the owl, the other by the cuckoo.—Ver, begin.

The Song

SPRING

>   When daisies pied and violets blue
>   And lady-smocks all silver-white
>   And cuckoo-buds of yellow hue
>   Do paint the meadows with delight,
>   The cuckoo then, on every tree,
>   Mocks married men; for thus sings he,
>   Cuckoo;
>   Cuckoo, cuckoo: Oh word of fear,
>   Unpleasing to a married ear!
>
>   When shepherds pipe on oaten straws,
>   And merry larks are ploughmen's clocks,
>   When turtles tread, and rooks, and daws,
>   And maidens bleach their summer smocks,
>   The cuckoo then, on every tree,
>   Mocks married men; for thus sings he,
>   Cuckoo;
>   Cuckoo, cuckoo: Oh word of fear,
>   Unpleasing to a married ear!

WINTER

When icicles hang by the wall,
And Dick the shepherd blows his nail,
And Tom bears logs into the hall,
And milk comes frozen home in pail,
When blood is nipp'd and ways be foul,
Then nightly sings the staring owl,
Tu-whit, tu-who,
A merry note,
While greasy Joan doth keel the pot.

When all aloud the wind doth blow,
And coughing drowns the parson's saw,
And birds sit brooding in the snow,
And Marian's nose looks red and raw,
When roasted crabs hiss in the bowl,
Then nightly sings the staring owl,
Tu-whit, tu-who,
A merry note,
While greasy Joan doth keel the pot.

ARMADO:

The words of Mercury are harsh after the songs of Apollo.
You that way,—we this way.   (*Exeunt.*)

Passages from *SONNETS*

XXI

I will not praise, that purpose not to sell.

XLIV

But, ah! thought kills me that I am not thought,
To leap large lengths of miles when thou art gone.

LIII

Wʜᴀᴛ is your substance, whereof are you made,
That millions of strange shadows on you tend?

LX

Time doth transfix the flourish set on youth,
And delves the parallels in beauty's brow,
Feeds on the rarities of nature's truth,
And nothing stands but for his scythe to mow:
 And yet to times in hope my verse shall stand,
 Praising thy worth, despite his cruel hand.

LXVI

Tɪʀᴇᴅ with all these, for restful death I cry,
As, to behold desert a beggar born,
And needy nothing trimm'd in jollity,
And purest faith unhappily forsworn,
And gilded honour shamefully misplac'd,
And maiden virtue rudely strumpeted,
And right perfection wrongfully disgrac'd,
And strength by limping sway disabled,
And art made tongue-tied by authority,
And folly, doctor-like, controlling skill,
And simple truth miscall'd simplicity,
And captive good attending captain ill:
 Tired with all these, from these would I be gone,
 Save that, to die, I leave my love alone.

LXXIV

My spirit is thine, the better part of me.

XC

If thou wilt leave me, do not leave me last,
When other petty griefs have done their spite,
But in the onset come: so shall I taste
At first the very worst of fortune's might.

XCIV

The summer's flower is to the summer sweet,
Though to itself it only live and die.

CIV

Ah, yet doth beauty, like a dial-hand,
Steal from his figure, and no pace perceiv'd.

CIX

For nothing this wide universe I call,
Save thou, my rose; in it thou art my all.

CXX

Oh! that our night of woe might have remember'd
My deepest sense, how hard true sorrow hits.

CXXVI

O THOU, my lovely boy, who in thy power
Dost hold Time's fickle glass, his fickle hour:
Who hast by waning grown, and therein show'st
Thy lovers withering, as thy sweet self grow'st;
If Nature, sovereign mistress over wrack,

As thou goest onwards, still will pluck thee back,
She keeps thee to this purpose, that her skill
May time disgrace, and wretched minutes kill.
Yet fear her, O thou minion of her pleasure!
She may detain, but not still keep, her treasure:
Her audit, though delay'd, answer'd must be,
And her quietus is to render thee.

CXLVI

Poor soul, the centre of my sinful earth,
Purse to these rebel powers that thee array,
Why dost thou pine within and suffer dearth,
Painting thy outward walls so costly gay?
Why so large cost, having so short a lease,
Dost thou upon thy fading mansion spend?
Shall worms, inheritors of this excess,
Eat up thy charge? is this thy body's end?
Then, soul, live thou upon thy servant's loss,
And let that pine to aggravate thy store;
Buy terms divine in selling hours of dross;
Within be fed, without be rich no more:
    So shalt thou feed on Death, that feeds on men,
    And Death once dead, there's no more dying then.

Note:

In the first known edition of the *Sonnets*, issued, as a quarto, in London in 1609, as "Never before Imprinted," this Sonnet's second line is printed:—

"My sinfull earth these rebell powres that thee array."

The two syllables, with which Shakespeare began the line, are gone. No manuscript has come down to us, or has yet been discovered, to give a clue to what Shakespeare wrote. Some unknown printer, not paying much attention, repeated the last three words of the opening line, and Mr. T. T. or whoever it may have been, who saw the book through the press, either did not notice or did not care.

A great many suggestions have been made for the missing words. Some of these are:—

Bled by.	Feeding.	Coin to.
Crushed by.		Slave to.
Fed by.		
Fooled by.		Spoil to.
Ruled by.		
Spent by.		
Spoiled by.		
Starved by.		
Sucked by.		

Others can be proposed by those who dislike these readings, and have some feeling for the Shakespearean Sonnet manners. It is most unlikely that Shakespeare's version will now come from the night of time to confound them.

Those who read or speak the Sonnet aloud often change the reading, to suit the mood of the moment.

When Mr. T. T. issued the book, Shakespeare was alive and certainly sometimes in London. It is possible that Mr. T. T. may have hesitated to consult him about the reading lest the publication of the book should have been stayed. We cannot suppose that Shakespeare had any hand in the arrangement of the volume: he may not have known that it was in the press.

POEMS

Line from *THE RAPE OF LUCRECE*

Night-wandering weasels shriek to see him there.

(Shakespeare seen in the tapestry.)

LUCRECE

For much imaginary work was there;
Conceit deceitful, so compact, so kind,
That for Achilles' image stood his spear
Grip'd in an armed hand; himself, behind,
Was left unseen, save to the eye of mind.

THE PHŒNIX AND TURTLE

Let the bird of loudest lay,
On the sole Arabian tree,
Herald sad and trumpet be,
To whose sound chaste wings obey.

But thou shrieking harbinger,
Foul precurrer of the fiend,
Augur of the fever's end,
To this troop come thou not near!

From this session interdict
Every fowl of tyrant wing,
Save the eagle, feather'd king:
Keep the obsequy so strict.

Let the priest in surplice white,
That defunctive music can,
Be the death-divining swan,
Lest the requiem lack his right.

And thou treble-dated crow,
That thy sable gender makest
With the breath thou giv'st and takest,
'Mongst our mourners shalt thou go.

Here the anthem doth commence:
Love and constancy is dead;
Phœnix and the turtle fled
In a mutual flame from hence.

So they lov'd, as love in twain
Had the essence but in one;
Two distincts, division none:
Number there in love was slain.

Hearts remote, yet not asunder;
Distance, and no space was seen
'Twixt the turtle and his queen:
But in them it were a wonder.

So between them love did shine,
That the turtle saw his right
Flaming in the phœnix' sight;
Either was the other's mine.

Property was thus appall'd,
That the self was not the same;
Single nature's double name
Neither two nor one was call'd.

Reason, in itself confounded,
Saw division grow together,
To themselves yet either neither,
Simple were so well compounded;

That it cried, How true a twain
Seemeth this concordant one!
Love hath reason, reason none,
If what parts can so remain.

Whereupon it made this threne
To the phœnix and the dove,
Co-supremes and stars of love,
As chorus to their tragic scene.

Threnos

Beauty, truth, and rarity,
Grace in all simplicity,
Here enclos'd in cinders lie.

Death is now the phœnix' nest;
And the turtle's loyal breast
To eternity doth rest,

Leaving no posterity:
'Twas not their infirmity,
It was married chastity.

Truth may seem, but cannot be;
Beauty brag, but 'tis not she;
Truth and beauty buried be.

To this urn let those repair
That are either true or fair;
For these dead birds sigh a prayer.

HENRY THE FOURTH. PT. II

Act II

SCENE IV

(A room in the Tavern. *Enter* HOSTESS and DOLL TEARSHEET.)

HOSTESS:

I'faith, sweetheart, methinks now you are in an excellent good temporality: your pulsidge beats as extraordinary as heart would desire; and your colour, I warrant you, is as red as any rose, in good truth, la! But, i'faith, you have drunk too much canaries; and that's a marvellous searching wine, and it perfumes the blood ere one can say 'What's this?' How do you now?

DOLL:

Better than I was: hem!

HOSTESS:

Why, that's well said; a good heart's worth gold. Lo, here comes Sir John.

(*Enter* FALSTAFF.)

FALSTAFF (*Singing*):
  'When Arthur first in court'—
  Empty the jordan.
  (*Singing*.)   'And was a worthy king.'—How now,
  Mistress Doll!

HOSTESS:
  Sick of a calm; yea, good faith.

FALSTAFF:
  So is all her sect; an they be once in a calm, they are sick.

DOLL:
  You muddy rascal, is that all the comfort you give me?

FALSTAFF:
  You make fat rascals, Mistress Doll.

DOLL:
  I make them! gluttony and diseases make them; I make them not.

FALSTAFF:
  If the cook help to make the gluttony, you help to make the diseases, Doll: we catch of you, Doll, we catch of you; grant that, my poor virtue, grant that.

DOLL:
  Yea, joy, our chains and our jewels.

FALSTAFF:
  'Your brooches, pearls and ouches:' for to serve bravely is to come halting off, you know; to come off the breach with his pike bent bravely, and to surgery bravely; to venture upon the charged chambers bravely. . . .

DOLL:
  Hang yourself, you muddy conger, hang yourself!

HOSTESS:

By my troth, this is the old fashion; you two never meet but you fall to some discord; you are both, i'good truth, as rheumatic as two dry toasts; you cannot one bear with another's confirmities. What the good-year! one must bear, and that must be you: you are the weaker vessel, as they say, the emptier vessel. . . .

DOLL:

Come, I'll be friends with thee, Jack: thou art going to the wars; and whether I shall ever see thee again or no, there is nobody cares.

(*Enter* FIRST DRAWER.)

FIRST DRAWER:

Sir, Ancient Pistol's below, and would speak with you.

DOLL:

Hang him, swaggering rascal! let him not come hither: it is the foul-mouthedst rogue in England.

HOSTESS:

If he swagger, let him not come here: no, by my faith; I must live among my neighbours; I'll no swaggerers; I am in good name and fame with the very best.—Shut the door; there comes no swaggerers here: I have not lived all this while, to have swaggering now: shut the door, I pray you.

FALSTAFF:

Dost thou hear, hostess?

HOSTESS:

Pray ye, pacify yourself, Sir John: there comes no swaggerers here.

FALSTAFF:

Dost thou hear? it is mine ancient.

HOSTESS:

Tilly-fally, Sir John, ne'er tell me: your ancient swaggerer comes not in my doors. I was before Master Tisick, the deputy, t'other day; and, as he said to me, 'twas no longer ago than Wednesday last, 'I'good faith, neighbour Quickly,' says he; Master Dumbe, our minister, was by then; 'neighbour Quickly,' says he, 'receive those that are civil; for,' said he, 'you are in an ill name:' now a' said so, I can tell whereupon; 'for,' says he, 'you are an honest woman, and well thought on; therefore take heed what guests you receive; receive,' says he, 'no swaggering companions.' There comes none here: you would bless you to hear what he said: no, I'll no swaggerers.

FALSTAFF:

He's no swaggerer, hostess: a tame cheater, you may stroke him as gently as a puppy greyhound; he'll not swagger with a Barbary hen, if her feathers turn back in any show of resistance. —Call him up, drawer.

(*Exit* FIRST DRAWER.)

HOSTESS:

Cheater, call you him? I will bar no honest man my house, nor no cheater: but I do not love swaggering, by my troth; I am the worse, when one says swagger:—feel, masters, how I shake; look you, I warrant you.

DOLL:

So you do, hostess.

HOSTESS:

Do I? yea, in very truth, do I, an 'twere an aspen leaf: I cannot abide swaggerers.

(Enter Pistol, Bardolph, *and* Page.*)*

PISTOL:

God save you, Sir John!

FALSTAFF:

Welcome, Ancient Pistol. Here, Pistol, I charge you with a cup of sack: do you discharge upon mine hostess.

PISTOL:

I will discharge upon her, Sir John, with two bullets.

FALSTAFF:

She is pistol-proof, sir; you shall hardly offend her.

HOSTESS:

Come, I'll drink no proofs nor no bullets: I'll drink no more than will do me good, for no man's pleasure, I.

PISTOL:

Then to you, Mistress Dorothy; I will charge you.

DOLL:

Charge me! I scorn you, scurvy companion. What! you poor, base, rascally, cheating, lack-linen mate! Away, you mouldy rogue, away! I am meat for your master.

PISTOL:

I know you, Mistress Dorothy.

DOLL:

Away, you cut-purse rascal: you filthy bung, away! by this wine, I'll thrust my knife in your mouldy chaps, an you play the saucy cuttle with me. Away, you bottle-ale rascal! you basket-hilt stale juggler, you! Since when, I pray you, sir? God's light, with two points on your shoulder? much!

PISTOL:

God let me not live, but I will murder your ruff for this.

FALSTAFF:

No more, Pistol; I would not have you go off here: discharge yourself of our company, Pistol.

HOSTESS:

No, good Captain Pistol; not here, sweet captain.

DOLL:

'Captain'! thou abominable damned cheater, art thou not ashamed to be called captain? An captains were of my mind, they would truncheon you out, for taking their names upon you before you have earned them. You a captain! you slave, for what? for tearing a poor whore's ruff in a bawdy-house?—He a captain! hang him, rogue! he lives upon mouldy stewed prunes and dried cakes. A captain! God's light, these villains will make the word as odious as the word 'occupy;' which was an excellent good word before it was ill sorted: therefore captains had need look to't.

FALSTAFF:

Hark thee hither, Mistress Doll.

BARDOLPH:

Pray thee, go down, good ancient.

PISTOL:

Not I: I tell thee what, Corporal Bardolph, I could tear her: I'll be revenged of her.

PAGE:

Pray thee, go down.

PISTOL:

I'll see thee damnèd first; to Pluto's damnèd lake, by this hand, to the infernal deep, with Erebus and tortures vile also.—Hold hook and line, say I. Down, down, dogs! down, faitors! Have we not Hiren here?

HOSTESS:

Good Captain Peesel, be quiet: 'tis very late, i'faith: I beseek you now, aggravate your choler.

PISTOL:

These be good humours, indeed! Shall pack-horses,
And hollow pamper'd jades of Asia,
Which cannot go but thirty mile a day,
Compare with Cæsars, and with Cannibals,
And Trojan Greeks? nay, rather damn them with
King Cerberus; and let the welkin roar.
Shall we fall foul for toys?

HOSTESS:

By my troth, Captain, these are very bitter words.

BARDOLPH:

Be gone, good ancient: this will grow to a brawl anon.

PISTOL:

Die men like dogs! give crowns like pins! Have we not Hiren here?

HOSTESS:

O' my word, captain, there's none such here. What the good-year! do you think I would deny her? For God's sake, be quiet.

PISTOL:

Then feed, and be fat, my fair Calipolis.
Come, give's some sack.
'Si fortuna me tormenta, sperato me contenta.'
Fear we broadsides? no, let the fiend give fire:
Give me some sack:—and, sweetheart, lie thou there.
(*Laying down his sword.*)
Come we to full points here; and are etceteras nothing?

FALSTAFF:

Pistol, I would be quiet.

PISTOL:

Sweet knight, I kiss thy neaf: what! we have seen the seven stars.

DOLL:

For God's sake, thrust him down stairs: I cannot endure such a fustian rascal.

PISTOL:

'Thrust him down stairs!' know we not Galloway nags?

FALSTAFF:

Quoit him down, Bardolph, like a shove-groat shilling: nay, an a'do nothing but speak nothing, a'shall be nothing here.

BARDOLPH:

Come, get you down stairs.

PISTOL:

What! shall we have incision? shall we imbrue?
                    (*Snatching up his sword.*)
Then death rock me asleep,
Abridge my doleful days!
Why, then, let grievous, ghastly, gaping wounds
Untwine the Sisters Three!—
Come, Atropos, I say!

HOSTESS:

Here's goodly stuff toward!

FALSTAFF:

Give me my rapier, boy.

DOLL:

I pray thee, Jack, I pray thee, do not draw.

FALSTAFF:

Get you down stairs.
                    (*Drawing, and making for* PISTOL.)

HOSTESS:

Here's a goodly tumult! I'll forswear keeping house, afore I'll be in these tirrits and frights. So; murder, I warrant now.—Alas, alas! put up your naked weapons, put up your naked weapons.

(*Exeunt* PISTOL and BARDOLPH.)

DOLL:

I pray thee, Jack, be quiet; the rascal's gone. Ah, you whoreson little valiant villain you!

HOSTESS:

Are you not hurt i'the groin? methought a'made a shrewd thrust at your belly.

(*Re-enter* BARDOLPH.)

FALSTAFF:

Have you turned him out o'doors?

BARDOLPH:

Yes, sir. The rascal's drunk: you have hurt him, sir, i' the shoulder.

FALSTAFF:

A rascal! to brave me!

DOLL:

Ah, you sweet little rogue, you! Alas, poor ape, how thou sweatest! come, let me wipe thy face; come on, you whoreson chops: ah, rogue! i'faith, I love thee: thou art as valorous as Hector of Troy, worth five of Agamemnon, and ten times better than the Nine Worthies: ah, villain!

FALSTAFF:

A rascally slave! I will toss the rogue in a blanket.

DOLL:

Do, an thou darest for thy heart: an thou dost, I'll canvass thee between a pair of sheets.

(*Enter* MUSICIANS.)

PAGE:
The music is come, sir.

FALSTAFF:
Let them play.—Play, sirs.—Sit on my knee, Doll. A rascal bragging slave! the rogue fled from me like quicksilver.

DOLL:
I'faith, and thou followedst him like a church. Thou whoreson little tidy Bartholomew boar-pig, when wilt thou leave fighting o' days and foining o' nights, and begin to patch up thine old body for heaven?

FALSTAFF:
Peace, good Doll! do not speak like a death's-head; do not bid me remember mine end.

Act V

SCENE III

(Gloucestershire: SHALLOW's orchard. *Enter* FALSTAFF, SHALLOW, SILENCE, DAVY, BARDOLPH, *and the* PAGE.)

SHALLOW:
Nay, you shall see mine orchard, where, in an arbour, we will eat a last year's pippin of my own graffing, with a dish of cara-ways, and so forth—come, cousin Silence—and then to bed.

FALSTAFF:
'Fore God, you have here a goodly dwelling and a rich.

SHALLOW:
Barren, barren, barren; beggars all, beggars all, Sir John: marry, good air.—Spread, Davy; spread, Davy; well said, Davy.

FALSTAFF:

This Davy serves you for good uses; he is your serving-man and your husband.

SHALLOW:

A good varlet, a good varlet, a very good varlet, Sir John: by the mass, I have drunk too much sack at supper: a good varlet. Now sit down, now sit down—come, cousin.

SILENCE:

Ah, sirrah! quoth-a, we shall
 (*Singing*.) 'Do nothing but eat, and make good cheer,
And praise God for the merry year;
When flesh is cheap and females dear,
And lusty lads roam here and there
So merrily,
And ever among so merrily.'

FALSTAFF:

There's a merry heart!—Good Master Silence, I'll give you a health for that anon.

SHALLOW:

Give Master Bardolph some wine, Davy.

DAVY:

Sweet sir, sit; I'll be with you anon; most sweet sir, sit.—Master page, good master page, sit.—Proface! What you want in meat, we'll have in drink: but you must bear; the heart's all. (*Exit*.)

SHALLOW:

Be merry, Master Bardolph; and, my little soldier there, be merry.

SILENCE (*Singing*):

   'Be merry, be merry, my wife has all;
   For women are shrews, both short and tall:
   'Tis merry in hall when beards wag all,
   And welcome merry Shrove-tide.
   Be merry, be merry.'

FALSTAFF:
I did not think Master Silence had been a man of this mettle.

SILENCE:
Who, I? I have been merry twice and once ere now.
        (*Re-enter* DAVY.)

DAVY (*To* BARDOLPH):
There's a dish of leather-coats for you.

SHALLOW:
Davy!

DAVY:
Your worship! I'll be with you straight. (*To* BARDOLPH.)
A cup of wine, sir?

SILENCE (*Singing*):
            'A cup of wine that's brisk and fine,
            And drink unto the leman mine;
            And a merry heart lives long-a.'

FALSTAFF:
Well said, Master Silence.

SILENCE:
An we shall be merry, now comes in the sweet o' the night.

FALSTAFF:
Health and long life to you, Master Silence.

SILENCE (*Singing*):
            'Fill the cup, and let it come;
            I'll pledge you a mile to the bottom.'

SHALLOW:
Honest Bardolph, welcome: if thou wantest any thing, and wilt
not call, beshrew thy heart. (*To the* PAGE.) Welcome, my little

tiny thief, and welcome indeed too.—I'll drink to Master Bardolph, and to all the cavaleros about London.

DAVY:
  I hope to see London once ere I die.

BARDOLPH:
  An I might see you there, Davy . . .

SHALLOW:
  By the mass, you'll crack a quart together, ha! will you not, Master Bardolph?

BARDOLPH:
  Yes, sir, in a pottle-pot.

SHALLOW:
  By God's liggens, I thank thee: the knave will stick by thee, I can assure thee that. A' will not out: he is true bred.

BARDOLPH:
  And I'll stick by him, sir.

SHALLOW:
  Why, there spoke a king. Lack nothing: be merry. (*Knocking within.*) Look who's at door there, ho! who knocks?
            (*Exit* DAVY.)

FALSTAFF:
  Why, now you have done me right.
            (*To* SILENCE, *seeing him take off a bumper.*)

SILENCE (*Singing*):
            'Do me right.
            And dub me knight,
            Samingo.'
  Is't not so?

FALSTAFF:
  'Tis so.

SILENCE:
Is't so? Why then, say an old man can do somewhat.
> (*Re-enter* DAVY.)

DAVY:
An 't please your worship, there's one Pistol come from the court with news.

FALSTAFF:
From the court! let him come in.
> (*Enter* PISTOL.)
How now, Pistol!

PISTOL:
Sir John, God save you!

FALSTAFF:
What wind blew you hither, Pistol?

PISTOL:
Not the ill wind which blows no man to good. Sweet knight, thou art now one of the greatest men in this realm.

SILENCE:
By'r lady, I think a'be, but goodman Puff of Barson.

PISTOL:
> 'Puff'!
> Puff in thy teeth, most recreant coward base!—
> Sir John, I am thy Pistol and thy friend,
> And helter-skelter have I rode to thee,
> And tidings do I bring and lucky joys
> And golden times and happy news of price.

FALSTAFF:
I pray thee now, deliver them like a man of this world.

PISTOL:
> A foutre for the world and wordlings base!
> I speak of Africa and golden joys.

FALSTAFF:

>O base Assyrian knight, what is thy news?
>Let King Cophetua know the truth thereof.

SILENCE (*Singing*):
>'And Robin Hood, Scarlet, and John.'

PISTOL:

>Shall dunghill curs confront the Helicons?
>And shall good news be baffled?
>Then, Pistol, lay thy head in Furies' lap.

SHALLOW:
>Honest gentleman, I know not your breeding.

PISTOL:
>Why then, lament therefore.

SHALLOW:
>Give me pardon, sir: if, sir, you come with news from the court, I take it there's but two ways, either to utter them, or to conceal them. I am, sir, under the king, in some authority.

PISTOL:
>Under which king, Besonian? speak, or die.

SHALLOW:
>Under King Harry.

PISTOL:

>Harry the fourth? or fifth?

SHALLOW:
>Harry the fourth.

PISTOL:

>A foutre for thine office!—

Sir John, thy tender lambkin now is king;
Harry the fifth's the man. I speak the truth:
When Pistol lies, do this; and fig me, like
The bragging Spaniard.

FALSTAFF:

What, is the old king dead?

PISTOL:

As nail in door: the things I speak are just.

FALSTAFF:

Away, Bardolph! saddle my horse.—Master Robert Shallow, choose what office thou wilt in the land, 'tis thine.—Pistol, I will double-charge thee with dignities.

BARDOLPH:

O joyful day!
I would not take a knighthood for my fortune.

PISTOL:

What! I do bring good news.

FALSTAFF:

Carry Master Silence to bed.—Master Shallow, my Lord Shallow—be what thou wilt; I am fortune's steward; get on thy boots: we'll ride all night.—O sweet Pistol!—Away, Bardolph! (*Exit* BARDOLPH.) Come, Pistol, utter more to me; and withal devise something to do thyself good.—Boot, boot, Master Shallow! I know the young king is sick for me. Let us take any man's horses; the laws of England are at my commandment. Blessed are they that have been my friends; and woe to my lord chief justice!

PISTOL:

Let vultures vile seize on his lungs also!
'Where is the life that late I led?' say they:
Why, here it is; welcome these pleasant days!
(*Exeunt.*)

HENRY V

Act II

Scene III

(London. Before a tavern. *Enter* Pistol, Hostess, Nym, Bardolph, and Boy.)

Hostess:
Prithee, honey-sweet husband, let me bring thee to Staines.

Pistol:
No; for my manly heart doth yearn.—
Bardolph, be blithe:—Nym, rouse thy vaunting veins:—
Boy, bristle thy courage up: for Falstaff he is dead,
And we must yearn therefore.

Bardolph:
Would I were with him, wheresome'er he is, either in heaven or in hell!

Hostess:
Nay, sure, he's not in hell: he's in Arthur's bosom, if ever man went to Arthur's bosom. A' made a finer end and went away an it had been any christom child; a' parted even just between twelve and one, even at the turning o' the tide: for after I saw him fumble with the sheets, and play with flowers, and smile upon his fingers' ends, I knew there was but one way; for his nose was as sharp as a pen, and a' babbled of green fields. 'How now, Sir John!' quoth I: 'what, man! be o' good cheer.' So a' cried out, 'God, God, God!' three or four times. So I, to comfort him, bid him a' should not think of God; I hoped there was no need to trouble himself with any such thoughts yet. So a' bad me lay more clothes on his feet: I put my hand into the bed and felt them, and they were as cold as any stone; then I felt to his knees, and they were as cold as any stone, and so upward and upward, and all was as cold as any stone.

Nym:
They say he cried out of sack.

Hostess:
Ay, that a' did.

Bardolph:
And of women.

Hostess:
Nay, that a' did not.

Boy:
Yes, that a' did; and said they were devils incarnate.

Hostess:
A' could never abide carnation; 'twas a colour he never liked.

Boy:
A' said once, the devil would have him about women.

Hostess:
A' did in some sort, indeed, handle women; but then he was rheumatic, and talked of the whore of Babylon.

Boy:
Do you not remember, a' saw a flea stick upon Bardolph's nose, and a' said it was a black soul burning in hell-fire?

Bardolph:
Well, the fuel is gone that maintained that fire: that's all the riches I got in his service.

Nym:
Shall we shog? the king will be gone from Southampton.

Pistol:
Come, let's away.—My love, give me thy lips.
Look to my chattels and my movables:

Let senses rule; the word is 'Pitch and Pay:'
Trust none;
For oaths are straw, men's faiths are wafer-cakes
And hold-fast is the only dog, my duck:
Therefore, Caveto be thy counsellor.
Go, clear thy crystals.—Yoke-fellows in arms,
Let us to France; like horse-leeches, my boys,
To suck, to suck, the very blood to suck!

BOY:
And that's but unwholesome food, they say.

PISTOL:
Touch her soft mouth, and march.

BARDOLPH:
Farewell, hostess.

NYM:
I cannot kiss, that is the humour of it; but, adieu.

PISTOL:
Let housewifery appear: keep close, I thee command.

HOSTESS:
Farewell; adieu. (*Exeunt.*)

TWELFTH NIGHT

Act II

SCENE IV

(The Duke's palace. *Enter* DUKE, VIOLA, CURIO, *and others.*)

DUKE:
Give me some music.—Now, good morrow, friends.—
Now, good Cesario, but that piece of song,
That old and antique song we heard last night:
Methought it did relieve my passion much,

More than light airs and recollected terms
Of these most brisk and giddy-paced times—
Come, but one verse.

CURIO:

He is not here, so please your lordship, that should sing it.

DUKE:

Who was it?

CURIO:

Feste, the jester, my lord; a fool that the lady Olivia's father
took much delight in. He is about the house.

DUKE:

    Seek him out, and play the tune the while.
        (*Exit* CURIO. *Music plays*.)
    Come hither, boy: if ever thou shalt love,
    In the sweet pangs of it remember me;
    For such as I am all true lovers are,
    Unstaid and skittish in all motions else,
    Save in the constant image of the creature
    That is belov'd. How dost thou like this tune?

VIOLA:

    It gives a very echo to the seat
    Where love is thron'd.

DUKE:

        Thou dost speak masterly:
    My life upon 't, young though thou art, thine eye
    Hath stay'd upon some favour that it loves:
    Hath it not, boy?

VIOLA:

    A little, by your favour.

DUKE:

    What kind of woman is 't?

VIOLA:

Of your complexion.

DUKE:

She is not worth thee, then. What years, i' faith?

VIOLA:

About your years, my lord.

DUKE:

Too old, by heaven: let still the woman take
An elder than herself; so wears she to him,
So sways she level in her husband's heart:
For, boy, however we do praise ourselves,
Our fancies are more giddy and unfirm,
More longing, wavering, sooner lost and won,
Than women's are.

VIOLA:

I think it well, my lord.

DUKE:

Then let thy love be younger than thyself,
Or thy affection cannot hold the bent;
For women are as roses, whose fair flower
Being once display'd, doth fall that very hour.

VIOLA:

And so they are: alas, that they are so;
To die, even when they to perfection grow!

(*Re-enter* CURIO and CLOWN.)

DUKE:

O fellow, come, the song we had last night.—
Mark it, Cesario, it is old and plain;
The spinsters and the knitters in the sun
And the free maids that weave their thread with bones
Do use to chant it: it is silly sooth,

And dallies with the innocence of love,
Like the old age.

CLOWN:

Are you ready, sir?

DUKE:

Ay; prithee, sing. (*Music.*) ·

SONG

CLOWN:

Come away, come away, death, ˙
And in sad cypress let me be laid;
Fly away, fly away, breath;
I am slain by a fair cruel maid.
My shroud of white, stuck all with yew,
Oh, prepare it!
My part of death, no one so true
Did share it.

Not a flower, not a flower sweet,
On my black coffin let there be strown;
Not a friend, not a friend greet
My poor corpse, where my bones shall be thrown:
A thousand thousand sighs to save,
Lay me, Oh, where
Sad true lover never find my grace,
To weep there!

DUKE:

There's for thy pains.

CLOWN:

No pains, sir; I take pleasure in singing, sir.

DUKE:

I'll pay thy pleasure then.

CLOWN:

Truly, sir, and pleasure will be paid, one time or another.

DUKE:

Give me now leave to leave thee.

CLOWN:

Now, the melancholy god protect thee; and the tailor make thy doublet of changeable taffeta, for thy mind is a very opal. I would have men of such constancy put to sea, that their business might be every thing and their intent every where; for that 's it that always makes a good voyage of nothing.—Farewell.

(*Exit.*)

DUKE:

  Let all the rest give place.
     (CURIO *and Attendants retire.*)
    Once more, Cesario,
  Get thee to yond same sovereign cruelty:
  Tell her, my love, more noble than the world,
  Prizes not quantity of dirty lands;
  The parts that fortune hath bestow'd upon her,
  Tell her, I hold as giddily as fortune;
  But 'tis that miracle and queen of gems
  That nature pranks her in attracts my soul.

VIOLA:

  But if she cannot love you, sir?

DUKE:

  I cannot be so answer'd.

VIOLA:

     Sooth, but you must.
  Say that some lady, as perhaps there is,
  Hath for your love as great a pang of heart
  As you have for Olivia: you cannot love her;
  You tell her so; must she not then be answer'd?

DUKE:

>There is no woman's sides
Can bide the beating of so strong a passion
As love doth give my heart; no woman's heart
So big, to hold so much; they lack retention.
Alas, their love may be call'd appetite—
No motion of the liver, but the palate—
That suffers surfeit, cloyment and revolt;
But mine is all as hungry as the sea,
And can digest as much: make no compare
Between that love a woman can bear me
And that I owe Olivia.

VIOLA:

>Ay, but I know . . .

DUKE:

What dost thou know?

VIOLA:

>Too well what love women to men may owe:
In faith, they are as true of heart as we.
My father had a daughter lov'd a man,
As it might be, perhaps, were I a woman,
I should your lordship.

DUKE:

>And what's her history?

VIOLA:

>A blank, my lord. She never told her love,
But let concealment, like a worm i' the bud,
Feed on her damask cheek: she pin'd in thought;
And with a green and yellow melancholy
She sat like patience on a monument,
Smiling at grief. Was not this love indeed?
We men may say more, swear more: but indeed

Our shows are more than will: for still we prove
Much in our vows, but little in our love.

Duke:

But died thy sister of her love, my boy?

Viola:

I am all the daughters of my father's house,
And all the brothers too—and yet I know not.—
Sir, shall I to this lady?

Duke:

Ay that's the theme.
To her in haste: give her this jewel: say,
My love can give no place, bide no denay.   (*Exeunt.*)

Act V

Scene i

Clown (*Sings*):

When that I was and a little tiny boy,
With hey, ho, the wind and the rain,
A foolish thing was but a toy,
For the rain it raineth every day.

But when I came to man's estate,
With hey, ho, the wind and the rain,
'Gainst knaves and thieves men shut their gate,
For the rain it raineth every day.

But when I came, alas! to wive,
With hey, ho, the wind and the rain
By swaggering could I never thrive,
For the rain it raineth every day.

> But when I came unto my beds,
> With hey, ho, the wind and the rain,
> With toss-pots still had drunken heads,
> For the rain it raineth every day.
>
> A great while ago the world begun,
> With hey, ho, the wind and the rain,
> But that's all one, our play is done,
> And we'll strive to please you every day.   (*Exit.*)

Note:

One of the old tunes still used on the stage with this song seems like a sailor's hauling-song, with two hauls and recoveries in each refrain. Let us hope that Shakespeare first heard the song sung thus, in a ship in the London River.

TIMON OF ATHENS

Act II

Scene ii

FLAVIUS:
> Ah, when the means are gone that buy this praise,
> The breath is gone whereof this praise is made:
> Fast-won, fast-lost; one cloud of winter showers,
> These flies are couch'd.

TIMON:
> Come, sermon me no further:
> No villainous bounty yet hath pass'd my heart;
> Unwisely, not ignobly, have I given.

Act IV

SCENE III

ALCIBIADES:

>How came the noble Timon to this change?

TIMON:

>As the moon does, by wanting light to give:
>But then renew I could not, like the moon;
>There were no suns to borrow of.

Act V

SCENE I

TIMON:

>If Alcibiades kill my countrymen,
>Let Alcibiades know this of Timon,
>That Timon cares not. But if he sack fair Athens
>Giving our holy virgins to the stain
>Of contumelious, beastly, mad-brain'd war;
>Then let him know, and tell him Timon speaks it,
>In pity of our aged and our youth.
>I cannot choose but tell him, that I care not,
>And let him take 't at worst; for their knives care not,
>While you have throats to answer: for myself,
>There's not a whittle in the unruly camp,
>But I do prize it at my love before
>The reverend'st throat in Athens. So I leave you
>To the protection of the prosperous gods,
>As thieves to keepers.

>Come not to me again: but say to Athens,
>Timon hath made his everlasting mansion

Upon the beached verge of the salt flood;
Who once a day with his embossèd froth
The turbulent surge shall cover: thither come,
And let my grave-stone be your oracle.—

Act V

Scene iv

ALCIBIADES (*Reads*):
    'Here lies a wretched corse,
    Of wretched soul bereft:
    Seek not my name: a plague consume
    You wicked caitiffs left!
    Here lie I. Timon; who, alive,
    All living men did hate:
    Pass by and curse thy fill; but pass
    And stay not here thy gait.'
    These well express in thee thy latter spirits:
    Though thou abhorr'dst in us our human griefs,
    Scorn'dst our brain's flow, and those our droplets which
    From niggard nature fall, yet rich conceit
    Taught thee to make vast Neptune weep for aye
    On thy low grave, on faults forgiven.—Dead
    Is noble Timon: of whose memory
    Hereafter more. Bring me into your city,
    And I will use the olive with my sword,
    Make war breed peace, make peace stint war, make each
    Prescribe to other as each other's leech.—
    Let our drums strike.   (*Exeunt.*)

MACBETH

Act II

Scene i

(Macbeth's Castle.   Banquo, Fleance.
Macbeth, *and a Servant.*)

Banquo:

                   Give me my sword.
Who's there?

Macbeth:

    A friend.

Banquo:

    What, sir, not yet at rest? The king's a-bed:
He hath been in unusual pleasure, and
Sent forth great largess to your officers:
This diamond he greets your wife withal,
By the name of most kind hostess; and shut up
In measureless content.

Macbeth:

               Being unprepar'd,
Our will became the servant to defect,
Which else should free have wrought.

Banquo:

                   All's well.
I dreamt last night of the three weird sisters:
To you they have show'd some truth.

Macbeth:

                  I think not of them:
Yet, when we can entreat an hour to serve,
We would spend it in some words upon that business,
If you would grant the time.

BANQUO:

>> At your kind'st leisure.

MACBETH:

> If you shall cleave to my consent, when 'tis,
> It shall make honour for you.

BANQUO:

>>> So I lose none
> In seeking to augment it, but still keep
> My bosom franchis'd and allegiance clear,
> I shall be counsell'd.

MACBETH:

>> Good repose the while!

BANQUO:

> Thanks, sir: the like to you!
>> (*Exeunt* BANQUO *and* FLEANCE.)

MACBETH:

> Go bid thy mistress, when my drink is ready,
> She strike upon the bell. Get thee to bed.
>> (*Exit Servant.*)
>
> Is this a dagger which I see before me,
> The handle toward my hand?—Come, let me clutch thee.
> I have thee not, and yet I see thee still.
> Art thou not, fatal vision, sensible
> To feeling as to sight? or art thou but
> A dagger of the mind, a false creation,
> Proceeding from the heat-oppressed brain?
> I see thee yet, in form as palpable
> As this which now I draw.
> Thou marshall'st me the way that I was going;
> And such an instrument I was to use.
> Mine eyes are made the fools o' the other senses,
> Or else worth all the rest: I see thee still;
> And on thy blade and dudgeon gouts of blood,

Which was not so before.—There's no such thing:
It is the bloody business which informs
Thus to mine eyes. Now o'er the one half world
Nature seems dead, and wicked dreams abuse
The curtain'd sleep; witchcraft celebrates
Pale Hecate's offerings; and wither'd murder,
Alarum'd by his sentinel, the wolf,
Whose howl's his watch, thus with his stealthy pace,
With Tarquin's ravishing strides, towards his design
Moves like a ghost.—Thou sure and firm-set earth,
Hear not my steps, which way they walk, for fear
Thy very stones prate of my whereabout,
And take the present horror from the time,
Which now suits with it.—Whiles I threat, he lives:
Words to the heat of deeds too cold breath gives.

(*A bell rings.*)

I go, and it is done: the bell invites me.—
Hear it not, Duncan, for it is a knell,
That summons thee to heaven, or to hell.

(*Exit.*)

SCENE II

(The same. *Enter* LADY MACBETH.)

LADY MACBETH:
That which hath made them drunk hath made me bold;
What hath quench'd them hath given me fire. Hark! Peace:
It was the owl that shriek'd, the fatal bellman,
Which gives the stern'st good-night. He is about it:
The doors are open, and the surfeited grooms
Do mock their charge with snores: I have drugg'd their possets,
That death and nature do contend about them,
Whether they live or die.

MACBETH:
Who's there? what, ho?

LADY MACBETH:

> Alack, I am afraid they have awak'd
> And 'tis not done: the attempt and not the deed
> Confounds us. Hark! I laid their daggers ready;
> He could not miss 'em. Had he not resembled
> My father as he slept, I had done 't.
>
> > *(Re-enter MACBETH.)*
> > My husband?

MACBETH:

> I have done the deed. Didst thou not hear a noise?

LADY MACBETH:

> I heard the owl scream and the crickets cry.
> Did not you speak?

MACBETH:

> When?

LADY MACBETH:

> Now.

MACBETH:

> As I descended?

LADY MACBETH:

> Ay.

MACBETH:

> Hark!
> Who lies i' the second chamber?

LADY MACBETH:

> > Donalbain.

MACBETH:

> This is a sorry sight.   *(Looking on his hands.)*

LADY MACBETH:

> A foolish thought, to say a sorry sight.

MACBETH:

There's one did laugh in 's sleep, and one cried 'Murder!'
That they did wake each other: I stood and heard them:
But they did say their prayers, and address'd them
Again to sleep.

LADY MACBETH:

There are two lodg'd together.

MACBETH:

One cried 'God bless us!' and 'Amen' the other,
As they had seen me with these hangman's hands:
Listening their fear, I could not say 'Amen,'
When they did say 'God bless us!'

LADY MACBETH:

Consider it not so deeply.

MACBETH:

But wherefore could not I pronounce 'Amen'?
I had most need of blessing, and 'Amen'
Stuck in my throat.

LADY MACBETH:

These deeds must not be thought
After these ways; so, it will make us mad.

MACBETH:

Methought I heard a voice cry 'Sleep no more!
Macbeth does murder sleep'—the innocent sleep,
Sleep that knits up the ravell'd sleave of care,
The death of each day's life, sore labour's bath,
Balm of hurt minds, great nature's second course,
Chief nourisher in life's feast,—

LADY MACBETH:

What do you mean?

MACBETH:

> Still it cried 'Sleep no more!' to all the house:
> 'Glamis hath murder'd sleep, and therefore Cawdor
> Shall sleep no more: Macbeth shall sleep no more.'

LADY MACBETH:

> Who was it that thus cried? Why worthy thane,
> You do unbend your noble strength, to think
> So brainsickly of things. Go get some water,
> And wash this filthy witness from your hand.
> Why did you bring these daggers from the place?
> They must lie there: go carry them, and smear
> The sleepy grooms with blood.

MACBETH:

> I'll go no more:
> I am afraid to think what I have done;
> Look on 't again I dare not.

LADY MACBETH:

> Infirm of purpose!
> Give me the daggers: the sleeping and the dead
> Are but as pictures: 'tis the eye of childhood
> That fears a painted devil. If he do bleed,
> I'll gild the faces of the grooms withal,
> For it must seem their guilt.
>
> (*Exit. Knocking within.*)

MACBETH:

> Whence is that knocking?
> How is 't with me, when every noise appals me?
> What hands are here? ha! they pluck out mine eyes!
> Will all great Neptune's ocean wash this blood
> Clean from my hand? No; this my hand will rather
> The multitudinous seas incarnadine,
> Making the green one red.
>
> (*Re-enter* LADY MACBETH.)

LADY MACBETH:

>My hands are of your colour, but I shame
>To wear a heart so white.   (*Knocking within.*)
>   I hear a knocking
>At the south entry: retire we to our chamber:
>A little water clears us of this deed:
>How easy is it then! Your constancy
>Hath left you unattended.   (*Knocking within.*)
>   Hark! more knocking:
>Get on your nightgown, lest occasion call us
>And show us to be watchers: be not lost
>So poorly in your thoughts.

MACBETH:

>To know my deed,   (*Knocking within.*)
>   'twere best not know myself.—
>Wake Duncan with thy knocking! I would thou couldst!
>   (*Exeunt.*)

Act III

SCENE IV

(The Banquet Scene.)

MACBETH:

>Blood hath been shed ere now, i' the olden time,
>Ere humane statute purg'd the gentle weal;
>Ay, and since too, murders have been perform'd
>Too terrible for the ear: the time has been,
>That, when the brains were out, the man would die,
>And there an end; but now they rise again,
>With twenty mortal murders on their crowns,
>And push us from our stools: this is more strange
>Than such a murder is.

Act III

(The end of the Banquet Scene.)

MACBETH:

    It will have blood, they say: blood will have blood:
    Stones have been known to move, and trees to speak;
    Augures, and understood relations, have
    By maggot-pies and choughs and rooks brought forth
    The secret'st man of blood. What is the night?

LADY MACBETH:

    Almost at odds with morning, which is which.

MACBETH:

    How say'st thou, that Macduff denies his person
    At our great bidding?

LADY MACBETH:

          Did you send to him, sir?

MACBETH:

    I hear it by the way, but I will send:
    There's not a one of them but in his house
    I keep a servant fee'd. I will to-morrow,
    And betimes I will, to the weird sisters:
    More shall they speak, for now I am bent to know,
    By the worst means, the worst. For mine own good
    All causes shall give way: I am in blood
    Stepp'd in so far that, should I wade no more,
    Returning were as tedious as go o'er:
    Strange things I have in head that will to hand,
    Which must be acted ere they may be scann'd.

Act IV

SCENE 1

(The three Witches at their cauldron.)

FIRST WITCH:
> Thrice the brinded cat hath mew'd.

SECOND WITCH:
> Thrice and once the hedge-pig whin'd.

THIRD WITCH:
> Harpier cries ' 'Tis time, 'tis time.'

FIRST WITCH:
> Round about the cauldron go:
> In the poison'd entrails throw.
> Toad, that under cold stone
> Days and nights has thirty one
> Swelter'd venom sleeping got,
> Boil thou first i' the charmed pot.

ALL:
> Double, double toil and trouble;
> Fire burn, and cauldron bubble.

SECOND WITCH:
> Fillet of a fenny snake,
> In the cauldron boil and bake;
> Eye of newt, and toe of frog,
> Wool of bat, and tongue of dog,
> Adder's fork, and blind-worm's sting,
> Lizard's leg, and howlet's wing,
> For a charm of powerful trouble,
> Like a hell-broth, boil and bubble.

ALL:

    Double, double toil and trouble:—
    Fire burn, and cauldron bubble.

THIRD WITCH:

    Scale of dragon, tooth of wolf,
    Witches' mummy, maw and gulf
    Of the ravin'd salt-sea shark,
    Root of hemlock digg'd i' the dark,
    Liver of blaspheming Jew,
    Gall of goat, and slips of yew
    Sliver'd in the moon's eclipse,
    Nose of Turk, and Tartar's lips,
    Finger of birth-strangled babe
    Ditch-deliver'd by a drab,
    Make the gruel thick and slab:
    Add thereto a tiger's chaudron,
    For the ingredients of our cauldron.

ALL:

    Double, double toil and trouble;
    Fire burn, and cauldron bubble.

SECOND WITCH:

    Cool it with a baboon's blood,
    Then the charm is firm and good.
    By the pricking of my thumbs,
    Something wicked this way comes:—
    Open, locks,
    Whoever knocks!

                      (Enter MACBETH.*)*

MACBETH:

    How now, you secret, black, and midnight hags!
    What is't you do?

ALL:

            A deed without a name.

MACBETH:

> I conjure you, by that which you profess,
> Howe'er you come to know it, answer me:
> Though you untie the winds and let them fight
> Against the churches; though the yesty waves
> Confound and swallow navigation up;
> Though bladed corn be lodg'd, and trees blown down;
> Though castles topple on their warders' heads;
> Though palaces and pyramids do slope
> Their heads to their foundations; though the treasure
> Of nature's germens tumble all together,
> Even till destruction sicken; answer me
> To what I ask you.

FIRST WITCH:

> Speak.

SECOND WITCH:

> Demand.

THIRD WITCH:

> We'll answer.

FIRST WITCH:

> Say, if thou 'dst rather hear it from our mouths,
> Or from our masters?

MACBETH:

> Call 'em, let me see 'em.

FIRST WITCH:

> Pour in sow's blood, that hath eaten
> Her nine farrow; grease that's sweaten
> From the murderer's gibbet throw
> Into the flame.

ALL:

> Come, high or low;
> Thyself and office deftly show!
> (*Thunder. First apparition: an armed Head.*)

MACBETH:
> Tell me, thou unknown power,—

FIRST WITCH:
> He knows thy thought:
> Hear his speech, but say thou nought.

FIRST APPARITION:
> Macbeth! Macbeth! Macbeth! beware Macduff;
> Beware the thane of Fife. Dismiss me: enough.
>
> (*Descends.*)

MACBETH:
> Whate'er thou art, for thy good caution, thanks;
> Thou hast harp'd my fear aright: but one word more—

FIRST WITCH:
> He will not be commanded: here's another,
> More potent than the first.
> (*Thunder. Second Apparition: a bloody Child.*)

SECOND APPARITION:
> Macbeth! Macbeth! Macbeth!

MACBETH:
> Had I three ears, I 'ld hear thee.

SECOND APPARITION:
> Be bloody, bold and resolute; laugh to scorn
> The power of man, for none of woman born
> Shall harm Macbeth.   (*Descends.*)

MACBETH:
> Then live, Macduff: what need I fear of thee?
> But yet I'll make assurance doubly sure,
> And take a bond of fate; thou shalt not live;
> That I may tell pale-hearted fear it lies,
> And sleep in spite of thunder.

(*Thunder. Third apparition: a Child crowned, with a tree in his hand.*)

What is this,
That rises like the issue of a king,
And wears upon his baby-brow the round
And top of sovereignty?

ALL:

Listen, but speak not to 't.

THIRD APPARITION:

Be lion-mettled, proud, and take no care
Who chafes, who frets, or where conspirers are:
Macbeth shall never vanquish'd be until
Great Birnam wood to high Dunsinane hill
Shall come against him.   (*Descends.*)

MACBETH:

That will never be:
Who can impress the forest, bid the tree
Unfix his earth-bound root? Sweet bodements! good!
Rebellion's head, rise never, till the wood
Of Birnam rise, and our high-plac'd Macbeth
Shall live the lease of nature, pay his breath
To time and mortal custom. Yet my heart
Throbs to know one thing: tell me, if your art
Can tell so much: shall Banquo's issue ever
Reign in this kingdom?

ALL:

Seek to know no more.

MACBETH:

I will be satisfied: deny me this,
And an eternal curse fall on you! Let me know:
Why sinks that cauldron? and what noise is this?

(*Hautboys.*)

FIRST WITCH:
> Show!

SECOND WITCH:
> Show!

THIRD WITCH:
> Show!

ALL:

> Show his eyes, and grieve his heart;
> Come like shadows, so depart!
> (*A show of eight Kings, the last with a glass in his hand;*
> BANQUO's *Ghost following.*)

MACBETH:

> Thou art too like the spirit of Banquo: down!
> Thy crown does sear mine eye-balls.—And thy hair,
> Thou other gold-bound brow, is like the first.—
> A third is like the former.—Filthy hags!
> Why do you show me this?—A fourth! Start, eyes!
> What, will the line stretch out to the crack of doom?
> Another yet! A seventh! I'll see no more:
> And yet the eighth appears, who bears a glass
> Which shows me many more; and some I see
> That two-fold balls and treble sceptres carry:
> Horrible sight! Now I see 'tis true;
> For the blood-bolter'd Banquo smiles upon me,
> And points at them for his.—What, is this so?

FIRST WITCH:
> Ay, sir, all this is so.
> > (*The Witches vanish.*)

MACBETH:
> Where are they? Gone? Let this pernicious hour
> Stand aye accursed in the calendar!—
> Come in, without there!
> > (*Enter* LENNOX.)

LENNOX:

What's your grace's will?

MACBETH:
Saw you the weird sisters?

LENNOX:

No, my lord.

MACBETH:
Came they not by you?

LENNOX:

No indeed, my lord.

MACBETH:
Infected be the air whereon they ride,
And damn'd all those that trust them! I did hear
The galloping of horse: who was't came by?

LENNOX:
'Tis two or three, my lord, that bring you word
Macduff is fled to England.

MACBETH:

'Fled to England.'

LENNOX:
Ay, my good lord.

MACBETH (*Aside*):
Time, thou anticipat'st my dread exploits:
The flighty purpose never is o'ertook
Unless the deed go with it: from this moment
The very firstlings of my heart shall be
The firstlings of my hand. And even now,
To crown my thoughts with acts, be it thought and done:

The castle of Macduff I will surprise;
Seize upon Fife; give to the edge o' the sword
His wife, his babes, and all unfortunate souls
That trace him in his line. No boasting like a fool;
This deed I'll do before this purpose cool:
But no more sights!—Where are these gentlemen?
Come, bring me where they are.   (*Exeunt.*)

OTHELLO

Act IV

SCENE III

DESDEMONA:

 Dost thou in conscience think,—tell me, Emilia,—
 That there be women do abuse their husbands
 In such gross kind?

EMILIA:

    There be some such, no question.

DESDEMONA:

 Wouldst thou do such a deed for all the world?

EMILIA:

 Why, would not you?

DESDEMONA:

    No, by this heavenly light!

EMILIA:

Nor I neither by this heavenly light; I might do 't as well i' the
dark.

DESDEMONA:

Woulds't thou do such a deed for all the world?

EMILIA:

The world's a huge thing: it is a great price
For a small vice.

DESDEMONA:

In troth, I think thou wouldst not.

EMILIA:

In troth, I think I should; and undo 't when I had done.
Marry, I would not do such a thing for a joint-ring, nor for
measures of lawn, nor for gowns, petticoats, nor caps, nor any
petty exhibition; but, for the whole world—why, who would not
make her husband a cuckold to make him a monarch? I should
venture purgatory for 't.

DESDEMONA:

Beshrew me, if I would do such a wrong
For the whole world.

EMILIA:

Why, the wrong is but a wrong i' the world; and having the
world for your labour, 'tis a wrong in your own world, and you
might quickly make it right.

DESDEMONA:

I do not think there is any such woman.

Act V

SCENE II

OTHELLO:

It is the very error of the moon;
She comes more nearer earth than she was wont,
And makes men mad. . . .

She's like a liar gone to burning hell:
'Twas I that kill'd her.

EMILIA:

Oh, the more angel she,
And you the blacker devil!

OTHELLO:

She turn'd to folly, and she was a whore.

EMILIA:

Thou dost belie her, and thou art a devil.

OTHELLO:

She was false as water.

EMILIA:

Thou art rash as fire, to say
That she was false: Oh, she was heavenly true!

OTHELLO:

Cassio did top her; ask thy husband else.
Oh, I were damn'd beneath all depth in hell,
But that I did proceed upon just grounds
To this extremity. Thy husband knew it all.

EMILIA:

My husband?

OTHELLO:

Thy husband.

EMILIA:

That she was false to wedlock?

OTHELLO:

    Ay, with Cassio. Nay, had she been true,
    If heaven would make me such another world
    Of one entire and perfect chrysolite,
    I 'ld not have sold her for it.

EMILIA:

    My husband?

OTHELLO:

        Ay, 'twas he that told me first:
    An honest man he is, and hates the slime
    That sticks on filthy deeds.

EMILIA:

        My husband?

OTHELLO:

    What needs this iteration? Woman, I say thy husband.

EMILIA:

    O mistress, villany hath made mocks with love!—
    My husband say that she was false!

OTHELLO:

        He, woman;
    I say thy husband, dost understand the word?
    My friend, thy husband, honest, honest Iago.

EMILIA:

    If he say so, may his pernicious soul
    Rot half a grain a day! he lies to the heart:
    She was too fond of her most filthy bargain.

OTHELLO:

Ha?

EMILIA:

Do thy worst:
This deed of thine is no more worthy heaven
Than thou wast worthy her.

OTHELLO:

Peace, you were best.

EMILIA:

Thou hast not half that power to do me harm
As I have to be hurt. O gull! O dolt!
As ignorant as dirt! thou hast done a deed—
I care not for thy sword; I'll make thee known,
Though I lost twenty lives. Help! help, ho! help!
The Moor hath kill'd my mistress! Murder! murder!

KING RICHARD THE SECOND

Act I

SCENE I

Old John of Gaunt, time-honoured Lancaster.

Act II

SCENE I

Eating the bitter bread of banishment.

ROMEO AND JULIET

Act V

SCENE III

ROMEO:

Thou art not conquered; beauty's ensign yet
Is crimson in thy lips and in thy cheeks,
And Death's pale flag is not advancèd there.

THE WINTER'S TALE

Act V

SCENE I

LEONTES:

. . . Stars, stars,
And all eyes else dead coals.

HAMLET, PRINCE OF DENMARK

Act I

SCENE I

MARCELLUS:

It faded on the crowing of the cock.
Some say that ever 'gainst that season comes
Wherein our Saviour's birth is celebrated,
The bird of dawning singeth all night long:
And then, they say, no spirit dare stir abroad;
The nights are wholesome; then no planets strike,
No fairy takes, nor witch hath power to charm,
So hallow'd and so gracious is that time.

Act V

SCENE II

FORTINBRAS:

> Let four captains
> Bear Hamlet, like a soldier, to the stage;
> For he was likely, had he been put on,
> To have prov'd most royal: and, for his passage,
> The soldiers' music and the rites of war
> Speak loudly for him.
> Take up the bodies: such a sight as this
> Becomes the field, but here shows much amiss.
> Go, bid the soldiers shoot.

THE TEMPEST

from *The Epilogue* spoken by PROSPERO.

> . . . . .   Now I want
> Spirits to enforce, art to enchant;
> And my ending is despair,
> Unless I be relieved by prayer,
> Which pierces so, that it assaults
> Mercy itself, and frees all faults.
>
> As you from crimes would pardoned be,
> Let your indulgence set me free.

William Shakespeare and John Fletcher

THE TWO NOBLE KINSMEN

Song at the opening of the play (for "a Boy in a white robe . . . singing and strewing Flowres.")

Roses, their sharp spines being gone,
Not royal in their smell alone,
But in their hue.
Maiden Pinks, of odour faint,
Daisies smell-less, yet most quaint
And sweet Thyme true.

Primrose, first-born child of Ver,
Merry Spring-time's harbinger,
With Hare-bells dim.
Oxlips, in their cradles growing,
Marigolds, on death-beds blowing,
Larks' Heels trim.

All dear Nature's children sweet
Lie 'fore Bride and Bridegroom's feet,
Blessing their sense.
Not an angel of the air,
Bird melodious or bird fair,
Be absent hence.

The Cow, the slandrous Cuckoo, nor
The boding Raven, nor Chough hoar,
Nor chattering Pie,
May on our Bride-house perch or sing,
Or with them any discord bring
But from it fly.

(The closing couplet at the end of Act One.)

THE THIRD QUEEN:
This world's a City full of straying streets,
And Death's the market-place where each one meets.

Thomas Nash

SUMMER'S LAST WILL AND TESTAMENT

(A play produced before Queen Elizabeth at the Palace of Archbishop Whitgift at Croydon during the (late summer) pestilence of 1593. It seems to have been played by amateurs with professional help.)

Enter Ver with his train, overlaid with suits of green moss, representing short grass, singing.

Spring, the sweet Spring, is the year's pleasant King;
Then blooms each thing, then maids dance in a ring,
Cold doth not sting, the pretty birds do sing,
Cuckoo, jugge, jugge, pu wee, to witta woo.

The Palm and May make country houses gay,
Lambs frisk and play, the Shepherds pipe all day,
And we hear aye birds tune this merry lay,
Cuckoo, jugge, jugge, pu wee, to witta woo.

The fields breathe sweet, the daisies kiss our feet,
Young lovers meet, old wives a-sunning sit,
In every street these tunes our ears do greet,
Cuckoo, jugge, jugge, pu wee, to witta woo.
Spring, the sweet Spring.

(*From the same.*)

SUMMER

Sing me some doleful ditty to the lute,
That may complain my near approaching death.

The Song

Adieu, farewell, Earth's bliss,
This world uncertain is,
Fond are life's lustful joys,
Death proves them all but toys:
None from his darts can fly;
I am sick, I must die:
    Lord, have mercy on us.

Rich men, trust not in wealth,
Gold cannot buy you health;
Physic himself must fade,
All things to end are made,
The plague full swift goes by:
I am sick, I must die:
    Lord, have mercy on us.

Beauty is but a flower,
Which wrinkles will devour;
Brightness falls from the air;
Queens have died young and fair,
Dust hath closed Helen's eye:
I am sick, I must die:
    Lord, have mercy on us.

Strength stoops unto the grave,
Worms feed on Hector brave,
Swords may not fight with fate,
Earth still holds ope her gate.
Come, come! the bells do cry;
I am sick, I must die:
    Lord, have mercy on us.

Wit, with his wanton-ness,
Tasteth Death's bitterness:
Hell's executioner

Hath no ears for to hear
What vain art can reply.
I am sick, I must die:
    Lord, have mercy on us.

Haste, therefore, each degree
To welcome Destiny:
Heaven is our heritage,
Earth but a player's stage.
Mount we unto the sky:
I am sick, I must die:
    Lord, have mercy on us.

Fair Summer droops, droop, men and beasts there-fore,
So fair a Summer look for never more:
All good things vanish, less than in a day,
Peace, plenty, pleasure, suddenly decay.
Go not yet away, bright soul of the sad year,
The Earth is hell when thou leav'st to appear.

What, shall those flowers that deckt thy garland erst,
Upon thy grave be wastefully disperst?
O trees, consume your sap in sorrow's source;
Streams, turn to tears your tributary course.
Go not yet hence, bright soul of the sad year,
The Earth is hell when thou leav'st to appear.

Francis Beaumont and John Fletcher

THE FAITHFUL SHEPHERDESS

Act I

SCENE 1

(The Wood before Clorin's Bower.
Enter CLORIN.)

CLORIN:

> Hail, holy earth, whose cold arms do embrace
> The truest man that ever fed his flocks
> By the fat plains of fruitful Thessaly!
> Thus I salute thy grave; thus do I pay
> My early vows and tribute of mine eyes
> To thy still-lovèd ashes; thus I free
> Myself from all ensuing heats and fires
> Of love; all sports, delights, and jolly games,
> That shepherds hold full dear, thus put I off:
> Now no more shall these smooth brows be begirt
> With youthful coronals, and lead the dance;
> No more the company of fresh fair maids
> And wanton shepherds be to me delightful,
> Nor the shrill pleasing sound of merry pipes
> Under some shady dell, when the cool wind
> Plays on the leaves: all be far away,
> Since thou art far away, by whose dear side
> How often have I sat crowned with fresh flowers
> For summer's queen, whilst every shepherd's boy
> Puts on his lusty green, with gaudy hook,
> And hanging scrip of finest cordevan.
> But thou art gone, and these are gone with thee,
> And all are dead but thy dear memory;

That shall outlive thee, and shall ever spring,
Whilst there are pipes or jolly shepherds sing.
And here will I, in honour of thy love,
Dwell by thy grave, forgetting all those joys
That former times made precious to mine eyes;
Only remembering what my youth did gain
In the dark, hidden virtuous use of herbs:
That will I practise, and as freely give
All my endeavours as I gained them free.
Of all green wounds I know the remedies
In men or cattle, be they stung with snakes,
Or charmed with powerful words of wicked art,
Or be they love-sick, or through too much heat
Grown wild or lunatic, their eyes or ears
Thickened with misty film of dulling rheum;
These I can cure, such secret virtue lies
In herbs applièd by a virgin's hand.
My meat shall be what these wild woods afford,
Berries and chestnuts, plantains, on whose cheeks
The sun sits smiling, and the lofty fruit
Pulled from the fair head of the straight-grown pine;
On these I'll feed with free content, and rest,
When night shall blind the world, by thy side blest

(*Enter* SATYR *with a Basket of Fruit.*)

SAT.:

Through yon same bending plain,
That flings his arms down to the main,
And through these thick woods, have I run,
Whose bottom never kissed the sun
Since the lusty spring began;
All to please my master Pan,
Have I trotted without rest
To get him fruit; for at a feast
He entertains, this coming night,
His paramour, the Syrinx bright.—
But, behold, a fairer sight!

(*Seeing* CLORIN *he stands amazed.*)

By that heavenly form of thine,
Brightest fair, thou art divine,
Sprung from great immortal race
Of the gods; for in thy face
Shines more awful majesty
Than dull weak mortality
Dare with misty eyes behold,
And live: therefore on this mould
Lowly do I bend my knee
In worship of thy deity.
Deign it, goddess, from my hand
To receive whate'er this land
From her fertile womb doth send
Of her choice fruits; and but lend
Belief to that the Satyr tells:
Fairer by the famous wells
To this present day ne'er grew,
Never better nor more true.
Here be grapes, whose lusty blood
Is the learnèd poets' good,
Sweeter yet did never crown
The head of Bacchus; nuts more brown
Than the squirrel's teeth that crack them:
Deign, O fairest fair, to take them!
For these black-eyèd Dryope
Hath oftentimes commanded me
With my claspèd knee to climb:
See how well the lusty time
Hath decked their rising cheeks in red
Such as on your lips is spread!
Here be berries for a queen,
Some be red, some be green;
These are of that luscious meat,
The great god Pan himself doth eat:
All these, and what the woods can yield,
The hanging mountain or the field,
I freely offer, and ere long
Will bring you more, more sweet and strong;

Till when, humbly leave I take,
Lest the great Pan do awake,
That sleeping lies in a deep glade,
Under a broad beech's shade.
I must go, I must run
Swifter than the fiery sun. (*Exit.*)

CLO.:

And all my fears go with thee!
What greatness, or what private hidden power,
Is there in me, to draw submission
From this rude man and beast? Sure I am mortal,
The daughter of a shepherd; he was mortal,
And she that bore me mortal: prick my hand,
And it will bleed; a fever shakes me, and
The self-same wind that makes the young lambs shrink
Makes me a-cold; my fear says I am mortal.
Yet I have heard (my mother told it me,
And now I do believe it), if I keep
My virgin-flower uncropt, pure, chaste, and fair,
No goblin, wood-god, fairy, elf, or fiend,
Satyr, or other power that haunts the groves,
Shall hurt my body, or by vain illusion
Draw me to wander after idle fires;
Or voices calling me in dead of night,
To make me follow, and so tole me on,
Through mire and standing pools, to find my ruin:
Else why should this rough thing, who never knew
Manners nor smooth humanity, whose heats
Are rougher than himself and more mis-shapen,
Thus mildly kneel to me? Sure there is a power
In that great name of virgin, that binds fast
All rude uncivil bloods, all appetites
That break their confines: then, strong chastity,
Be thou my strongest guard, for here I'll dwell
In opposition against fate and hell!

(*Retires into the bower.*)

THE MAD LOVER

Act IV

Song

To the fair fields where loves eternal dwell
There's none that come, but first they pass thro' hell. . . .

Now in cold frosts, now scorching fires
They sit, and curse their lost desires;
Nor shall these souls be free from pains and fears,
Till women waft them over in their tears.

RULE A WIFE AND HAVE A WIFE

Act III

LEON:

I cast my cloud off, and appear myself,
The master of this little piece of mischief.

PEREZ:

There's an old woman . . . .
The true proportion of an old smoked Sibyl;
There is a young thing, too, that Nature meant
For a maid-servant, but 'tis now a monster;
She has a husk about her like a chestnut
With laziness and living under the line here;
And these two make a hollow sound together,
Like frogs, or winds between two doors that murmur.

Act V

DUKE:

Preserve me but this once.

MARGARITA:

There's a deep well
In the next yard, if you dare venture drowning:
It is but death.

THE ELDER BROTHER

Act II, Scene III

EUSTACE:

And read a little unbaked poetry
Such as the dabblers of our time contrive.

Act IV, Scene II

Like a ring of bells, whose sound the wind still alters.

THE HONEST MAN'S FORTUNE

Act IV, Scene I

CHARLOTTE:

That soul's most stout
That, bearing all mischance, dares last it out.

THE SPANISH CURATE

Act III, Scene III

The stewed cock shall crow COCK-A-LOODLE-LOO
A loud COCK-A-LOODLE shall he crow.

Note: Long admiration for Fletcher's power of cheerful folly compels
me to include this.

THE CHANCES

Act II, Scene III

CONSTANTIA:

Our own desires
Are our own fates, our own stars all our fortunes,
Which, as we sway 'em, so abuse or bless us.

A WIFE FOR A MONTH

Act I, Scene I

FREDERICK:

No rose—
Nor lily, nor no glorious hyacinth,
Are of that sweetness, whiteness, tenderness,
Softness, and satisfying blessedness.

Act IV, Scene I

EVANTHE:

Pray, Captain, tell the King
They that are sad on earth in Heaven shall sing.

THE QUEEN OF CORINTH

Act III, Scene III

AGENOR:
>Like a green meadow on an April day.

THE SCORNFUL LADY

Act IV

YOUNG LOVELESS:
>Ale is their eating and their drinking solely.

PHILASTER

Act III

PHILASTER:
>Sweet as Arabian winds, when fruits are ripe.

THE NIGHT-WALKER: OR THE LITTLE THIEF

Act II, Scene I

ALATHE:
>I've walked through all the lodgings
>A silence, as if death dwelt there, inhabits . . . .

LURCHER:
>Are they all asleep?

ALATHE:

> I think so, and sound asleep, unless it be
> Some women that keep watch in a low parlour,
> And drink, and weep, I know not to what end.

Act II, Scene II

NURSE:

> O 'tis a sad time. All the burnt wine's drunk.

TOBY:

> > The canary's gone, too . . . .
> > I cannot mourn in beer.

George Chapman

BUSSY D'AMBOIS

Act II, Scene I

BUSSY:

                Since I am free,
Offending no just law, let no law make,
By any wrong it does, my life her slave:
When I am wronged, and that law fails to right me,
Let me be King myself, as man was made.
And do a justice that exceeds the law.
If my wrong pass the power of single valour
To right and expiate, then be, you, my King,
And do a right exceeding law and nature.

Who to himself is law, no law doth need,
Offends no law, and is a King indeed.

THE CONSPIRACY OF CHARLES, DUKE OF BYRON

Act I, Scene I

BYRON:

To fear a violent good, abuseth goodness;
'Tis immortality to die aspiring,
As if a man were taken quick to Heaven.
What will not hold perfection, let it burst.

What force hath any cannon, not being charged,
Or being not discharged?
                              To have stuff and form,
And to lie idle, fearful, and unused,
Nor form nor stuff shows. . . . .
. . . .   Happiness
Denies comparison of less or more,
And not at most is nothing. Like the shaft
Shot at the sun by angry Hercules,
And into shivers by the thunder broken,
Will I be, if I burst; and in my heart
This shall be written:—"Yet 'twas high and right."

The end of *Act III*.

BYRON:

    Give me a spirit that on this life's rough sea
    Loves t' have his sails filled with lusty wind,
    Even till his sail-yards tremble, his masts crack,
    And his rapt ship runs on her side so low
    That she drinks water, and her keel plows air.

    There is no danger to a man that knows
    What life and death is; there's not any law
    Exceeds his knowledge; neither is it lawful
    That he should stoop to any other law.

    He goes before them, and commands them all,
    That to himself is a law rational.

THE TRAGEDY OF CHARLES, DUKE OF BYRON

The last speech.

BYRON:
     And so, farewell for ever. Never more
Shall any hope of my revival see me.
Such is the endless exile of dead men.
Summer succeeds the Spring; Autumn the Summer;
The frosts of Winter the fall'n leaves of Autumn:
All these, and all fruits in them, yearly fade,
And every year return: but cursèd Man
Shall never more renew his vanished face.

Fall on your knees, then, Statists, ere ye fall
That you may rise again: knees bent too late,
Stick you in earth like statues: see, in me,
How you are poured down from your clearest Heavens;
Fall lower yet, mixt with th' unmovèd centre,
That your own shadows may no longer mock ye.

Strike, strike, O strike: fly, fly, commanding Soul,
And on thy wings, for this thy body's breath,
Bear the eternal victory of Death.

John Ford

THE LOVER'S MELANCHOLY

Act IV, Scene II

MELEANDER:

> A lamentable tale of things
> Done long ago, and ill done.

Act IV, Scene III

PALADOR:

> Parthenophil is lost, and I would see him,
> For he is like to something I remember
> A great while since, a long, long time ago.

Act V, Scene I

MELEANDER:

> The cunning arts man
> Faltered not in a line. Could he have fashioned
> A little hollow space here, and blown breath
> To have made it move and whisper, it had been excellent. . . .
> But, faith, 'tis well: 'tis very well as 'tis;
> Passing, most passing well.

LINES TO JOHN WEBSTER
on his play *The Duchess of Malfi*

Crown him a poet, whom nor Rome nor Greece
Transcend, in all their's, for a master-piece.

Ben Jonson

THE ALCHEMIST

Act IV, Scene IV

ANANIAS:
> Thou lookst like Antichrist, in that lewd hat.

THE SAD SHEPHERD

Act I, Scene I

ÆGLAMOUR:
> The world may find the Spring by following her.

EPITAPH ON THE COUNTESS OF PEMBROKE

Underneath this sable hearse
Lies the subject of all verse;
Sidney's Sister, Pembroke's Mother;
Death, ere Thou hast slain another,
Learn'd, and fair, and good as she,
Time shall throw a dart at thee.

TO WILLIAM CAMDEN

Camden, most reverend head, to whom I owe
All that I am in arts, all that I know.

EPIGRAM CI
Inviting a Friend to Supper

Tonight, grave Sir, both my poor house and I
Do equally desire your company:
Not that we think us worthy such a guest,
But that your worth will dignify our feast. . . . .

It is the fair acceptance, Sir, creates
The entertainment perfect, not the cates;
Yet shall you have, to rectify your palate,
An olive, capers, or some better salad
Ushering the mutton—with a short-legged hen,
If we can get her full of eggs, and then
Lemons, and wine for sauce: to these, a coney
Is not to be despaired of, for our money;
And though fowl may be scarce, yet there are clerks,
(The sky not falling) think we may have larks.

I'll tell you of more (and lie) so you will come:
Of partridge, pheasant, woodcock, of which some
May yet be there: and godwit if we can:
Knot, rail and ruff, too.

                              How so'er, my man
Shall read a piece of Virgil, Tacitus,
Livy, or of some better book to us.
Of which we'll speak our minds, amidst our meat:
And I'll profess no verses to repeat.

To this, if aught appear which I not know of,
That will the pastry, not my paper, show of.
Digestive cheese and fruit there sure will be.

But that which most doth take my Muse and me,
Is a pure cup of rich Canary wine,
Which is the Mermaid's now, but shall be mine,

Of which had Horace or Anacreon tasted,
Their lives, as do their lines, till now had lasted.
Tobacco, nectar, or the Thespian spring
Are all but Luther's beer, to this I sing.
. . . .
. . . .
Nor shall our cups make any guilty men:
But, at our parting, we will be, as when
We innocently met. No simple word
That shall be uttered at our mirthful board,
Shall make us sad next morning, or affright
The liberty that we'd enjoy tonight.

UNDERWOODS

To the Memory of my beloved Master William Shakespeare, and what he hath left us.

To draw no envy, Shakespeare, on thy name,
Am I thus ample to thy book and fame;
While I confess thy writings to be such
As neither Man nor Muse can praise too much.
. . . .
. . . .
I therefore will begin: Soul of the age,
The applause; delight; the wonder of our stage.
My Shakespeare, rise. I will not lodge thee by
Chaucer, or Spenser, or bid Beaumont lie
A little further off, to make thee room.
Thou art a monument without a tomb,
And art alive still, while thy book doth live,
And we have wits to read and praise to give.
. . . .
. . . . How far thou didst our Lyly outshine,
Or sporting Kyd, or Marlowe's mighty line. . . .
. . . .

Sweet Swan of Avon, what a sight it were
To see thee in our water yet appear,
And make those flights upon the banks of Thames
That so did take Eliza and our James.

John Webster

THE WHITE DEVIL

FLAMINEO:
>   Glories, like glow-worms, afar off shine bright,
>   But, looked-to, near, have neither heat nor light.

(This couplet appears also in *The Duchess of Malfi*, IV. 2.)

SONG

>   Call for the robin red-breast and the wren,
>   Since o'er shady groves they hover,
>   And with leaves and flowers do cover
>   The friendless bodies of unburied men.

FLAMINEO:
>   We think caged birds sing, when, indeed, they cry.

THE DUCHESS OF MALFI

Act III, Scene V

DUCHESS:
>   There's no deep valley but near some great hill.

Sir John Davies

NOSCE TEIPSUM

. . . We seek to know the moving of each sphere,
  And the strange cause of th'ebbs and floods of Nile;
  But of that Clock, which in our breasts we bear,
  The subtle motions we forget the while!

We that acquaint ourselves with every zone,
  And pass both tropics, and behold both poles;
  When we come home, are to ourselves unknown
  And unacquainted still with our own souls! . . .

If ought can teach us ought, Affliction's looks
  (Making us look into ourselves so near)
  Teach us to *know ourselves*, beyond all books,
  Or all the learned Schools that ever were!

This Mistress, lately, plucked me by the ear,
  And many a golden lesson hath me taught,
  Hath made my Senses quick, and Reason clear,
  Reformed my Will, and rectified my Thought . . .

Neither Minerva, nor the learned Muse,
  Nor Rules of Art, nor Precepts of the Wise,
  Could in my brain those beams of skill infuse,
  As but the glance of this Dame's angry eyes.

She, within lists, my ranging mind hath brought,
  That now beyond myself I list not go;
  Myself am Centre of my circling thought,
  Only Myself, I study, learn, and know.

I *know* my Body's of so frail a kind,
  As force without, fevers within, can kill;

I *know* the heavenly nature of my Mind;
But 'tis corrupted, both in Wit and Will.

I *know* my Soul hath power to know all things,
    Yet she is blind and ignorant in all;
    I *know* I am one of Nature's little kings,
    Yet to the least and vilest things am thrall!

I *know* my Life's a pain, and but a span;
    I *know* my Sense is mocked in every thing:
    And to conclude, I *know* myself a Man;
    Which is a proud, and yet a wretched thing! . . .

O ignorant poor Man! what dost thou bear,
    Locked up within the casket of thy breast;
    What jewels, and what riches hast thou there,
    What heavenly treasure in so weak a chest!

Look in thy Soul! and thou shalt beauties find,
    Like those which drowned NARCISSUS in the flood;
    Honour and Pleasure both are in thy Mind,
    And all that in the world is counted Good.

Think of her worth! and think that GOD did mean
    This worthy Mind should worthy things embrace!
    Blot not her beauties, with thy thoughts unclean;
    Nor her dishonour with thy Passions base.

Kill not her Quick'ning Power with surfeitings!
    Mar not her Sense with sensualities!
    Cast not her serious Wit on idle things!
    Make not her free Will slave to vanities!

And when thou thinkest of her Eternity;
    Think not that Death against her nature is;
    Think it a Birth! and, when thou goest to die,
    Sing like a swan, as if thou wentst to bliss!

And if thou, like a child, didst fear before,
    Being in the dark, when thou didst nothing see;
    Now I have brought thee Torch-light, fear no more,
    Now, when thou diest, thou canst not hoodwinked be.

And thou, my Soul! which turn'st thy curious eye,
    To view the beams of thine own form divine;
    Know, that thou canst know nothing perfectly,
    While thou art *clouded* with this flesh of mine.

Take heed of *overweening!* and compare
    Thy peacock's feet, with thy gay peacock's train;
    Study the *best* and *highest* things that are;
    But of thyself, an humble thought retain!

Cast down thyself! and only strive to raise
    The glory of thy Maker's sacred name!
    Use all thy powers, that Blessed Power to praise,
    Which gives thee power to Be, and Use the same.

John Donne

ELEGY

On His Mistress

By our first strange and fatal interview,
By all desires which thereof did ensue,
By our long starving hopes, by that remorse
Which my words' masculine persuasive force
Begot in thee, and by the memory
Of hurts, which spies and rivals threatened me,
I calmly beg. But by thy father's wrath,
By all pains, which want and divorcement hath,
I conjure thee, and all the oaths which I
And thou have sworn to seal joint constancy,
Here I unswear, and overswear them thus;
Thou shalt not love by ways so dangerous.
Temper, O fair Love, love's impetuous rage,
Be my true Mistress still, not my feigned Page;
I'll go, and, by thy kind leave, leave behind
Thee, only worthy to nurse in my mind
Thirst to come back. O if thou die before,
My soul from other lands to thee shall soar.
Thy else almighty beauty cannot move
Rage from the seas, nor thy love teach them love,
Nor tame wild Boreas' harshness. Thou hast read
How roughly he in pieces shiverèd
Fair Orithea, whom he swore he loved.
Fall ill or good, 'tis madness to have proved
Dangers unurged; feed on this flattery,
That absent lovers one in th'other be.
Dissemble nothing, not a boy, nor change
Thy body's habit, nor mind's; be not strange
To thyself only; all will spy in thy face
A blushing womanly discovering grace.

Richly clothed apes are called Apes, and as soon
Eclipsed as bright we call the Moon the Moon.
Men of France, changeable chameleons,
Spitals of diseases, shops of fashions,
Love's fuellers, and the rightest company
Of Players, which upon the world's stage be,
Will quickly know thee, and no less, alas!
Th'indifferent Italian, as we pass
His warm land, well content to think thee Page,
Will hunt thee with such lust, and hideous rage,
As Lot's fair guests were vext. But none of these
Nor spongy hydroptic Dutch shall thee displease,
If thou stay here. O stay here, for to thee
England is only a worthy Gallerie,
To walk in expectation, till from thence
Our greatest King call thee to His presence.
When I am gone, dream me some happiness,
Nor let thy looks our long-hid love confess,
Nor praise, nor dispraise me, nor bless nor curse
Openly love's force, nor in bed fright thy Nurse
With midnight startings, crying out, "O, O,
Nurse, O my love is slain, I saw him go
O'er the white Alps alone; I saw him, I,
Assail'd, fight, taken, stabb'd, bleed, fall, and die."
Augur me better chance, except great JOVE
Think it enough for me to have had thy love.

OF THE PROGRESS OF THE SOUL

The Second Anniversary

. . . . Her pure and eloquent blood
Spoke in her cheeks, and so distinctly wrought,
That one might almost say, her body thought.

THE OBSEQUIES OF THE LORD HARRINGTON

Thou seest me here at midnight: now all rest;
Time's dead low-water, when all minds divest
Tomorrow's business; when the labourers have
Such rest in bed, that their last churchyard grave,
Subject to change, will scarce be a type of this:
Now, when the client, whose last hearing is
Tomorrow, sleeps; when the condemned man,
Who, when he opes his eyes, must shut them than
Again by death, although sad watch he keep,
Doth practice dying by a little sleep.

SONNET IV

O my black Soul! now thou art summonèd
By sickness, Death's herald and champion;
Thou art like a Pilgrim, which abroad hath done
Treason, and durst not turn to whence he is fled,
Or like a thief, which till death's doom be read,
Wisheth himself delivered from prison;
But damned and haled to execution,
Wisheth that still he might be imprisonèd.
Yet grace, if thou repent, thou canst not lack;
But who shall give thee that grace, to begin?
O, make thy self with holy mourning black,
And red with blushing, as thou art with sin;
Or wash thee in Christ's blood, which hath this might
That being red, it dyes red souls to white.

SONNET V

I am a little world made cunningly
Of Elements, and an Angelic Sprite,
But black sin hath betrayed to endless night

My world's both parts, and O, both parts must die.
You, which beyond that Heaven which was most high,
Have found new spheres, and of new lands can write,
Pour new seas in mine eyes, that so I might
Drown my world with my weeping earnestly;
Or wash it, if it must be drown'd no more.
But O, it must be burnt! alas, the fire
Of lust and envy have burnt it heretofore,
And made it fouler; let their flames retire,
And burn me, O Lord, with a fiery zeal
Of Thee and Thy House, which doth in eating heal.

SONNET VI

This is my play's last scene, here Heavens appoint
My pilgrimage's last mile; and my race
Idly, yet quickly run, hath this last pace;
My span's last inch, my minute's latest point,
And gluttonous Death, will instantly unjoint
My body, and soul, and I shall sleep a space;
But my ever-waking part shall see that Face,
Whose fear already shakes my every joint:
Then, as my soul to Heaven, her first seat, takes flight,
And earth-born body in the earth shall dwell,
So, fall my sins, that all may have their right,
To where they are bred, and would press me, to Hell.
Impute me righteous, thus purged of evil,
For thus I leave the world, the flesh, the devil.

SONNET VII

At the round Earth's imagined corners, blow
Your trumpets, Angels, and arise, arise,
From Death, you numberless infinities
Of souls, and to your scattered bodies go,

All whom the Flood did, and fire shall o'erthrow,
All whom war, dearth, age, agues, tyrannies,
Despair, law, chance, hath slain, and you whose eyes
Shall behold God, and never taste Death's woe.
But let them sleep, Lord, and me mourn a space;
For if, above all these, my sins abound,
'Tis late to ask abundance of Thy Grace,
When we are there. Here, on this lowly ground,
Teach me how to repent; for that's as good
As if Thou hadst seal'd my pardon with Thy Blood.

SONNET X

Death be not proud, though some have callèd thee
Mighty and dreadful, for thou art not so;
For those, whom thou think'st thou dost overthrow,
Die not, poor Death, nor yet canst thou kill me.
From rest and sleep, which but thy pictures be,
Much pleasure, then from thee much more must flow,
And soonest our best men with thee do go,
Rest of their bones, and soul's delivery.
Thou art slave to Fate, Chance, Kings, and desperate men,
And dost with poison, war, and sickness dwell,
And poppy, or charms can make us sleep as well,
And better than thy stroke; why swell'st thou then?
One short sleep past, we wake eternally,
And Death shall be no more; Death, thou shalt die.

A FEVER

These burning fits but meteors be,
  Whose matter in thee is soon spent.
Thy beauty, and all parts, which are thee,
  Are unchangeable firmament.

LOVE'S DEITY

I long to talk with some old lover's ghost,
   Who died before the god of Love was born:

THE RELIC

When my grave is broke up again
   Some second guest to entertain,
   (For graves have learn'd that woman-head
   To be to more than one a Bed)
      And he that digs it, spies
A bracelet of bright hair about the bone,
      Will not he let us alone,
And think that there a loving couple lies,
Who thought that this device might be some way
To make their souls, at the last busy day,
Meet at this grave, and make a little stay?

If this fall in a time, or land,
   Where mis-devotion doth command,
   Then, he that digs us up, will bring
   Us, to the Bishop, or the King,
      To make us Relics; then
Thou shalt be a Mary Magdalen, and I
      A something else thereby;
All women shall adore us, and some men;
And, since at such time miracles are sought,
I would have that age by this paper taught
What miracles we harmless lovers wrought.

First, we loved well and faithfully,
   Yet knew not what we loved, nor why;
   Difference of sex no more we knew,
   Than our Guardian Angels do;

Coming and going, we
Perchance might kiss, but not between those meals;
     Our hands ne'r toucht the seals,
Which Nature, injured by late law, sets free:
These miracles we did; but now alas,
All measure, and all language, I should pass,
Should I tell what a miracle she was.

ELEGY

The Autumnal

No SPRING, nor SUMMER Beauty hath such grace,
     As I have seen in one AUTUMNAL face. . . .

If we love things long sought, AGE is a thing
     Which we are fifty years in compassing.

THE ANATOMY OF THE WORLD

The First Anniversary

She, she is dead; she's dead: when thou knowst this,
Thou knowst how lame a cripple this world is.

1 353   Sight is the noblest sense of any one;
     Yet sight hath only colour to feed on,
     And colour is decayed: summer's robe grows
     Dusky, and like an oft dyed garment shows.
     Our blushing red, which used in cheeks to spread,
     Is inward sunk, and only our souls are red.
     Perchance the world might have recoverèd,
     If she whom we lament had not been dead.

But she, in whom all white, and red, and blue
(Beauty's ingredients) voluntary grew,
As in an unvext Paradise; from whom
Did all things verdure, and their lustre come;
Whose composition was miraculous,
Being all colour, all diaphanous,
(For Air and Fire but thick gross bodies were,
And liveliest stones but drowsy and pale to her,)
She, she, is dead; she's dead: when thou know'st this,
Thou knowst how wan a Ghost this our world is:

John Dennys

THE SECRETS OF ANGLING (1613)

Let me live harmlessly, and near the brink
Of Trent or Avon have a dwelling-place;
Where I may see my quill, or cork, down sink
With eager bite of Perch, or Bleak, or Dace;
And on the world and my Creator think:
Whilst some men strive ill-gotten goods t' embrace;
And others spend their time in base excess
Of wine; or worse, in war and wanton-ness.

Let them that list these pastimes still pursue,
And on such pleasing fancies feed their fill;
So I the fields and meadows green may view,
And daily by fresh rivers walk at will,
Among the daisies and the violets blue,
Red hyacinth, and yellow daffodil,
Purple narcissus like the morning rays,
Pale gander-grass and azure culver-keys.

The lofty woods, the forests wide and long,
Adorned with leaves and branches fresh and green,
In whose cool bowers the birds with many a song
Do welcome with their quire the summer's Queen;
The meadows fair, where Flora's gifts among
Are intermixt, with verdant grass between;
The silver-scalèd fish that softly swim
Within the sweet brook's crystal, watery stream.

All these, and many more of His creation
That made the Heavens, the angler oft doth see;
Taking therein no little delectation,
To think how strange, how wonderful they be;

Framing thereof an inward contemplation
To set his heart from other fancies free;
And whilst he looks on these with joyful eye,
His mind is rapt above the starry sky.

Note:

Some think that gander-grass or gander-glas was ragwort,
which is not a spring flower, nor by any means pale. Culverkeys,
or culverkayes, are the wild hyacinths, or bluebells. The name is
sometimes given to cowslips and oxlips.

Sir Henry Wotton

ON HIS MISTRESS, THE QUEEN OF BOHEMIA

You meaner beauties of the night,
That poorly satisfy our eyes
More by your number than your light;
You common people of the skies:
What are you when the moon shall rise?

You curious chanters of the wood,
That warble forth Dame Nature's lays,
Thinking your passions understood
By your weak accents: what's your praise
When Philomel her voice shall raise?

You violets that first appear,
By your pure purple mantles known,
Like the proud virgins of the year,
As if the Spring were all your own;
What are you when the Rose is blown?

So, when my Mistress shall be seen
In form and beauty of Her mind
By Virtue first, then Choice, a Queen;
Tell me, if She was not designed
Th' eclipse and glory of Her kind?

As he wrote to this rare Queen, "the Memory of Your swee
and Royal Virtue is the last thing that will die in me".

ON THE BANK AS I SAT A-FISHING

And now all Nature seemed to love,
The lusty sap began to move;
New juice did stir th' embracing vines,
And birds had drawn their valentines.
 The jealous trout, that low did lie,
Rose at a well-dissembled fly.

 Already were the eaves possest
Of the swift pilgrim's daubèd nest;
The groves already did rejoice
In Philomel's triumphing voice:
The showers were short, the weather mild,
The morning fresh, the evening smiled.
 Joan takes her neat-rubbed pail, and now
She trips to milk the sand-red cow.

The fields and gardens were beset
With tulip, crocus, violet;

Thus all looked gay, all full of cheer,
To welcome the new liveried year.

THE HAPPY LIFE

 How happy is he born and taught
That serveth not another's will;
Whose armour is his honest thought,
And simple truth his utmost skill. . . .

 Who God doth late and early pray
More of His Grace than gifts to lend,
And entertains the harmless day
With a religious book or friend.

This man is freed from servile bands
Of hope to rise, or fear to fall,
Lord of himself, though not of lands,
And having nothing, yet hath all.

Richard Lovelace

FEMALE GLORY

'Mongst the world's wonders, there doth yet remain
One greater than the rest, that's all those o'er again,
And her own self beside: a Lady, whose soft breast
Is with vast Honour's soul and Virtue's life possesst.

Fair as original light first from the Chaos shot,
When Day, in virgin-beams, triumphed, and Night was not,
And as that breath infused in the new-breather Good,
When Ill, unknown, was dumb, and Bad not understood;
Cheerful, as that aspèct at this world's finishing
When Cherubims clapped wings, and the Sons of Heaven did sing;
Chaste as th' Arabian Bird, who all the air denies
And even in flames expires, when with herself she lies.

Oh, she's as kind as drops of new-faln April showers,
That on each gentle breast spring fresh perfuming flowers;
She's constant, generous, fixed; she's calm, she is the all
We can of virtue, honour, faith or glory call,
And she is (whom I thus transmit to endless fame)
Mistress o'th' world and me, and Laura is her name.

John Milton

LYCIDAS

Yet once more, O ye laurels, and once more
Ye myrtles brown, with ivy never sere,
I come to pluck your berries harsh and crude,
And with forc'd fingers rude,
Shatter your leaves before the mellowing year.
Bitter constraint, and sad occasion dear,
Compels me to disturb your season due:
For Lycidas is dead, dead ere his prime,
Young Lycidas, and hath not left his peer:
Who would not sing for Lycidas? He knew
Himself to sing, and build the lofty rhyme.
He must not float upon his watery bier
Unwept, and welter to the parching wind,
Without the meed of some melodious tear.
  Begin, then, Sisters of the sacred well,
That from beneath the seat of Jove doth spring,
Begin, and somewhat loudly sweep the string.
Hence with denial vain, and coy excuse,
So may some gentle Muse
With lucky words favour my destin'd urn,
And as he passes turn,
And bid fair peace be to my sable shroud.
For we were nurs'd upon the self-same hill,
Fed the same flock by fountain, shade, and rill.
  Together both, ere the high lawns appear'd
Under the opening eyelids of the morn,
We drove a field, and both together heard
What time the gray-fly winds her sultry horn,
Batt'ning our flocks with the fresh dews of night,
Oft till the star that rose, at evening, bright,
Toward heav'n's descent had slop'd his west'ring wheel.

Meanwhile the rural ditties were not mute,
Temper'd to th'oaten flute,
Rough Satyrs danc'd, and Fauns with cloven heel
From the glad sound would not be absent long,
And old Damœtas lov'd to hear our song.

But, O the heavy change, now thou art gone,
Now thou art gone, and never must return!
Thee, Shepherd, thee the woods, and desert caves
With wild thyme and the gadding vine o'ergrown,
And all their echoes mourn.
The willows, and the hazel copses green,
Shall now no more be seen,
Fanning their joyous leaves to thy soft lays.
As killing as the canker to the rose,
Or taint-worm to the weanling herds that graze,
Or frost to flow'rs, that their gay wardrobe wear,
When first the white-thorn blows;
Such, Lycidas, thy loss to shepherd's ear.

Where were ye, Nymphs, when the remorseless deep
Clos'd o'er the head of your lov'd Lycidas?
For neither were ye playing on the steep,
Where your old Bards, the famous Druids, lie,
Nor on the shaggy top of Mona high,
Nor yet where Deva spreads her wisard stream:
Ay me! I fondly dream!
Had ye been there, for what could that have done?
What could the Muse herself that Orpheus bore,
The Muse herself for her inchanting son,
Whom universal nature did lament,
When by the rout that made the hideous roar,
His goary visage down the stream was sent,
Down the swift Hebrus to the Lesbian shore?

Alas! what boots it with incessant care
To tend the homely slighted shepherd's trade,
And strictly meditate the thankless Muse?
Were it not better done as others use,
To sport with Amaryllis in the shade,
Or with the tangles of Neæra's hair?

Fame is the spur that the clear spirit doth raise
(That last infirmity of noble mind)
To scorn delights, and live laborious days;
But the fair guerdon when we hope to find,
And think to burst out into sudden blaze,
Comes the blind Fury with th'abhorred shears,
And slits the thin-spun life. But not the praise,
Phœbus replied, and touch'd my trembling ears;
Fame is no plant that grows on mortal soil,
Nor in the glist'ring foil
Set off to th'world, nor in broad rumour lies;
But lives and spreads aloft by those pure eyes,
And perfect witness of all-judging Jove;
As he pronounces lastly on each deed,
Of so much fame in heav'n expect thy meed.

O fountain Arethuse, and thou honour'd flood,
Smooth-sliding Mincius, crown'd with vocal reeds,
That strain I heard was of a higher mood:
But now my oat proceeds,
And listens to the herald of the sea
That came in Neptune's plea;
He ask'd the waves, and ask'd the felon winds,
What hard mishap hath doom'd this gentle swain?
And question'd every gust of rugged wings
That blows from off each beaked promontory:
They knew not of his story,
And sage Hippotades their answer brings,
That not a blast was from his dungeon stray'd,
The air was calm, and on the level brine
Sleek Panope with all her sisters play'd.
It was that fatal and perfidious bark,
Built in th'eclipse, and rigg'd with curses dark,
That sunk so low that sacred head of thine.

Next Camus, reverend sire, went footing slow,
His mantle hairy, and his bonnet sedge,
Inwrought with figures dim, and on the edge
Like to that sanguine flow'r inscrib'd with woe.
Ah! Who hath reft (quoth he) my dearest pledge?

Last came, and last did go,
The pilot of the Galilean lake;
Two massy keys he bore of metals twain,
(The golden opes, the iron shuts amain)
He shook his mitred locks, and stern bespake,
How well could I have spar'd for thee, young swain,
Enow of such as for their bellies' sake
Creep, and intrude, and climb into the fold?
Of other care they little reckoning make,
Than how to scramble at the shearer's feast,
And shove away the worthy bidden guest;
Blind mouths! that scarce themselves know how to hold
A sheep-hook, or have learn'd aught else the least
That to the faithful herdman's art belongs!
What recks it them? What need they? They are sped;
And when they list, their lean and flashy songs
Grate on their scrannel pipes of wretched straw;
The hungry sheep look up, and are not fed,
But swoln with wind, and the rank mist they draw,
Rot inwardly, and foul contagion spread;
Besides what the grim wolf with privy paw
Daily devours apace, and nothing said;
But that two-handed engine at the door
Stands ready to smite once, and smite no more.

   Return, Alpheus, the dread voice is past,
That shrunk thy streams; return, Sicilian Muse,
And call the vales, and bid them hither cast
Their bells, and flow'rets of a thousand hues.
Ye valleys low, where the mild whispers use
Of shades, and wanton winds, and gushing brooks,
On whose fresh lap the swart-star sparely looks:
Throw hither all your quaint enamell'd eyes,
That on the green turf suck the honied showers,
And purple all the ground with vernal flowers.
Bring the rathe primrose that forsaken dies,
The tufted crow-toe, and pale jessamine,
The white pink, and the pansy freak'd with jet,
The glowing violet,

The musk-rose, and the well-attir'd woodbine,
With cowslips wan that hang the pensive head,
And every flower that sad embroidery wears:
Bid amaranthus all his beauty shed,
And daffadillies fill their cups with tears,
To strew the laureate herse where Lycid lies.
For so to interpose a little ease,
Let our frail thoughts dally with false surmise.
Ay me! Whilst thee the shores, and sounding seas
Wash far away, where'er thy bones are hurl'd,
Whether beyond the stormy Hebrides,
Where thou perhaps under the whelming tide
Visit'st the bottom of the monstrous world;
Or whether thou to our moist vows denied,
Sleep'st by the fable of Bellerus old,
Where the great vision of the guarded mount
Looks toward Namancos and Bayona's hold;
Look homeward Angel now, and melt with ruth:
And, O ye dolphins, waft the hapless youth.

Weep no more, woful Shepherds, weep no more,
For Lycidas your sorrow is not dead,
Sunk though he be beneath the watery floor;
So sinks the day-star in the ocean bed,
And yet anon repairs his drooping head,
And tricks his beams, and with new spangled ore
Flames in the forehead of the morning sky;
So Lycidas sunk low, but mounted high,
Thro' the dear might of him that walk'd the waves,
Where other groves, and other streams along,
With nectar pure his oozy locks he laves,
And hears the unexpressive nuptial song,
In the blest kingdoms meek of joy and love.
There entertain him all the saints above,
In solemn troops, and sweet societies,
That sing, and singing in their glory move,
And wipe the tears for ever from his eyes.
Now, Lycidas, the shepherds weep no more;
Henceforth thou art the Genius of the shore,

In thy large recompense, and shalt be good
To all that wander in that perilous flood.
    Thus sang the uncouth swain to th'oaks and rills,
While the still morn went out with sandals gray,
He touch'd the tender stops of various quills,
With eager thought warbling his Doric lay;
And now the sun had stretch'd out all the hills,
And now was dropt into the western bay;
At last he rose, and twitch'd his mantle blue:
To-morrow to fresh woods, and pastures new.

L'ALLEGRO

Hence, loathed Melancholy,
  Of Cerberus and blackest Midnight born,
In Stygian cave forlorn
  'Mongst horrid shapes, and shrieks, and sights unholy,
Find out some uncouth cell,
  Where brooding Darkness spreads his jealous wings,
And the night-raven sings;
  There under ebon shades, and low-brow'd rocks,
As ragged as thy locks,
  In dark Cimmerian desert ever dwell.
But come thou Goddess fair and free,
In heav'n y-clep'd Euphrosyne,
And by Men, heart-easing Mirth,
Whom lovely Venus at a birth
With two sister Graces more,
To ivy-crowned Bacchus bore;
Or whether (as some sager sing)
The frolic wind that breathes the spring,
Zephyr with Aurora playing,
As he met her once a Maying;
There on beds of violets blue,
And fresh-blown roses wash'd in dew
Fill'd her with thee a daughter fair,

So buxom, blithe, and debonair.
   Haste thee, Nymph, and bring with thee
Jest, and youthful Jollity,
Quips, and Cranks, and wanton Wiles,
Nods, and Becks, and wreathed Smiles,
Such as hang on Hebe's cheek,
And love to live in dimple sleek;
Sport that wrinkled Care derides,
And Laughter holding both his sides.
Come, and trip it as you go,
On the light fantastic toe;
And in thy right hand lead with thee
The mountain nymph, sweet Liberty;
And if I give thee honour due,
Mirth, admit me of thy crew,
To live with her, and live with thee,
In unreproved pleasures free;
To hear the lark begin his flight,
And singing startle the dull night,
From his watch-tow'r in the skies,
Till the dappled dawn doth rise;
Then to come in spite of sorrow,
And at my window bid good morrow,
Through the sweet-briar, or the vine,
Or the twisted eglantine:
While the cock with lively din
Scatters the rear of darkness thin,
And to the stack, or the barn-door,
Stoutly struts his dames before:
Oft list'ning how the hounds and horn
Cheerly rouse the slumb'ring morn,
From the side of some hoar hill,
Through the high wood echoing shrill:
Some time walking, not unseen,
By hedge-row elms, on hillocks green,
Right against the eastern gate,
Where the great sun begins his state,
Rob'd in flames, and amber light,

The clouds in thousand liveries dight:
While the ploughman near at hand
Whistles o'er the furrow'd land,
And the milkmaid singeth blithe,
And the mower whets his scythe,
And every shepherd tells his tale
Under the hawthorn in the dale.
Straight mine eye hath caught new pleasures
Whilst the landscape round it measures;
Russet lawns, and fallows gray,
Where the nibbling flocks do stray,
Mountains, on whose barren breast
The lab'ring clouds do often rest;
Meadows trim with daisies pied,
Shallow brooks, and rivers wide.
Towers and battlements it sees
Bosom'd high in tufted trees,
Where perhaps some Beauty lies,
The Cynosure of neighb'ring eyes.
Hard by, a cottage chimney smokes,
From betwixt two aged oaks,
Where Corydon and Thyrsis met,
Are at their savoury dinner set
Of herbs, and other country messes,
Which the neat-handed Phillis dresses;
And then in haste the bow'r she leaves,
With Thestylis to bind the sheaves;
Or, if the earlier season lead,
To the tann'd haycock in the mead,
Sometimes with secure delight
The upland hamlets will invite,
When the merry bells ring round,
And the jocund rebecks sound
To many a youth, and many a maid,
Dancing in the chequer'd shade;
And young and old come forth to play
On a sunshine holiday,
Till the live-long daylight fail;

Then to the spicy nut-brown ale,
With stories told of many a feat,
How fairy Mab the junkets eat;
She was pinch'd, and pull'd, she said.
And he by friar's lanthorn led
Tells how the drudging Goblin sweat,
To earn his cream-bowl duly set,
When in one night, ere glimpse of morn,
His shadowy flail hath thresh'd the corn,
That ten day-lab'rers could not end;
Then lies him down the lubber fiend,
And stretch'd out all the chimney's length,
Basks at the fire his hairy strength,
And crop-full out of doors he flings,
Ere the first cock his matin rings.
Thus done the tales, to bed they creep,
By whispering winds soon lull'd asleep.
Tower'd cities please us then,
And the busy hum of men,
Where throngs of knights and barons bold
In weeds of peace high triumphs hold,
With store of ladies, whose bright eyes
Rain influence, and judge the prize
Of wit, or arms, while both contend
To win her grace, whom all commend.
There let Hymen oft appear
In saffron robe, with taper clear,
And pomp, and feast, and revelry,
With mask, and antique pageantry,
Such sights as youthful poets dream
On summer eves by haunted stream.
Then to the well-trod stage anon,
If Jonson's learned sock be on,
Or sweetest Shakespeare, Fancy's child,
Warble his native wood-notes wild.
And ever against eating cares,
Lap me in soft Lydian airs,
Married to immortal verse,

Such as the meeting soul may pierce
In notes, with many a winding bout
Of linked sweetness long drawn out,
With wanton heed and giddy cunning,
The melting voice through mazes running,
Untwisting all the chains that tie
The hidden soul of harmony;
That Orpheus' self may heave his head
From golden slumber on a bed
Of heap'd Elysian flowers, and hear
Such strains as would have won the ear
Of Pluto, to have quite set free
His half regain'd Eurydice.
    These delights if thou canst give,
Mirth, with thee I mean to live.

IL PENSEROSO

Hence, vain deluding joys,
    The brood of folly without father bred,
How little you bestead,
    Or fill the fixed mind with all your toys!
Dwell in some idle brain,
    And fancies fond with gaudy shapes possess,
As thick and numberless
    As the gay motes that people the sunbeams,
Or likest hovering dreams
    The fickle pensioners of Morpheus' train.
But hail thou Goddess, sage and holy,
Hail divinest Melancholy,
Whose saintly visage is too bright
To hit the sense of human sight,
And therefore to our weaker view
O'erlaid with black, staid wisdom's hue;
Black, but such as in esteem
Prince Memnon's sister might beseem,

Or that starr'd Ethiop queen that strove
To set her beauty's praise above
The Sea-Nymphs, and their pow'rs offended:
Yet thou art higher far descended;
Thee bright-hair'd Vesta, long of yore,
To solitary Saturn bore;
His daughter she (in Saturn's reign,
Such mixture was not held a stain).
Oft in glimmering bow'rs and glades
He met her, and in secret shades
Of woody Ida's inmost grove,
While yet there was no fear of Jove.
Come, pensive Nun, devout and pure,
Sober, steadfast, and demure,
All in a robe of darkest grain,
Flowing with majestic train,
And sable stole of cyprus lawn,
Over thy decent shoulders drawn.
Come, but keep thy wonted state,
With even step, and musing gait,
And looks commercing with the skies,
Thy rapt soul sitting in thine eyes:
There held in holy passion still,
Forget thyself to marble, till
With a sad leaden downward cast
Thou fix them on the earth as fast:
And join with thee calm Peace, and Quiet,
Spare Fast, that oft with Gods doth diet,
And hears the Muses in a ring
Aye round about Jove's altar sing:
And add to these retired Leisure,
That in trim gardens takes his pleasure;
But first, and chiefest, with thee bring,
Him that yon soars on golden wing,
Guiding the fiery-wheeled throne,
The Cherub Contemplation;
And the mute Silence hist along,
'Less Philomel will deign a song,

In her sweetest, saddest plight,
Smoothing the rugged brow of night,
While Cynthia checks her dragon yoke,
Gently o'er th'accustom'd oak;
Sweet bird, that shunn'st the noise of folly,
Most musical, most melancholy!
Thee, chauntress, oft the woods among
I woo, to hear thy even-song;
And missing thee, I walk unseen
On the dry smooth-shaven green,
To behold the wandering moon,
Riding near her highest noon,
Like one that had been led astray
Through the heav'n's wide pathless way;
And oft, as if her head she bow'd,
Stooping through a fleecy cloud.
Oft on a plat of rising ground,
I hear the far-off curfew sound,
Over some wide-water'd shore,
Swinging slow with sullen roar;
Or if the air will not permit,
Some still removed place will fit,
Where glowing embers through the room
Teach light to counterfeit a gloom;
Far from all resort of mirth,
Save the cricket on the hearth,
Or the bellman's drowsy charm,
To bless the doors from nightly harm:
Or let my lamp at midnight hour
Be seen in some high lonely tow'r,
Where I may oft out-watch the Bear,
With thrice-great Hermes, or unsphere
The spirit of Plato, to unfold
What worlds, or what vast regions hold
The immortal mind, that hath forsook
Her mansion in this fleshly nook:
And of those Demons that are found
In fire, air, flood, or under ground,

Whose power hath a true consent
With planet, or with element.
Sometime let gorgeous tragedy
In sceptred pall come sweeping by,
Presenting Thebes, or Pelops' line,
Or the tale of Troy divine,
Or what (though rare) of later age
Ennobled hath the buskin'd stage.
But, O sad Virgin, that thy power
Might raise Musæus from his bower,
Or bid the soul of Orpheus sing
Such notes as warbled to the string.
Drew iron tears down Pluto's cheek,
And made Hell grant what love did seek.
Or call up him that left half told
The story of Cambuscan bold,
Of Camball, and of Algarsife,
And who had Canace to wife,
That own'd the virtuous ring and glass,
And of the wondrous horse of brass,
On which the Tartar king did ride;
And if aught else great bards beside
In sage and solemn tunes have sung,
Of turneys and of trophies hung,
Of forests, and inchantments drear,
Where more is meant than meets the ear.
Thus night oft see me in thy pale career,
Till civil-suited morn appear,
Not trick'd and frounc'd as she was wont.
With the Attic boy to hunt,
But kerchef'd in a comely cloud,
While rocking winds are piping loud,
Or usher'd with a shower still,
When the gust hath blown his fill,
Ending on the rustling leaves,
With minute drops from off the eaves.
And when the sun begins to fling
His flaring beams, me, Goddess, bring

To arched walks of twilight groves,
And shadows brown that Sylvan loves
Of pine, or monumental oak,
Where the rude axe with heaved stroke
Was never heard the Nymphs to daunt,
Or fright them from their hallow'd haunt.
There in close covert by some brook,
Where no profaner eye may look,
Hide me from day's garish eye,
While the bee with honied thigh,
That at her flowery work doth sing,
And the waters murmuring
With such consort as they keep,
Entice the dewy-feather'd sleep;
And let some strange mysterious dream
Wave at his wings in airy stream
Of lively portraiture display'd,
Softly on my eyelids laid.
And as I wake, sweet music breathe
Above, about, or underneath,
Sent by some Spirit to mortals good,
Or th'unseen Genius of the wood.
But let my due feet never fail
To walk the studious cloisters pale,
And love the high embowed roof,
With antic pillars massy proof,
And storied windows richly dight,
Casting a dim religious light:
There let the pealing organ blow,
To the full voic'd quire below,
In service high, and anthems clear,
As may with sweetness, through mine ear,
Dissolve me into ecstasies,
And bring all heav'n before mine eyes.
And may at last my weary age
Find out the peaceful hermitage,
The hairy gown and mossy cell,
Where I may sit and rightly spell

Of every star that heav'n doth show,
And every herb that sips the dew;
Till old experience do attain
To something like prophetic strain.
These pleasures, Melancholy, give,
And I with thee will choose to live.

SONNET I

To the Nightingale

O Nightingale, that on yon bloomy spray
   Warblest at eve, when all the woods are still,
   Thou with fresh hope the lover's heart dost fill,
   While the jolly hours lead on propitious May.
Thy liquid notes that close the eye of day,
   First heard before the shallow cuckoo's bill,
   Portend success in love; O if Jove's will
   Have link'd that amorous power to thy soft lay,
Now timely sing, ere the rude bird of hate
   Foretell my hopeless doom in some grove nigh;
   As thou from year to year hast sung too late
For my relief, yet hadst no reason why:
   Whether the Muse, or Love call thee his mate,
   Both them I serve, and of their train am I.

SONNET XX

To Mr. Lawrence

Lawrence, of virtuous father virtuous son,
   Now that the fields are dank, and ways are mire,
   Where shall we sometimes meet, and by the fire
   Help waste a sullen day, what may be won

From the hard season gaining? Time will run
   On smoother, till Favonius re-inspire
   The frozen earth, and clothe in fresh attire
   The lily and rose, that neither sow'd nor spun.
What neat repast shall feast us, light and choice,
   Of Attic taste, with wine, whence we may rise
   To hear the lute well touch'd, or artful voice
Warble immortal notes and Tuscan air?
   He who of those delights can judge, and spare
   To interpose them oft, is not unwise.

From *COMUS*

SPIRIT. . . . .
   There is a gentle nymph not far from hence,
That with moist curb sways the smooth Severn stream,
Sabrina is her name, a virgin pure;
Whileome she was the daughter of Locrine,
That had the sceptre from his father Brute.
She, guiltless damsel, flying the mad pursuit
Of her enraged stepdame Guendolen,
Commended her fair innocence to the flood,
That stay'd her flight with his cross-flowing course.
The water nymphs, that in the bottom play'd,
Held up their pearled wrists, and took her in,
Bearing her straight to aged Nereus' hall,
Who piteous of her woes, rear'd her lank head,
And gave her to his daughters to imbathe
In nectar'd lavers strow'd with asphodel,
And through the porch and inlet of each sense
Dropp'd in ambrosial oils, till she reviv'd,
And underwent a quick immortal change,
Made Goddess of the river: still she retains
Her maiden gentleness, and oft at eve
Visits the herds along the twilight meadows,
Helping all urchin blasts, and ill-luck signs

That the shrewd meddling elf delights to make,
Which she with precious vial'd liquors heals.
For which the shepherds at their festivals
Carol her goodness loud in rustic lays,
And throw sweet garland wreaths into her stream
Of pansies, pinks, and gaudy daffodils.
And, as the old swain said, she can unlock
The clasping charm, and thaw the numbing spell,
If she be right invok'd in warbled song,
For maidenhood she loves, and will be swift
To aid a virgin, such as was herself,
In hard-besetting need; this will I try,
And add the pow'r of some adjuring verse.

Song

Sabrina fair,
   Listen where thou art sitting
Under the glassy, cool, translucent wave,
   In twisted braids of lilies knitting
The loose train of thy amber-dropping hair;
   Listen for dear honour's sake,
   Goddess of the silver lake,
     Listen and save.
Listen and appear to us
In name of great Oceanus,
By th'earth-shaking Neptune's mace,
And Tethys' grave majestic pace,
By hoary Nereus' wrinkled look,
And the Carpathian wisard's hook,
By scaly Triton's winding shell,
And old soothsaying Glaucus' spell,
By Leucothea's lovely hands,
And her son that rules the strands,
By Thetis' tinsel-slipper'd feet,
And the songs of Sirens sweet,
By dead Parthenope's dear tomb,

And fair Ligea's golden comb,
Wherewith she sits on diamond rocks,
Sleeking her soft alluring locks,
By all the nymphs that nightly dance
Upon thy streams with wily glance,
Rise, rise, and heave thy rosy head
From thy coral-paven bed,
And bridle in thy headlong wave,
Till thou our summons answer'd have.

                       Listen and save.

  SABRINA: By the rushy-fringed bank,
Where grows the willow and the osier dank,
  My sliding chariot stays,
Thick set with agate, and the azurn sheen
Of turkis blue, and emerald green,
  That in the channel strays;
Whilst from off the waters fleet,
Thus I set my printless feet
O'er the cowslip's velvet head,
  That bends not as I tread;
Gentle Swain, at thy request
  I am here.

  SPIRIT: Goddess dear,
We implore thy pow'rful hand
To undo the charmed band
Of true virgin here distrest,
Through the force, and through the wile
Of unblest inchanter vile.

  SABRINA: Shepherd, 'tis my office best
To help insnared chastity:
Brightest Lady, look on me;
Thus I sprinkle on thy breast
Drops that from my fountain pure
I have kept of precious cure,
Thrice upon thy finger's tip,
Thrice upon thy rubied lip;
Next this marble venom'd seat,
Smear'd with gums of glutinous heat,

I touch with chaste palms moist and cold:
Now the spell hath lost his hold;
And I must haste ere morning hour
To wait in Amphitrite's bow'r.

    SPIRIT: Virgin, daughter of Locrine
Sprung of old Anchises' line,
May thy brimmed waves for this
Their full tribute never miss
From a thousand petty rills,
That tumble down the snowy hills:
Summer drouth or singed air
Never scorch thy tresses fair,
Nor wet October's torrent flood
Thy molten crystal fill with mud;
May thy billows roll ashore
The beryl, and the golden ore;
May thy lofty head be crown'd
With many a tow'r and terrace round,
And here and there thy banks upon
With groves of myrrh and cinnamon.

LATER POEMS

PARADISE LOST

BOOK I.   44

    . . . . Him the almighty Power
Hurl'd headlong flaming from th'ethereal sky,
With hideous ruin and combustion, down
To bottomless perdition, there to dwell
In adamantine chains and penal fire,
Who durst defy th'Omnipotent to arms.
Nine times the space that measures day and night
To mortal men, he with his horrid crew
Lay vanquish'd, rolling in the fiery gulf,
Confounded though immortal: but his doom
Reserv'd him to more wrath; for now the thought

Both of lost happiness and lasting pain
Torments him; round he throws his baleful eyes,
That witness'd huge affliction and dismay,
Mix'd with obdurate pride and stedfast hate.
At once, as far as angels ken, he views
The dismal situation waste and wild;
A dungeon horrible, on all sides round,
As one great furnace, flam'd; yet from those flames
No light, but rather darkness visible
Serv'd only to discover sights of woe,
Regions of sorrow, doleful shades, where peace
And rest can never dwell, hope never comes
That comes to all; but torture without end
Still urges, and a fiery deluge, fed
With ever-burning sulphur unconsum'd.
Such place eternal justice had prepar'd
For those rebellious; here their prison ordain'd
In utter darkness, and their portion set
As far remov'd from God and light of heav'n,
As from the centre thrice to th'utmost pole.
O how unlike the place from whence they fell!
There the companions of his fall, o'erwhelm'd
With floods and whirlwinds of tempestuous fire,
He soon discerns, and welt'ring by his side
One next himself in power, and next in crime,
Long after known in Palestine, and nam'd
Beelzebub. To whom th'arch-enemy,
And thence in heav'n call'd Satan, with bold words
Breaking the horrid silence, thus began.

If thou beest he—But O how fall'n! how chang'd
From him, who in the happy realms of light,
Cloath'd with transcendent brightness, didst outshine
Myriads, though bright! If he, whom mutual league,
United thoughts and counsels, equal hope.
And hazard in the glorious enterprize,
Join'd with me once, now misery hath join'd
In equal ruin: into what pit thou seest
From what height fall'n, so much the stronger prov'd

He with his thunder; and till then who knew
The force of those dire arms? yet not for those,
Nor what the potent victor in his rage
Can else inflict, do I repent, or change,
Though chang'd in outward lustre, that fix'd mind
And high disdain from sense of injur'd merit,
That with the Mightiest rais'd me to contend,
And to the fierce contention brought along
Innumerable force of Spirits arm'd,
That durst dislike his reign; and, me preferring,
His utmost power with adverse power oppos'd
In dubious battel on the plains of heav'n,
And shook his throne. What though the field be lost?
All is not lost; th'unconquerable will,
And study of revenge, immortal hate
And courage never to submit or yield,
And what is else not to be overcome;
That glory never shall his wrath or might
Extort from me: to bow and sue for grace
With suppliant knee, and deify his power,
Who from the terror of this arm so late
Doubted his empire, that were low indeed,
That were an ignominy and shame beneath
This downfall; since by fate the strength of Gods
And this empyreal substance cannot fail;
Since through experience of this great event,
In arms not worse, in foresight much advanc'd,
We may with more successful hope resolve
To wage by force or guile eternal war,
Irreconcileable to our grand foe,
Who now triumphs, and in th'excess of joy
Sole reigning holds the tyranny of heav'n.

So spake th'apostate Angel, though in pain,
Vaunting aloud, but rack'd with deep despair:
And him thus answer'd soon his bold compeer.

O Prince, O chief of many throned Powers,
That led th'imbattell'd Seraphim to war
Under thy conduct, and, in dreadful deeds

Fearless, endanger'd heav'n's perpetual King,
And put to proof his high supremacy;
Whether upheld by strength, or chance, or fate,
Too well I see and rue the dire event,
That with sad overthrow and foul defeat
Hath lost us heav'n, and all this mighty host
In horrible destruction laid thus low,
As far as Gods and heavenly essences
Can perish: for the mind and spirit remains
Invincible, and vigour soon returns,
Though all our glory extinct, and happy state
Here swallow'd up in endless misery.
But what if he our conqueror, whom I now
Of force believe almighty, since no less
Than such could have o'erpower'd such force as ours,
Have left us this our spirit and strength entire,
Strongly to suffer and support our pains,
That we may so suffice his vengeful ire,
Or do him mightier service, as his thralls
By right of war, whate'er his business be,
Here in the heart of hell to work in fire,
Or do his errands in the gloomy deep:
What can it then avail, though yet we feel
Strength undiminish'd, or eternal being
To undergo eternal punishment?
Whereto with speedy words th'Arch-fiend reply'd.

   Fall'n Cherub, to be weak is miserable,
Doing or suffering: but of this be sure,
To do ought good never will be our task,
But ever to do ill our sole delight;
As being the contrary to his high will,
Whom we resist. If then his providence
Out of our evil seek to bring forth good,
Our labour must be to pervert that end,
And out of good still to find means of evil;
Which oft-times may succeed, so as perhaps
Shall grieve him, if I fail not, and disturb
His inmost counsels from their destin'd aim.

But see! the angry victor hath recall'd
His ministers of vengeance and pursuit
Back to the gates of heav'n: the sulphurous hail,
Shot after us in storm, o'erblown hath laid
The fiery surge, that from the precipice
Of heav'n receiv'd us falling, and the thunder,
Wing'd with red lightning and impetuous rage,
Perhaps hath spent his shafts, and ceases now
To bellow through the vast and boundless deep.
Let us not slip th'occasion, whether scorn
Or satiate fury yield it from our foe.
Seest thou yon dreary plain, forlorn and wild,
The seat of desolation, void of light,
Save what the glimmering of these livid flames
Casts pale and dreadful? thither let us tend
From off the tossing of these fiery waves,
There rest, if any rest can harbour there,
And, reassembling our afflicted powers,
Consult how we may henceforth most offend
Our enemy, our own loss how repair,
How overcome this dire calamity,
What reinforcement we may gain from hope,
If not, what resolution from despair.

Book i.   242

Is this the region, this the soil, the clime,
Said then the lost Arch-Angel, this the seat
That we must change for heav'n, this mournful gloom
For that celestial light? Be it so, since he,
Who now is Sov'reign, can dispose and bid
What shall be right: farthest from him is best,
Whom reason hath equall'd, force hath made supreme
Above his equals. Farewell happy fields,
Where joy for ever dwells: hail horrors; hail
Infernal world; and thou profoundest hell
Receive thy new possessor; one who brings

A mind not to be chang'd by place or time.
The mind is its own place, and in itself
Can make a heav'n of hell, a hell of heav'n.
What matter where, if I be still the same,
And what I should be, all but less than he
Whom thunder hath made greater? here at least
We shall be free: th'Almighty hath not built
Here for his envy, will not drive us hence:
Here we may reign secure, and in my choice
To reign is worth ambition, though in hell:
Better to reign in hell, than serve in heav'n.
But wherefore let we then our faithful friends,
Th'associates and copartners of our loss,
Lie thus astonish'd on th'oblivious pool,
And call them not to share with us their part
In this unhappy mansion; or once more
With rallied arms to try what may be yet
Regain'd in heav'n, or what more lost in hell?

Book i. 522

All these and more came flocking; but with looks
Down-cast and damp, yet such wherein appear'd
Obscure some glimpse of joy, to have found their chief
Not in despair, to have found themselves not lost
In loss itself; which on his count'nance cast
Like doubtful hue: but he, his wonted pride
Soon recollecting, with high words, that bore
Semblance of worth not substance, gently rais'd
Their fainted courage, and dispell'd their fears.
Then straight commands, that at the warlike sound
Of trumpets loud and clarions be uprear'd
His mighty standard: that proud honour claim'd
Azazel as his right, a cherub tall;
Who forthwith from the glittering staff unfurl'd
Th'imperial ensign, which, full high advanc'd,
Shone like a meteor, streaming to the wind,

With gems and golden lustre rich imblaz'd,
Seraphic arms and trophies; all the while
Sonorous metal blowing martial sounds:
At which the universal host up sent
A shout that tore hell's concave, and beyond
Frighted the reign of Chaos and old Night.
All in a moment through the gloom were seen
Ten thousand banners rise into the air
With orient colour waving: with them rose
A forest huge of spears; and thronging helms
Appear'd, and serried shields in thick array
Of depth immeasurable: anon they move
In perfect phalanx to the Dorian mood
Of flutes and soft recorders; such as rais'd
To highth of noblest temper heroes old
Arming to battle; and instead of rage
Deliberate valor breath'd, firm, and unmov'd
With dread of death to flight or foul retreat;
Nor wanting power to mitigate and swage
With solemn touches troubled thoughts, and chase
Anguish, and doubt, and fear, and sorrow, and pain,
From mortal or immortal minds. Thus they,
Breathing united force, with fixed thought,
Mov'd on in silence to soft pipes, that charm'd
Their painful steps o'er the burnt soil; and now
Advanc'd in view they stand, a horrid front
Of dreadful length and dazzling arms, in guise
Of warriors old with order'd spear and shield,
Awaiting what command their mighty chief
Had to impose: he through the armed files
Darts his experienc'd eye, and soon traverse
The whole battalion views; their order due,
Their visages and stature as of Gods;
Their number last he sums.

Book ii.   546

. . . . Others more mild,
Retreated in a silent valley, sing
With notes angelical to many a harp
Their own heroic deeds and hapless fall
By doom of battel; and complain that fate
Free virtue should inthral to force or chance.
Their song was partial; but the harmony,
What could it less when spirits immortal sing?
Suspended hell, and took with ravishment
The thronging audience. In discourse more sweet,
For eloquence the soul, song charms the sense,
Others apart sat on a hill retir'd,
In thoughts more elevate, and reason'd high
Of providence, foreknowledge, will, and fate.
Fix'd fate, free will, foreknowledge absolute;
And found no end, in wand'ring mazes lost.
Of good and evil much they argued then,
Of happiness and final misery,
Passion and apathy, and glory and shame,
Vain wisdom all, and false philosophy:
Yet with a pleasing sorcery could charm
Pain for a while or anguish, and excite
Fallacious hope, or arm th'obdured breast
With stubborn patience as with triple steel.
Another part in squadrons and gross bands,
On bold adventure to discover wide
That dismal world, if any clime perhaps,
Might yield them easier habitation, bend
Four ways their flying march, along the banks
Of four infernal rivers, that disgorge
Into the burning lake their baleful streams;
Abhorred Styx, the flood of deadly hate;
Sad Acheron of sorrow, black and deep;
Cocytus, nam'd of lamentation loud
Heard on the rueful stream; fierce Phlegeton,

Whose waves of torrent fire inflame with rage.
Far off from these a slow and silent stream,
Lethe the river of oblivion, rolls
Her wat'ry labyrinth, whereof who drinks,
Forthwith his former state and being forgets,
Forgets both joy and grief, pleasure, and pain.
Beyond this flood a frozen continent
Lies, dark and wild, beat with perpetual storms
Of whirlwind and dire hail; which on firm land
Thaws not, but gathers heap, and ruin seems
Of antient pile; all else deep snow and ice;
A gulf profound as that Serbonian bog
Betwixt Damiata and mount Casius old,
Where armies whole have sunk: the parching air
Burns frore, and cold performs th'effect of fire.
Thither by harpy-footed Furies hal'd
At certain revolutions all the damn'd
Are brought; and feel by turns the bitter change
Of fierce extremes, extremes by change more fierce,
From beds of raging fire to starve in ice
Their soft ethereal warmth, and there to pine
Immovable, infix'd, and frozen round,
Periods of time; thence hurried back to fire.
They ferry over this Lethean sound
Both to and fro, their sorrow to augment,
And wish and struggle, as they pass to reach
The tempting stream, with one small drop to lose
In sweet forgetfulness all pain and woe,
All in one moment, and so near the brink:
But fate withstands, and to oppose th'attempt
Medusa with Gorgonian terror guards
The ford, and of itself the water flies
All taste of living wight, as once it fled
The lip of Tantalus. Thus roving on
In confus'd march forlorn, th'advent'rous bands,
With shudd'ring horror pale, and eyes agast,
View'd first their lamentable lot, and found
No rest: through many a dark and dreary vale

They pass'd, and many a region dolorous,
O'er many a frozen, many a fiery Alp,
Rocks, caves, lakes, fens, bogs, dens, and shades of death,
A universe of death, which God by curse
Created evil, for evil only good,
Where all life dies, death lives, and nature breeds,
Perverse, all monstrous, all prodigious things,
Abominable, inutterable, and worse
Than fables yet have feign'd, or fear conceiv'd.

BOOK XII.   552 (the End)

He ended; and thus Adam last reply'd.
How soon hath thy prediction, Seer bless'd,
Measur'd this transient world, the race of time,
Till time stand fix'd! beyond is all abyss,
Eternity, whose end no eye can reach:
Greatly instructed I shall hence depart,
Greatly in peace of thought, and have my fill
Of knowledge, what this vessel can contain;
Beyond which was my folly to aspire.
Henceforth I learn that to obey is best,
And love with fear the only God, to walk
As in his presence, ever to observe
His providence, and on him sole depend,
Merciful over all his works, with good
Still overcoming evil; and by small
Accomplishing great things, by things deem'd weak
Subverting worldly strong, and worldly wise
By simply meek; that suffering for truth's sake
Is fortitude to highest victory
And to the faithful death the gate of life;
Taught this by his example, whom I now
Acknowledge my Redeemer ever bless'd.

To whom thus also th'angel last reply'd.
This having learn'd, thou hast attain'd the sum

Of wisdom; hope no higher, though all the stars
Thou knew'st by name, and all th'ethereal powers
All secrets of the deep, all nature's works,
Or works of God in heav'n, air, earth, or sea,
And all the riches of this world enjoy'dst,
And all the rule, one empire; only add
Deeds to thy knowledge answerable, add faith,
Add virtue, patience, temperance, add love,
By name to come call'd charity, the soul
Of all the rest; then wilt thou not be loath
To leave this paradise, but shalt possess
A paradise within thee, happier far.
Let us descend now therefore from this top
Of speculation; for the hour precise
Exacts our parting hence; and see the guards,
By me encamp'd on yonder hill, expect
Their motion, at whose front a flaming sword,
In signal of remove, waves fiercely round;
We may no longer stay: go, waken Eve;
Her also I with gentle dreams have calm'd
Portending good, and all her spirits compos'd
To meek submission: thou at season fit
Let her with thee partake what thou hast heard,
Chiefly what may concern her faith to know,
The great deliverance by her seed to come,
For by the woman's seed, on all mankind.
That ye may live, which will be many days,
Both in one faith unanimous, though sad
With cause for evils past; yet much more cheer'd
With meditation on the happy end.

   He ended, and they both descend the hill;
Descended, Adam to the bower, where Eve
Lay sleeping, ran before, but found her wak'd;
And thus with words not sad she him receiv'd.

   Whence thou return'st, and whither went'st, I know;
For God is also in sleep, and dreams advise,
Which he hath sent propitious, some great good
Presaging, since with sorrow and heart's distress

Wearied I fell asleep: but now lead on;
In me is no delay; with thee to go
Is to stay here; without thee here to stay
Is to go hence unwilling; thou to me
Art all things under heav'n, all places thou,
Who for my wilful crime art banish'd hence.
This further consolation yet secure
I carry hence; though all by me is lost,
Such favour I unworthy am vouchsaf'd,
By me the promis'd seed shall all restore.

  So spake our mother Eve, and Adam heard
Well pleas'd, but answer'd not; for now too nigh
Th'archangel stood, and from the other hill
To their fix'd station all in bright array
The Cherubim descended; on the ground
Gliding meteorous, as ev'ning mist
Ris'n from a river o'er the marish glides,
And gathers ground fast at the labourer's heel
Homeward returning. High in front advanc'd
The brandish'd sword of God before them blaz'd
Fierce as a comet; which with torrid heat,
And vapour as the Libyan air adust,
Began to parch that temperate clime: whereat
In either hand th'hast'ning angel caught
Our ling'ring parents, and to the eastern gate
Led them direct, and down the cliff as fast
To the subjected plain; then disappear'd.
They looking back all th'eastern side beheld
Of paradise, so late their happy seat,
Wav'd over by that flaming brand, the gate
With dreadful faces throng'd and fiery arms:
Some natural tears they dropp'd, but wip'd them soon;
The world was all before them, where to choose
Their place of rest, and providence their guide.
They, hand in hand with wand'ring steps and slow,
Through Eden took their solitary way.

From *SAMSON AGONISTES*

CHORUS: All is best, though we oft doubt,
What th'unsearchable dispose
Of highest wisdom brings about,
And ever best found in the close.
Oft he seems to hide his face,
But unexpectedly returns. . . .
His servants he, with new acquist
Of true experience from this great event,
With peace and consolation hath dismiss'd,
And calm of mind, all passion spent.

Occasional Lines

PARADISE LOST

BOOK I.   330

Awake, arise, or be for ever fall'n.

BOOK II.   146

For who would lose,
Though full of pain, this intellectual being,
Those thoughts that wander through eternity?

BOOK IV.   677

Millions of spiritual creatures walk the earth
Unseen, both when we wake, and when we sleep.

BOOK IV.   846

Abasht the Devil stood,
And felt how awful goodness is, and saw
Virtue in her shape how lovely; saw, and pined.

BOOK XI.   399

Mombaza, and Quiloa, and Melind.

Robert Herrick

HESPERIDES

I sing of brooks, of blossoms, birds and bowers,
Of April, May, of June and July flowers;
I sing of May-poles, Hock-carts, Wassails, Wakes,
Of bride-grooms, brides and of their bridal-cakes;
I write of youth, of love, and have access
By these, to sing of cleanly wanton-ness;
I sing of dews, of rains, and piece by piece
Of balm, of oil, of spice and ambergris;
I sing of Time's trans-shifting, and I write
How roses first came red and lilies white;
I write of groves, of twilights, and I sing
The Court of Mab, and of the Fairy King;
I write of Hell; I sing (and ever shall)
Of Heaven, and hope to have it after all.

UPON JULIA'S VOICE

So smooth, so sweet, so silvery is thy voice
As, could they hear, the damned would make no noise,
But listen to thee walking in thy chamber
Melting melodious words to lutes of amber.

HIS PARTING WITH MRS. DOROTHY KENNEDY

Prithee (lest maids should censure thee) but say
Thou shed'st one tear, whenas I went away;
And that will please me somewhat: though I know,
(And Love will swear 't) my dearest did not so.

TO LIVE MERRILY AND TO TRUST TO GOOD VERSES

Now is the time for mirth,
Nor cheek or tongue be dumb;
For, with the flowery earth,
The golden pomp is come.

TO A GENTLEWOMAN OBJECTING TO HIM HIS GRAY HAIRS

Am I despised because, you say,
(And I dare swear), that I am gray?
Know, Lady, you have but your day:
And time will come when you shall wear
Such frost and snow upon your hair;
And when (though long, it comes to pass)
You question with your looking-glass,
And in that sincere crystal seek,
But find no rose-bud in your cheek . . . .
Ah, then, too late, close in your chamber keeping,
    It will be told
    That you are old,
By those true tears y' are weeping.

CHOP-CHERRY

Thou gav'st me leave to kiss;
Thou gav'st me leave to woo;
Thou mad'st me think, by this
And that, thou lovdst me too.

But I shall ne'er forget
How, for to make thee merry,
Thou mad'st me chop, but yet
Another snapp'd the cherry.

Note:

  Chop-Cherry, or Bob-cherry, a game in which the players try to catch (with their mouths alone) a cherry dangling from a thread.

FAIR DAYS: or *DAWNS DECEITFUL*

Fair was the dawn, and, but e'en now, the skies
Showd like to cream inspired with strawberries.

A COUNTRY LIFE

And the brisk mouse may feast herself with crumbs
Till that the green-eyed Kitling comes.

TO VIOLETS

Welcome, Maids of Honour,
You do bring
In the Spring
And wait upon her.

She has virgins many,
Fresh and fair:
Yet you are
More sweet than any. . . .

HIS POETRY—HIS PILLAR

Only a little more
I have to write,
Then I'll give o'er,
And bid the world good-night.

Behold this living stone
I rear for me,

Ne'er to be thrown
Down, envious Time, by Thee.

Pillars let some set up
If so they please:
Here is my hope
And my Pyramides.

TO MEADOWS

Ye have been fresh and green,
Ye have been filled with flowers,
And ye the walks have been
Where maids have spent their hours. . . .

THE APPARITION OF HIS MISTRESS CALLING HIM TO ELYSIUM

575   Here in green meadows sits eternal May.

444   The gum
That shines upon the bluer plum.

A TERNARY OF LITTLES, UPON A PIPKIN OF JELLY SENT TO A LADY

A little Saint best fits a little shrine,
A little prop best fits a little vine:
As my small cruse best fits my little wine.

A little hearth best fits a little fire,
A little chapel fits a little quire,
As my small bell best fits my little spire.
. . . . . etc.

From *NOBLE NUMBERS*

43   *Cock-Crow*

Bellman of Night, if I about shall go
For to deny my Master, do thou crow.
Thou stopp'st St Peter in the midst of sin;
Stay me, by crowing, ere I do begin.

71   *Alms*

Give, if thou canst, an alms; if not, afford,
Instead of that, a sweet and gentle word.

96   The Chorus from *A Christmas Carol*

We see Him come, and know Him ours,
Who, with His sunshine and His showers,
Turns all the patient ground to flowers.

Andrew Marvell

From *BERMUDAS*

He hangs in shades the Orange bright
Like golden lamps in a green night.

John Dryden

ALL FOR LOVE, or *THE WORLD WELL LOST*

The last Scene of Act III

CHARMIAN:

She comes. She's here.

IRAS:

Fly, Madam. Cæsar's Sister.

CLEOPATRA:

Were she the Sister of the Thunderer, Jove,
And bore her Brother's Lightning in her eyes,
Thus would I face my rival.   (OCTAVIA *enters.*)

OCTAVIA:

I need not ask, if you are Cleopatra . . . . .
Your haughty carriage. . . .

CLEOPATRA:

Shows I am a Queen . . .
Nor need I ask you who you are.

OCTAVIA:

A Roman:
A name that makes, and can unmake a Queen.

CLEOPATRA:

Your Lord, the man who serves me, is a Roman.

OCTAVIA:

He *was* a Roman, till he lost that name
To be a slave in Egypt; but I come
To free him thence.

CLEOPATRA:

                Peace, peace, my lover's Juno.
When he grew weary of that household clog
He chose my easier bonds.

OCTAVIA:

      Your bonds are easy; you have long been practised
In that lascivious art: he's not the first
For whom you spread your snares: let Cæsar witness.

CLEOPATRA:

      I loved not Cæsar: 'twas but gratitude
I paid his love. The worst your malice can,
Is but to say the greatest of mankind
Has been my slave. The next, but far above him
In my esteem, is he whom law calls yours,
But whom his love made mine.

OCTAVIA:

                I would view nearer
That face, which has so long usurped my right,
To find the inevitable charms, that catch
Mankind, so sure; that ruined my dear Lord.

CLEOPATRA:

      O you do well to search; for had you known
But half these charms, you had not lost his heart.

OCTAVIA:

      Far be their knowledge from a Roman lady.
Far from a modest wife. Shame of our sex,
Dost thou not blush, to own those black endearments
That make sin pleasing?

CLEOPATRA:

          You may blush, who want 'em.
If bounteous Nature, if indulgent Heaven,
Have given me charms to please the bravest men,

Should I not thank 'em? Should I be ashamed,
And not be proud? I am, that he has loved me.
And, when I love not him, Heaven change this face
For one like that.

OCTAVIA:

Thou lov'st him not so well.

CLEOPATRA:

I love him better and deserve him more.

OCTAVIA:

You do not: cannot. You have been his ruin.
Who made him cheap at Rome, but Cleopatra?
Who made him scorned abroad, but Cleopatra?
At Actium, who betrayed him? Cleopatra.
Who made his children orphans? and poor me
A wretched widow? only Cleopatra.

CLEOPATRA:

Yet she who loves him best is Cleopatra.

Alexander Pope

From *THE RAPE OF THE LOCK*

She said: then, raging to Sir Plume repairs,
And bids her beau demand the precious hairs;
(Sir Plume, of amber snuff-box justly vain,
And the nice conduct of a clouded cane),
With earnest eyes, and round, unthinking face,
He first the snuff-box opened, then the case,
And thus broke out:—

            "My Lord, why, what the devil?
Zounds! Damn the lock. 'Fore 'Gad, you must be civil . . .
Plague on 't, 'tis past a jest . . . nay, prythee . . . pox . . .
Give her the hair" . . .

            he spoke, and rapped his box.
"It grieves me much" (replied the peer again)
"Who speaks so well should ever speak in vain . . .
But by this lock, this sacred lock, I swear . . . .
This hand, which won it, shall forever wear."

Matthew Prior

Lines and Stanzas from *DOWN HALL*

"Come here, my sweet Landlady, pray, how d'ye do?
Where is Cicely so cleanly, and Prudence, and Sue?
And where is the Widow that dwelt here below?
And the Ostler that sang, about eight years ago?

And where is your Sister, so mild and so dear?
Whose voice to her maids like a trumpet was clear."

"By my troth," she replies, "You grow younger, I think . . .
And pray, Sir, what wine does the gentleman drink?

Why, now, let me die, Sir, or live upon trust,
If I know to which question to answer you first:
Why, things, since I saw you, most strangely have varied:
The Ostler is hanged, and the Widow is married.

And Prue left a child for the parish to nurse,
And Cicely went off with a gentleman's purse;
And as to my Sister, so mild and so dear,
She has lain in the church-yard full many a year."

A line from *DOWN HALL*, earlier in the poem than the above

But Matthew thought better, for Matthew thought right.

Christopher Smart

From *A SONG TO DAVID*

Strong is the horse upon his speed;
Strong in pursuit the rapid glede,
Which makes at once his game:
Strong the tall ostrich on the ground;
Strong through the turbulent profound
Shoots Xiphias to his aim.

Strong is the lion:—like a coal
His eyeball:—like a bastion's mole
His chest against the foes:
Strong the gier-eagle on his sail,
Strong, against tide, th' enormous whale
Emerges as he goes.

But stronger still, in earth and air,
And in the sea, the Man of Pray'r,
And far beneath the tide:
And in the seat to Faith assigned,
Where Ask is Have, where Seek is Find,
Where Knock is Open Wide.

Glede: A kite or lesser bird of prey.
Xiphias: A sword-fish.
Gier-Eagle: A vulture.

Thomas Gray

ELEGY WRITTEN IN A COUNTRY CHURCH-YARD

The curfew tolls the knell of parting day,
  The lowing herd winds slowly o'er the lea,
The ploughman homeward plods his weary way,
  And leaves the world to darkness and to me.

Now fades the glimmering landscape on the sight,
  And all the air a solemn stillness holds,
Save where the beetle wheels his droning flight,
  And drowsy tinklings lull the distant folds:

Save that from yonder ivy-mantled tow'r
  The moping owl does to the moon complain
Of such as, wand'ring near her secret bow'r,
  Molest her ancient solitary reign.

Beneath those rugged elms, that yew-tree's shade,
  Where heaves the turf in many a mould'ring heap,
Each in his narrow cell for ever laid,
  The rude forefathers of the hamlet sleep.

The breezy call of incense-breathing morn,
  The swallow twitt'ring from the straw-built shed,
The cock's shrill clarion, or the echoing horn,
  No more shall rouse them from their lowly bed.

For them no more the blazing hearth shall burn,
  Or busy housewife ply her evening care;
No children run to lisp their sire's return,
  Or climb his knees the envied kiss to share.

Oft did the harvest to their sickle yield,
  Their furrow oft the stubborn glebe has broke:
How jocund did they drive their team afield!
  How bow'd the woods beneath their sturdy stroke!

Let not ambition mock their useful toil,
 Their homely joys, and destiny obscure;
Nor grandeur hear with a disdainful smile
 The short and simple annals of the poor.

The boast of heraldry, the pomp of pow'r,
 And all that beauty, all that wealth e'er gave,
Await alike th'inevitable hour.
 The paths of glory lead but to the grave.

Nor you, ye proud, impute to these the fault,
 If memory o'er their tomb no trophies raise,
Where through the long-drawn isle and fretted vault
 The pealing anthem swells the note of praise.

Can storied urn, or animated bust,
 Back to its mansion call the fleeting breath?
Can honour's voice provoke the silent dust,
 Or flatt'ry soothe the dull cold ear of death?

Perhaps in this neglected spot is laid
 Some heart once pregnant with celestial fire;
Hands, that the rod of empire might have sway'd,
 Or wak'd to ecstasy the living lyre.

But knowledge to their eyes her ample page
 Rich with the spoils of time did ne'er unroll;
Chill penury repress'd their noble rage,
 And froze the genial current of the soul.

Full many a gem of purest ray serene
 The dark unfathom'd caves of ocean bear:
Full many a flower is born to blush unseen,
 And waste its sweetness on the desert air.

Some village-Hampden, that, with dauntless breast,
  The little tyrant of his fields withstood,
Some mute inglorious Milton here may rest,
  Some Cromwell guiltless of his country's blood.

Th'applause of list'ning senates to command,
  The threats of pain and ruin to despise,
To scatter plenty o'er a smiling land,
  And read their history in a nation's eyes,

Their lot forbad: nor circumscrib'd alone
  Their growing virtues, but their crimes confin'd;
Forbad to wade thro' slaughter to a throne,
  And shut the gates of mercy on mankind,

The struggling pangs of conscious truth to hide,
  To quench the blushes of ingenuous shame,
Or heap the shrine of luxury and pride
  With incense kindled at the Muse's flame.

Far from the madding crowd's ignoble strife,
  Their sober wishes never learn'd to stray;
Along the cool sequester'd vale of life
  They kept the noiseless tenor of their way.

Yet ev'n these bones from insult to protect
  Some frail memorial still erected nigh,
With uncouth rhymes and shapeless sculpture deck'd,
  Implores the passing tribute of a sigh.

Their name, their years, spelt by th'unletter'd Muse,
  The place of fame and elegy supply:
And many a holy text around she strews,
  That teach the rustic moralist to die.

For who, to dumb forgetfulness a prey,
  This pleasing anxious being e'er resign'd,
Left the warm precincts of the cheerful day,
  Nor cast one longing ling'ring look behind?

On some fond breast the parting soul relies,
  Some pious drops the closing eye requires;
E'en from the tomb the voice of nature cries,
  E'en in our ashes live their wonted fires.

For thee, who, mindful of th'unhonour'd dead,
  Dost in these lines their artless tale relate;
If chance, by lonely contemplation led,
  Some kindred spirit shall enquire thy fate,—

Haply some hoary-headed swain may say,
  "Oft have we seen him at the peep of dawn
Brushing with hasty steps the dews away,
  To meet the sun upon the upland lawn:

"There at the foot of yonder nodding beech,
  That wreathes its old fantastic roots so high,
His listless length at noontide would he stretch,
  And pore upon the brook that babbles by.

"Hard by yon wood, now smiling as in scorn,
  Mutt'ring his wayward fancies he would rove;
Now drooping, woful-wan, like one forlorn,
  Or craz'd with care, or cross'd in hopeless love.

"One morn I miss'd him on the custom'd hill,
  Along the heath, and near his fav'rite tree;
Another came; nor yet beside the rill,
  Nor up the lawn, nor at the wood was he:

"The next, with dirges due in sad array
  Slow through the church-way path we saw him borne:—
Approach and read (for thou can'st read) the lay
  Grav'd on the stone beneath yon aged thorn."

The Epitaph

Here rests his head upon the lap of earth
A youth, to fortune and to fame unknown:
Fair science frown'd not on his humble birth,
And melancholy mark'd him for her own.

Large was his bounty, and his soul sincere,
Heaven did a recompense as largely send:
He gave to mis'ry (all he had) a tear,
He gain'd from heav'n ('twas all he wish'd) a friend.

No farther seek his merits to disclose,
Or draw his frailties from their dread abode,
(There they alike in trembling hope repose,)
The bosom of his Father and his God.

" 'There scatter'd oft, the earliest of the year,
By hands unseen are show'rs of violets found;
The redbreast loves to build and warble there,
And little footsteps lightly print the ground.' "

Note: This last stanza formerly preceded the Epitaph.

TOPHET

An Epigram

Thus Tophet look'd; so grinn'd the brawling fiend,
Whilst frighted prelates bow'd and call'd him friend.
Our mother-church, with half-averted sight,
Blush'd as she bless'd her griesly proselyte;
Hosannas rung through hell's tremendous borders,
And Satan's self had thoughts of taking orders.

IMPROMPTU

Old, and abandon'd by each venal friend,
   Here H——d form'd the pious resolution
To smuggle a few years, and strive to mend
   A broken character and constitution.

On this congenial spot he fix'd his choice;
   Earl Goodwin trembled for his neighbouring sand;
Here sea-gulls scream, and cormorants rejoice,
   And mariners, though shipwreck'd, dread to land.

Here reign the blustering North and blighting East,
   No tree is heard to whisper, bird to sing;
Yet Nature could not furnish out the feast,
   Art he invokes new horrors still to bring.

Here mouldering fanes and battlements arise,
   Turrets and arches nodding to their fall,
Unpeopled monast'ries delude our eyes,
   And mimic desolation covers all.

"Ah!" said the sighing peer, "had B—te been true,
   Nor M—'s, R—'s, B—'s friendship vain,
Far better scenes than these had blest our view,
   And realiz'd the beauties which we feign:

"Purg'd by the sword, and purified by fire,
   Then had we seen proud London's hated walls;
Owls would have hooted in St. Peter's choir,
   And foxes stunk and litter'd in St. Paul's."

Holland
Bute
Mungo
Rigby
Bradshaw

William Cowper

From *THE CONTRITE HEART*
(*Olney Hymns* IX)

Thy Saints are comforted, I know,
And love Thy house of pray'r;
I therefore go where others go,
But find no comfort there.

O make this heart rejoice or ache;
Decide this doubt for me;
And if it be not broken, break,
And heal it, if it be.

ON THE LOSS OF THE ROYAL GEORGE

(written when the news arrived, to the tune of the Dead March in
Scipio, the Opera by Handel.)

Toll for the brave!
The brave that are no more!
All sunk beneath the wave,
Fast by their native shore!

Eight hundred of the brave,
Whose courage well was tried,
Had made the vessel heel,
And laid her on her side.

A land-breeze shook the shrouds,
And she was overset;
Down went the *Royal George*
With all her crew complete.

Toll for the brave!
Brave Kempenfelt is gone;
His last sea-fight is fought;
His work of glory done.

It was not in the battle;
No tempest gave the shock;
She sprang no fatal leak;
She ran upon no rock.

His sword was in its sheath;
His fingers held the pen,
When Kempenfelt went down
With twice four hundred men.

Weigh the vessel up,
Once dreaded by our foes!
And mingle with our cup
The tears that England owes.

Her timbers yet are sound,
And she may float again
Full charged with England's thunder,
And plough the distant main.

But Kempenfelt is gone,
His victories are o'er;
And he and his eight hundred
Shall plough the wave no more.

September, 1782.

H.M.S. *Royal George* was a first-rate Man of War of 100 gun
She was built at Woolwich, and first floated there (not launched
in 1755. She was built to carry a very heavy armament: and ver
heavily sparred and rigged. On August 19th, 1782, she wa
heeled while at anchor at Spithead, so that her sea-cock might b
repaired. Various little causes added to her list, and sudden

he went over on her side and sank, taking with her a sloop, the *ark*, then lying alongside. Most of the men on deck at the time were saved, but almost all those below, with many women visitors, between 900 and 1000 people in all, were drowned. It is thought that the immediate cause of her loss was the breaking of her main beam, through strain and rottenness. Her wreck was blown up many years later. Admiral Kempenfelt, a distinguished Swede in our Navy, was among the drowned.

William Blake

The Little Black Boy

My Mother bore me in the southern wild,
And I am black, but O, my soul is white.
White as an angel is the English child,
But I am black, as if bereaved of light.

My Mother taught me underneath a tree,
And, sitting down before the heat of day,
She took me on her lap and kissèd me,
And, pointing to the East, began to say:—

"Look on the rising Sun: there God does live,
And gives His light, and gives His heat away,
And flowers and trees, and beasts and men, receive
Comfort in morning, joy in the noon-day.

"And we are put on Earth a little space,
That we may learn to bear the beams of Love;
And these black bodies and this sunburnt face
Are but a cloud, and like a shady grove.

"For, when our souls have learned the heat to bear,
The cloud will vanish, we shall hear His voice,
Saying, 'Come out from the grove, my love and care,
And round my golden tent like lambs rejoice.'"

Thus did my Mother say, and kissèd me,
And thus I say to little English boy.
When I from black, and he from white cloud free,
And round the tent of God like lambs we joy,

I'll shade him from the heat till he can bear
To lean in joy upon our Father's knee;
And then I'll stand and stroke his silver hair,
And be like him, and he will then love me.

Night

The Sun descending in the West,
The Evening Star does shine;
The birds are silent in their nest,
And I must seek for mine.

The moon, like a flower,
In Heaven's high bower,
With silent delight
Sits and smiles on the night.

Farewell, green fields and happy groves,
Where flocks have took delight.
Where lambs have nibbled, silent moves
The feet of angels bright:
Unseen, they pour blessing,
And joy without ceasing,
On each bud and blossom,
And each sleeping bosom.

They look in every thoughtless nest
Where birds are covered warm;
They visit caves of every beast,
To keep them all from harm.
If they see any weeping
That should have been sleeping,
They pour sleep on their head
And sit down by their bed.

When wolves and tigers howl for prey,
They pitying stand and weep;
Seeking to drive their thirst away,
And keep them from the sheep.
    But, if they rush dreadful,
    The angels, most heedful,
    Receive each mild spirit.
    New worlds to inherit.

And there the Lion's ruddy eyes
Shall flow with tears of gold:
And pitying the tender cries,
And walking round the fold:
    Saying:—"Wrath, by His meekness,
    And, by His health, sickness,
    Is driven away
    From our immortal Day . . .

"And now, beside thee, bleating lamb,
I can lie down and sleep,
Or think on Him who bore thy name,
Graze after thee, and weep.
    For, washed in Life's river,
    My bright mane for ever
    Shall shine like the gold
    As I guard o'er the fold."

SONGS OF EXPERIENCE

The Tiger

Tiger, tiger, burning bright
In the forests of the night,
What immortal hand or eye
Could frame thy fearful symmetry?

In what distant deeps or skies
Burnt the fire of thine eyes?
On what wings dare he aspire?
What the hand dare seize the fire?

And what shoulder and what art
Could twist the sinews of thy heart?
And, when thy heart began to beat,
What dread hand and what dread feet?

What the hammer? What the chain?
In what furnace was thy brain?
What the anvil? What dread grasp
Dare its deadly terrors clasp?

When the stars threw down their spears,
And watered Heaven with their tears,
Did He smile His work to see?
Did He who made the lamb make thee?

Tiger, tiger, burning bright
In the forests of the night,
What immortal hand or eye
Dare frame thy fearful symmetry?

WILLIAM BOND

Ideas of Good and Evil

I wonder whether the girls are mad,
And I wonder whether they mean to kill,
And I wonder if William Bond will die,
For assuredly he is very ill.

He went to Church on a May morning,
Attended by fairies, one, two and three,
But the Angels of Providence drove them away,
And he returned home in misery.

He went not out to the field nor fold,
He went not out to the village nor town,
But he came home in a black, black cloud,
And took to his bed, and there lay down.

And an Angel of Providence at his feet,
And an Angel of Providence at his head,
And in the midst, a black, black cloud,
And in the midst, the sick man on his bed.

And on his right hand was Mary Green,
And on his left hand was his Sister Jane,
And their tears fell through the black, black cloud
To drive away the sick man's pain.

"O, William, if thou dost another love,
Dost another love, better than poor Mary,
Go, and take that other to be thy Wife,
And Mary Green shall her servant be."

"Yes, Mary; I do another love,
Another I love far better than thee,
And another I will have for my wife:
Then what have I to do with thee?

For thou art melancholy pale,
And on thy head is the cold moon's shine,
But she is ruddy and bright as day,
And the sunbeams dazzle from her eyne."

Mary trembled, and Mary chilled,
And Mary fell down on the right-hand floor,
That William Bond and his Sister Jane
Scarce could recover Mary more.

When Mary woke and found her laid
On the right hand of her William dear,
On the right hand of his loved bed,
And saw her William Bond so near;

The fairies that fled from William Bond
Danced around her shining head;
They danced over the pillow white,
And the Angels of Providence left the bed.

"I thought Love lived in the hot sunshine,
But O he lives in the moony light.
I thought to find Love in the heat of day,
But sweet Love is the comforter of night.

Seek Love in the pity of others' woe,
In the gentle relief of another's care,
In the darkness of night and the winter's snow,
With the naked and outcast:—seek Love there."

George Crabbe

SIR EUSTACE GREY

Patient

And shall I then the fact deny?
  I was—thou know'st—I was begone,
Like him who fill'd the eastern throne,
  To whom the Watcher cried aloud;
That royal wretch of Babylon,
  Who was so guilty and so proud.

Like him, with haughty, stubborn mind,
  I, in my state, my comforts sought;
Delight and praise I hoped to find,
  In what I builded, planted, bought!
Oh! arrogance! by misery taught—
  Soon came a voice! I felt it come;
"Full be his cup, with evil fraught,
  Demons his guides, and death his doom!"

Then was I cast from out my state;
  Two fiends of darkness led my way;
They waked me early, watch'd me late,
  My dread by night, my plague by day!
Oh! I was made their sport, their play,
  Through many a stormy troubled year;
And how they used their passive prey
  Is sad to tell:—but you shall hear.

And first before they sent me forth,
  Through this unpitying world to run,
They robb'd Sir Eustace of his worth,
  Lands, manors, lordships, every one;

So was that gracious man undone,
    Was spurn'd as vile, was scorn'd as poor,
Whom every former friend would shun,
    And menials drove from every door.

Then those ill-favour'd Ones, whom none
    But my unhappy eyes could view,
Led me, with wild emotion, on,
    And, with resistless terror, drew.
Through lands we fled, o'er seas we flew,
    And halted on a boundless plain;
Where nothing fed, nor breathed, nor grew,
    But silence ruled the still domain.

Upon that boundless plain, below,
    The setting sun's last rays were shed,
And gave a mild and sober glow,
    Where all were still, asleep, or dead;
Vast ruins in the midst were spread,
    Pillars and pediments sublime,
Where the grey moss had form'd a bed,
    And clothed the crumbling spoils of time.

There was I fix'd, I know not how,
    Condemn'd for untold years to stay:
Yet years were not;—one dreadful Now
    Endured no change of night or day;
The same mild evening's sleeping ray
    Shone softly solemn and serene,
And all that time I gazed away,
    The setting sun's sad rays were seen.

At length a moment's sleep stole on,—
    Again came my commission'd foes:
Again through sea and land we're gone;
    No peace, no respite, no repose:
Above the dark broad sea we rose,
    We ran through bleak and frozen land;
I had no strength their strength t' oppose,
    An infant in a giant's hand.

They placed me where those streamers play,
　Those nimble beams of brilliant light;
It would the stoutest heart dismay,
　To see, to feel, that dreadful sight:
So swift, so pure, so cold, so bright,
　They pierced my frame with icy wound;
And all that half-year's polar night,
　Those dancing streamers wrapp'd me round.

Slowly that darkness pass'd away,
　When down upon the earth I fell,—
Some hurried sleep was mine by day;
　But, soon as toll'd the evening bell,
They forced me on, where ever dwell
　Far-distant men in cities fair,
Cities of whom no travellers tell,
　Nor feet but mine were wanderers there.

Their watchmen stare, and stand aghast,
　As on we hurry through the dark;
The watch-light blinks as we go past,
　The watch-dog shrinks and fears to bark;
The watch-tower's bell sounds shrill; and, hark!
　The free wind blows—we've left the town—
A wide sepulchral ground I mark,
　And on a tombstone place me down.

What monuments of mighty dead!
　What tombs of various kind are found!
And stones erect their shadows shed
　On humble graves, with wickers bound,
Some risen fresh, above the ground,
　Some level with the native clay:
What sleeping millions wait the sound,
　"Arise, ye dead, and come away!"

Those fiends upon a shaking fen
   Fix'd me, in dark tempestuous night
There never trod the foot of men,
   There flock'd the fowl in wint'ry flight;
There danced the moor's deceitful light
   Above the pool where sedges grow;
And when the morning-sun shone bright,
   It shone upon a field of snow.

They hung me on a bough so small,
   The rook could build her nest no higher;
They fix'd me on the trembling ball
   That crowns the steeple's quiv'ring spire;
They set me where the seas retire,
   But drown with their returning tide;
And made me flee the mountain's fire,
   When rolling from its burning side.

I've hung upon the ridgy steep
   Of cliffs and held the rambling brier;
I've plunged below the billowy deep,
   Where air was sent me to respire;
I've been where hungry wolves retire;
   And (to complete my woes) I've ran
Where Bedlam's crazy crew conspire
   Against the life of reasoning man.

I've furl'd in storms the flapping sail,
   By hanging from the topmast-head;
I've served the vilest slaves in jail,
   And pick'd the dunghill's spoil for bread:
I've made the badger's hole my bed,
   I've wander'd with a gipsy crew;
I've dreaded all the guilty dread,
   And done what they would fear to do.

William Wordsworth

THERE WAS A BOY

There was a Boy; ye knew him well, ye cliffs
And islands of Winander!—many a time,
At evening, when the earliest stars began
To move along the edges of the hills,
Rising or setting, would he stand alone,
Beneath the trees, or by the glimmering lake;
And there, with fingers interwoven, both hands
Pressed closely palm to palm and to his mouth
Uplifted, he, as through an instrument,
Blew mimic hootings to the silent owls,
That they might answer him.—And they would shout
Across the watery vale, and shout again,
Responsive to his call,—with quivering peals,
And long halloos, and screams, and echoes loud
Redoubled and redoubled; concourse wild
Of jocund din! And, when there came a pause
Of silence such as baffled his best skill:
Then, sometimes, in that silence, while he hung
Listening, a gentle shock of mild surprise
Has carried far into his heart the voice
Of mountain-torrents; or the visible scene
Would enter unawares into his mind
With all its solemn imagery, its rocks,
Its woods, and that uncertain heaven received
Into the bosom of the steady lake.

    This boy was taken from his mates, and died
In childhood, ere he was full twelve years old.
Pre-eminent in beauty is the vale
Where he was born and bred: the church-yard hangs
Upon a slope above the village-school;
And, through that church-yard when my way has led

On summer-evenings, I believe, that there
A long half-hour together I have stood
Mute—looking at the grave in which he lies!

THE PRELUDE

. . . And in the frosty season, when the sun
Was set, and visible for many a mile
The cottage windows blazed through twilight gloom,
I heeded not their summons: happy time
It was indeed for all of us—for me
It was a time of rapture! Clear and loud
The village clock tolled six,—I wheeled about,
Proud and exulting like an untired horse
That cares not for his home. All shod with steel,
We hissed along the polished ice in games
Confederate, imitative of the chase
And woodland pleasures,—the resounding horn,
The pack loud chiming, and the hunted hare.
So through the darkness and the cold we flew,
And not a voice was idle; with the din
Smitten, the precipices rang aloud;
The leafless trees and every icy crag
Tinkled like iron; while far distant hills
Into the tumult sent an alien sound
Of melancholy not unnoticed, while the stars
Eastward were sparkling clear, and in the west
The orange sky of evening died away.

. . . One summer evening (led by her) I found
A little boat tied to a willow tree
Within a rocky cave, its usual home.

Straight I unloosed her chain, and stepping in
Pushed from the shore. It was an act of stealth
And troubled pleasure, nor without the voice
Of mountain-echoes did my boat move on;
Leaving behind her still, on either side,
Small circles glittering idly in the moon,
Until they melted all into one track
Of sparkling light. But now, like one who rows,
Proud of his skill, to reach a chosen point
With an unswerving line, I fixed my view
Upon the summit of a craggy ridge,
The horizon's utmost boundary: far above
Was nothing but the stars and the grey sky.
She was an elfin pinnace; lustily
I dipped my oars into the silent lake,
And, as I rose upon the stroke, my boat
Went heaving through the water like a swan;
When, from behind that craggy steep till then
The horizon's bound, a huge peak, black and huge,
As if with voluntary power instinct,
Upreared its head. I struck and struck again,
And growing still in stature the grim shape
Towered up between me and the stars, and still,
For so it seemed, with purpose of its own
And measured motion like a living thing,
Strode after me. With trembling oars I turned,
And through the silent water stole my way
Back to the covert of the willow tree;
There in her mooring-place I left my bark,—
And through the meadows homeward went, in grave
And serious mood; but after I had seen
That spectacle, for many days, my brain
Worked with a dim and undetermined sense
Of unknown modes of being . . .

PERSONAL TALK

I am not One who much or oft delight
To season my fireside with personal talk—
Of friends, who live within an easy walk,
Or neighbours, daily, weekly, in my sight:
And, for my chance-acquaintance, ladies bright,
Sons, mothers, maidens withering on the stalk,
These all wear out of me, like Forms, with chalk
Painted on rich men's floors, for one feast-night.
Better than such discourse doth silence long,
Long, barren silence, square with my desire;
To sit without emotion, hope or aim,
In the loved presence of my cottage-fire,
And listen to the flapping of the flame,
Or kettle whispering its faint undersong.

SONNET XIV

To Sleep

A flock of sheep that leisurely pass by,
One after one; the sound of rain, and bees
Murmuring; the fall of rivers, winds and seas,
Smooth fields, white sheets of water, and pure sky;
I have thought of all by turns, and yet do lie
Sleepless! and soon the small birds' melodies
Must hear, first uttered from my orchard trees;
And the first cuckoo's melancholy cry.
Even thus last night, and two nights more, I lay,
And could not win thee, Sleep! by any stealth:
So do not let me wear to-night away:
Without Thee what is all the morning's wealth?
Come, blessed barrier between day and day,
Dear mother of fresh thoughts and joyous health!

ELEGIAC STANZAS

*Suggested by a picture of Peele Castle, in a storm, painted by Sir
George Beaumont*

I was thy neighbour once, thou rugged Pile!
Four summer weeks I dwelt in sight of thee:
I saw thee every day; and all the while
Thy Form was sleeping on a glassy sea.

So pure the sky, so quiet was the air!
So like, so very like, was day to day!
Whene'er I looked, thy Image still was there;
It trembled, but it never passed away.

How perfect was the calm! it seemed no sleep;
No mood, which season takes away or brings:
I could have fancied that the mighty Deep
Was even the gentlest of all gentle Things.

Ah! THEN, if mine had been the Painter's hand,
To express what then I saw; and add the gleam,
The light that never was, on sea or land,
The consecration, and the Poet's dream;

I would have planted thee, thou hoary Pile
Amid a world how different from this!
Beside a sea that could not cease to smile;
On tranquil land, beneath a sky of bliss.

Thou shouldst have seemed a treasure-house divine
Of peaceful years; a chronicle of heaven;—
Of all the sunbeams that did ever shine
The very sweetest had to thee been given.

A Picture had it been of lasting ease,
Elysian quiet, without toil or strife;
No motion but the moving tide, a breeze,
Or merely silent Nature's breathing life.

Such, in the fond illusion of my heart,
Such Picture would I at that time have made:
And seen the soul of truth in every part,
A stedfast peace that might not be betrayed.

So once it would have been,—'tis so no more;
I have submitted to a new control:
A power is gone, which nothing can restore;
A deep distress hath humanised my Soul.

Not for a moment could I now behold
A smiling sea, and be what I have been:
The feeling of my loss will ne'er be old;
This, which I know, I speak with mind serene.

Then, Beaumont, Friend! who would have been the Friend,
If he had lived, of Him whom I deplore,
This work of thine I blame not, but commend;
This sea in anger, and that dismal shore.

O 'tis a passionate Work!—yet wise and well,
Well chosen is the spirit that is here;
That Hulk which labours in the deadly swell,
This rueful sky, this pageantry of fear!

And this huge Castle, standing here sublime,
I love to see the look with which it braves,
Cased in the unfeeling armour of old time,
The lightning, the fierce wind, and trampling waves.

Farewell, farewell the heart that lives alone,
Housed in a dream, at distance from the Kind!
Such happiness, wherever it be known,
Is to be pitied; for 'tis surely blind.

But welcome fortitude, and patient cheer,
And frequent sights of what is to be borne!
Such sights, or worse, as are before me here.—
Not without hope we suffer and we mourn.

AMONG ALL LOVELY THINGS MY LOVE HAD BEEN

Among all lovely things my Love had been;
Had noted well the stars, all flowers that grew
About her home; but she had never seen
A glow-worm, never one, and this I knew.

While riding near her home one stormy night
A single glow-worm did I chance to espy;
I gave a fervent welcome to the sight,
And from my horse I leapt; great joy had I.

Upon a leaf the glow-worm did I lay,
To bear it with me through the stormy night:
And, as before, it shone without dismay;
Albeit putting forth a fainter light.

When to the dwelling of my Love I came,
I went into the orchard quietly;
And left the glow-worm, blessing it by name,
Laid safely by itself, beneath a tree.

The whole next day, I hoped, and hoped with fear;
At night the glow-worm shone beneath the tree;
I led my Lucy to the spot, "Look here."
Oh! joy it was for her, and joy for me!

HART-LEAP WELL

The Knight had ridden down from Wensley Moor
With the slow motion of a summer's cloud,
And now, as he approached a vassal's door,
"Bring forth another horse!" he cried aloud.

"Another horse!"—That shout the vassal heard
And saddled his best Steed, a comely grey;
Sir Walter mounted him; he was the third
Which he had mounted on that glorious day.

Joy sparkled in the prancing courser's eyes;
The horse and horseman are a happy pair;
But, though Sir Walter like a falcon flies,
There is a doleful silence in the air.

A rout this morning left Sir Walter's Hall,
That as they galloped made the echoes roar;
But horse and man are vanished, one and all;
Such race, I think, was never seen before.

Sir Walter, restless as a veering wind,
Calls to the few tired dogs that yet remain:
Blanch, Swift, and Music, noblest of their kind,
Follow, and up the weary mountain strain.

The Knight hallooed, he cheered and chid them on
With suppliant gestures and upbraidings stern;
But breath and eyesight fail; and, one by one,
The dogs are stretched among the mountain fern.

Where is the throng, the tumult of the race?
The bugles that so joyfully were blown?
—This chase it looks not like an earthly chase;
Sir Walter and the Hart are left alone.

The poor Hart toils along the mountainside;
I will not stop to tell how far he fled,
Nor will I mention by what death he died;
But now the Knight beholds him lying dead.

Dismounting, then, he leaned against a thorn;
He had no follower, dog, nor man, nor boy:
He neither cracked his whip, nor blew his horn,
But gazed upon the spoil with silent joy.

Close to the thorn on which Sir Walter leaned,
Stood his dumb partner in this glorious feat;
Weak as a lamb the hour that it is yeaned;
And white with foam as if with cleaving sleet.

Upon his side the Hart was lying stretched:
His nostril touched a spring beneath a hill,
And with the last deep groan his breath had fetched
The waters of the spring were trembling still.

And now, too happy for repose or rest,
(Never had living man such joyful lot!)
Sir Walter walked all round, north, south, and west,
And gazed and gazed upon that darling spot.

And climbing up the hill—(it was at least
Four roods of sheer ascent) Sir Walter found
Three several hoof-marks which the hunted Beast
Had left imprinted on the grassy ground.

Sir Walter wiped his face, and cried, "Till now
Such sight was never seen by human eyes:
Three leaps have borne him from this lofty brow
Down to the very fountain where he lies.

"I'll build a pleasure-house upon this spot,
And a small arbour, made for rural joy;
'Twill be the traveller's shed, the pilgrim's cot,
A place of love for damsels that are coy.

"A cunning artist will I have to frame
A basin for that fountain in the dell!
And they who do make mention of the same,
From this day forth, shall call it HART-LEAP WELL.

"And, gallant Stag! to make thy praises known,
Another monument shall here be raised;
Three several pillars, each a rough-hewn stone,
And planted where thy hoofs the turf have grazed.

"And, in the summer-time when days are long,
I will come hither with my Paramour;
And with the dancers and the minstrel's song
We will make merry in that pleasant bower.

"Till the foundations of the mountains fail
My mansion with its arbour shall endure;—
The joy of them who till the fields of Swale,
And them who dwell among the woods of Ure!"

Then home he went, and left the Hart, stone-dead,
With breathless nostrils stretched above the spring
—Soon did the Knight perform what he had said;
And far and wide the fame thereof did ring.

Ere thrice the Moon into her port had steered,
A cup of stone received the living well;
Three pillars of rude stone Sir Walter reared,
And built a house of pleasure in the dell.

And near the fountain, flowers of stature tall
With trailing plants and trees were intertwined,—
Which soon composed a little sylvan hall,
A leafy shelter from the sun and wind.

And thither, when the summer days were long,
Sir Walter led his wondering Paramour;
And with the dancers and the minstrel's song
Made merriment within that pleasant bower.

The Knight, Sir Walter, died in course of time,
And his bones lie in his paternal vale.—
But there is matter for a second rhyme,
And I to this would add another tale.

Part Second

The moving accident is not my trade:
To freeze the blood I have no ready arts:
'Tis my delight, alone in summer shade
To pipe a simple song for thinking hearts.

As I from Hawes to Richmond did repair,
It chanced that I saw standing in a dell
Three aspens at three corners of a square;
And one, not four yards distant, near a well.

What this imported I could ill divine:
And, pulling now the rein my horse to stop,
I saw three pillars standing in a line,—
The last stone-pillar on a dark hill-top.

The trees were grey, with neither arms nor head;
Half wasted the square mound of tawny green;
So that you just might say, as then I said,
"Here in old time the hand of man hath been".

I looked upon the hill both far and near,
More doleful place did never eye survey;
It seemed as if the spring-time came not here,
And Nature here were willing to decay.

I stood in various thoughts and fancies lost,
When one, who was in shepherd's garb attired,
Came up the hollow:—him did I accost,
And what this place might be I then inquired.

The Shepherd stopped, and that same story told
Which in my former rhyme I have rehearsed.
"A jolly place," said he, "in times of old!
But something ails it now: the spot is curst.

"You see these lifeless stumps of aspen wood—
Some say that they are beeches, others elms—
These were the bower; and here a mansion stood,
The finest palace of a hundred realms!

"The arbour does its own condition tell;
You see the stones, the fountain, and the stream;
But as to the great Lodge! you might as well
Hunt half a day for a forgotten dream.

"There's neither dog nor heifer, horse nor sheep,
Will wet his lips within that cup of stone;
And oftentimes, when all are fast asleep,
This water doth send forth a dolorous groan.

"Some say that here a murder has been done,
And blood cries out for blood: but, for my part,
I've guessed, when I've been sitting in the sun,
That it was all for that unhappy Hart.

"What thoughts must through the creature's brain have past!
Even from the topmost stone, upon the steep,
Are but three bounds—and look, Sir, at this last—
O Master! it has been a cruel leap.

"For thirteen hours he ran a desperate race;
And in my simple mind we cannot tell
What cause the Hart might have to love this place,
And come and make his deathbed near the well.

"Here on the grass perhaps asleep he sank,
Lulled by the fountain in the summer-tide;
This water was perhaps the first he drank
When he had wandered from his mother's side.

"In April here beneath the flowering thorn
He heard the birds their morning carols sing;
And he, perhaps, for aught we know, was born
Not half a furlong from that self-same spring.

"Now here is neither grass nor pleasant shade;
The sun on drearier hollow never shone;
So will it be, as I have often said,
Till trees, and stones, and fountain, all are gone."

"Grey-headed Shepherd, thou hast spoken well;
Small difference lies between thy creed and mine:
This Beast not unobserved by Nature fell;
His death was mourned by sympathy divine.

"The Being, that is in the clouds and air,
That is in the green leaves among the groves,
Maintains a deep and reverential care
For the unoffending creatures whom he loves.

"The pleasure-house is dust:—behind, before,
This is no common waste, no common gloom;
But Nature, in due course of time, once more
Shall here put on her beauty and her bloom.

"She leaves these objects to a slow decay,
That what we are, and have been, may be known;
But at the coming of the milder day,
These monuments shall all be overgrown.

"One lesson, Shepherd, let us two divide,
Taught both by what she shows, and what conceals;
Never to blend our pleasure or our pride
With sorrow of the meanest thing that feels."

EXTEMPORE EFFUSION UPON THE DEATH OF JAMES HOGG

When first, descending from the moorlands,
I saw the Stream of Yarrow glide
Along a bare and open valley,
The Ettrick Shepherd was my guide.

When last along its banks I wandered,
Through groves that had begun to shed
Their golden leaves upon the pathways,
My steps the Border-Minstrel led.

The mighty Minstrel breathes no longer,
'Mid mouldering ruins low he lies;
And death upon the braes of Yarrow,
Has closed the Shepherd-poet's eyes:

Nor has the rolling year twice measured,
From sign to sign, its steadfast course,
Since every mortal power of Coleridge
Was frozen at its marvellous source;

The rapt One, of the godlike forehead,
The heaven-eyed creature sleeps in earth:
And Lamb, the frolic and the gentle,
Has vanished from his lonely hearth.

Like clouds that rake the mountain summits,
Or waves that own no curbing hand,
How fast has brother followed brother
From sunshine to the sunless land!

Yet I, whose lids from infant slumber
Were earlier raised, remain to hear
A timid voice, that asks in whispers,
"Who next will drop and disappear?"

Our haughty life is crowned with darkness,
Like London with its own black wreath,
On which with thee, O Crabbe! forth-looking,
I gazed from Hampstead's breezy heath.

As if but yesterday departed,
Thou too art gone before; but why,
O'er ripe fruit, seasonably gathered,
Should frail survivors heave a sigh?

Mourn rather for that holy Spirit,
Sweet as the spring, as ocean deep;
For Her who, ere her summer faded,
Has sunk into a breathless sleep.

No more of old romantic sorrows,
For slaughtered Youth or love-lorn Maid!
With sharper grief is Yarrow smitten,
And Ettrick mourns with her their Poet dead.

Occasional Lines

From the Sonnet *MUTABILITY*

. . . . drop like the tower sublime
Of Yesterday, which royally did wear
His crown of weeds, but could not even sustain
Some casual shout that broke the silent air,
Or the unimaginable touch of Time.

From the Poem *THE SMALL CELANDINE*

This neither is its courage nor its choice,
But its necessity in being old.

From *THE IDIOT BOY*

"The cocks did crow to-whoo, to-whoo,
And the sun did shine so cold."

From *PETER BELL*

The towns in Saturn are decayed,
And melancholy spectres throng them.
. . . .
. . . .
. . . . . deep and low the hamlets lie
Beneath their little patch of sky
And little lot of stars.

. . . The ass did lengthen out . . .
The hard dry see-saw of his horrible bray.

From *THE FOUNTAIN*

About the crazy old church-clock,
And the bewildered chimes.

From *RUTH*

And many an endless, endless lake
With all its fairy crowds
Of islands that together lie
As quietly as spots of sky
Among the evening clouds.

From *FIDELITY*

[A scene on Helvellyn]
There sometimes doth a leaping fish
Send through the tarn a lonely cheer.

From *THE PRELUDE*

BOOK x. *Residence in France*. [Sleeping in Paris, during the Revolution, Oct. 1792.]

> That night
> I felt most deeply in what world I was.
> . . . .
> The fear gone by,
> Pressed on me almost like a fear to come.
> I thought of those September massacres,
> Divided from me by one little month.

Lord Byron

OCCASIONAL PIECES

So, We'll Go No More A-Roving (1817)

So, we'll go no more a-roving
So late into the night,
Though the heart be still as loving,
And the moon be still as bright.

For the sword outwears its sheath,
And the soul wears out the breast,
And the heart must pause to breathe,
And love itself have rest.

Though the night was made for loving,
And the day returns too soon,
Yet we'll go no more a-roving
By the light of the moon.

Samuel Taylor Coleridge

THE RIME OF THE ANCIENT MARINER

From *Part I*

"The ship was cheered, the harbour cleared,
Merrily did we drop
Below the Kirk, below the hill,
Below the light-house top.

The sun came up upon the left,
Out of the sea came he:
And he shone bright, and on the right
Went down into the sea.

Higher and higher every day,
Till over the mast at noon . . ."
The Wedding-Guest here beat his breast,
For he heard the loud bassoon.

The bride hath paced into the hall,
Red as a rose is she;
Nodding their heads before her goes
The merry minstrelsy.

From *Part II*

The fair breeze blew, the white foam flew,
The furrow followed free;
We were the first that ever burst
Into that silent sea.

Down dropt the breeze, the sails dropt down,
'Twas sad as sad could be;
And we did speak only to break
The silence of the sea.

All in a hot and copper sky,
The bloody Sun, at noon,
Right up above the mast did stand,
No bigger than the Moon.

Day after day, day after day,
We stuck, nor breath nor motion;
As idle as a painted ship
Upon a painted ocean.

Water, water, every where,
And all the boards did shrink;
Water, water, every where,
Nor any drop to drink.

The very deep did rot: O Christ,
That ever this should be.
Yea, slimy things did crawl with legs
Upon the slimy sea.

About, about, in reel and rout
The death-fires danced at night;
The water, like a witch's oils,
Burnt green, and blue, and white.

From *Part III*

The Sun's rim dips: the stars rush out:
At one stride comes the dark. . . .

The hornèd Moon, with one bright star
Within the nether tip.

From *Part IV*

Alone, alone, all, all alone,
Alone on a wide, wide sea.
And never a saint took pity on
My soul in agony.

The many men, so beautiful,
And they all dead did lie. . . .

Beyond the shadow of the ship,
I watched the water-snakes:
They moved in tracks of shining white,
And when they reared, the elfish light
Fell off in hoary flakes.

Within the shadow of the ship
I watched their rich attire:
Blue, glossy green, and velvet black,
They coiled and swam; and every track
Was a flash of golden fire.

O happy living things! no tongue
Their beauty might declare:
A spring of love gushed from my heart,
And I blessed them unaware:
Sure my kind saint took pity on me,
And I blessed them unaware.

From *Part V*

O, Sleep, it is a gentle thing,
Beloved from pole to pole.
To Mary Queen the praise be given:
She sent the gentle sleep from Heaven,
That slid into my soul. . . .

Around, around, flew each sweet sound,
Then darted to the Sun;
Slowly the sounds came back again,
Now mixed, now one by one.

Sometimes a-dropping from the sky
I heard the skylark sing;
Sometimes all little birds that are,
How they seemed to fill the sea and air
With their sweet jargoning.

And now 'twas like all instruments;
Now like a lonely flute:
And now it is an angel's song,
That makes the heavens be mute.

It ceased; yet still the sails made on
A pleasant noise till noon,
A noise like of a hidden brook
In the leafy month of June,
That to the sleeping woods all night
Singeth a quiet tune.

From *Part VI*

The harbour-bay was clear as glass,
So smoothly it was strewn:
And on the bay the moonlight lay
And the shadow of the moon.

The rock shone **bright**, the Kirk no less,
That stands above the rock:
The moonlight steeped in silentness
The steady weathercock.

From *Part VII*

Farewell, farewell; but this I tell,
To thee, thou Wedding Guest:
He prayeth well, who loveth well
Both man and bird and beast.

He prayeth best, who loveth best
All things both great and small;
For the dear God who loveth us,
He made and loveth all.

From *CHRISTABEL*

Part I

The neck that made that white robe wan.

Carved with figures strange and sweet
All made out of the carver's brain.

Part II

For she belike hath drunken deep
Of all the blessedness of sleep.

From *PHANTOM*

She, she herself, and only she,
Shone thro' her body visibly.

From *FEARS IN SOLITUDE*

O'er stiller place
No singing skylark ever poised himself.

KUBLA KHAN: OR, A VISION IN A DREAM

(Coleridge, who was nearly 25 when the poem was written, gives the following account of its creation.)

"In the summer of the year 1797, the Author, then in ill-health, had retired to a lonely farm-house between Porlock and Linton, on the Exmoor confines of Somerset and Devonshire.

In consequence of a slight indisposition, an anodyne had been prescribed, from the effects of which he fell asleep in his chair at the moment that he was reading the following sentence, or words of the same substance, in 'Purchas's Pilgrimage':

'Here the Khan Kubla commanded a palace to be built, and a stately garden thereunto. And thus ten miles of fertile ground were inclosed with a wall'.

The Author continued for about three hours in a profound sleep, at least of the external senses, during which time he has the most vivid confidence, that he could not have composed less than from two to three hundred lines; if that indeed can be called composition in which all the images rose up before him as *things*, with a parallel production of the correspondent expressions, without any sensation or consciousness of effort. On awaking, he appeared to himself to have a distinct recollection of the whole, and taking his pen, ink and paper, instantly and eagerly wrote down the lines that are here preserved.

At this moment he was unfortunately called out by a person on business from Porlock, and detained by him above an hour, and on his return to his room, found, to his no small surprise and mortification, that though he still retained some vague and dim recollection of the general purport of the vision, yet, with the exception of some eight or ten scattered lines and images, all the rest had passed away . . ."

KUBLA KHAN

In Xanadu did Kubla Khan
A stately pleasure-dome decree:
Where Alph, the sacred river, ran
Through caverns measureless to man
Down to a sunless sea.
So twice five miles of fertile ground
With walls and towers were girdled round.
And there were gardens bright with sinuous rills
Where blossomed many an incense-bearing tree;
And here were forests ancient as the hills,
Enfolding sunny spots of greenery.

But, oh, that deep romantic chasm which slanted
Down the green hill athwart a cedarn cover:
A savage place, as holy and enchanted
As e'er beneath a waning moon was haunted
By woman wailing for her demon-lover.
And from this chasm, with ceaseless turmoil seething,
As if this earth in fast thick pants were breathing,
A mightly fountain momently was forced:
Amid whose swift half-intermitted burst
Huge fragments vaulted like rebounding hail,
Or chaffy grain beneath the thresher's flail:
And mid these dancing rocks at once and ever
It flung up momently the sacred river.
Five miles meandering with a mazy motion
Through wood and dale the sacred river ran,
Then reached the caverns measureless to man,
And sank in tumult to a lifeless ocean:
And 'mid this tumult Kubla heard from far
Ancestral voices prophesying war.

The shadow of the dome of pleasure
Floated midway on the waves;
Where was heard the mingled measure

John Keats

From *I STOOD TIP-TOE*

11   A little noiseless noise among the leaves.

65   How silent comes the water round that bend;
        Not the minutest whisper does it send
        To the o'erhanging sallows; blades of grass
        Slowly across the chequer'd shadows pass.
        Why, you might read two sonnets, ere they reach
        To where the hurrying freshnesses aye preach
        A natural sermon o'er their pebbly beds;
        Where swarms of minnows show their little heads,
        Staying their wavy bodies 'gainst the streams,
        To taste the luxury of sunny beams
        Temper'd with coolness. How they ever wrestle
        With their own sweet delight, and ever nestle
        Their silver bellies on the pebbly sand.

From *ENDYMION*

Book iv.   782

                                    The spirit culls
        Unfaded amaranth, when wild it strays
        Through the old garden-ground of boyish days.

Book iv.   819

                Perhaps ye are too happy to be glad.

From *HYPERION*

Book i

> Deep in the shady sadness of a vale
> Far sunken from the healthy breath of morn
> Far from the fiery noon, and eve's one star,
> Sat gray-hair'd Saturn, quiet as a stone,
> Still as the silence round about his lair;
> Forest on forest hung about his head
> Like cloud on cloud. No stir of air was there,
> Not so much life as on a summer's day
> Robs not one light seed from the feather'd grass,
> But where the dead leaf fell, there did it rest.
> A stream went voiceless by, still deadened more
> By reason of his fallen divinity
> Spreading a shade: the Naiad 'mid her reeds
> Press'd her cold finger closer to her lips.

> Along the margin-sand large foot-marks went,
> No further than to where his feet had stray'd
> And slept there since. Upon the sodden ground
> His old right hand lay nerveless, listless, dead,
> Unsceptred; and his realmless eyes were closed;
> While his bow'd head seem'd list'ning to the Earth,
> His ancient mother, for some comfort yet.

Book i.   72

> As when, upon a tranced summer-night,
> Those green-rob'd senators of mighty woods,
> Tall oaks, branch-charmed by the earnest stars,
> Dream, and so dream all night without a stir,
> Save from one gradual solitary gust
> Which comes upon the silence, and dies off
> As if the ebbing air had but one wave.

Book ii. 33

> Scarce images of life, one here, one there,
> Lay vast and edgeways; like a dismal cirque
> Of Druid stones, upon a forlorn moor,
> When the chill rain begins at shut of eve.

Book ii. 116

> There is a roaring in the bleak-grown pines
> When Winter lifts his voice; there is a noise
> Among immortals when a God gives sign,
> With hushing finger, how he means to load
> His tongue with the full weight of utterless thought,
> With thunder, and with music, and with pomp:
> Such noise is like the roar of bleak-grown pines.

Book ii. 351

>   He look'd upon them all,
> And in each face he saw a gleam of light,
> But splendider in Saturn's, whose hoar locks
> Shone like the bubbling foam about a keel
> When the prow sweeps into a midnight cove.
> In pale and silver silence they remain'd,
> Till suddenly a splendour, like the morn,
> Pervaded all the beetling gloomy steeps,
> All the sad spaces of oblivion,
> And every gulf, and every chasm old,
> And every height, and every sullen depth,
> Voiceless, or hoarse with loud tormented streams:
> And all the everlasting cataracts,
> And all the headlong torrents far and near,
> Mantled before in darkness and huge shade,
> Now saw the light and made it terrible.

Book ii. 389

Saturn sat near the Mother of the Gods,
In whose face was no joy, though all the Gods
Gave from their hollow throats the name of "Saturn!"

THE EVE OF ST. AGNES

I.   St. Agnes' Eve—Ah, bitter chill it was!
        The owl, for all his feathers, was a-cold;
        The hare limp'd trembling through the frozen grass,
        And silent was the flock in woolly fold:
        Numb were the Beadsman's fingers, while he told
        His rosary, and while his frosted breath,
        Like pious incense from a censer old,
        Seem'd taking flight for heaven, without a death,
   Past the sweet Virgin's picture, while his prayer he saith.

II.   His prayer he saith, this patient, holy man;
        Then takes his lamp, and riseth from his knees,
        And back returneth, meagre, barefoot, wan,
        Along the chapel aisle by slow degrees:
        The sculptur'd dead, on each side, seem to freeze,
        Emprison'd in black, purgatorial rails:
        Knights, ladies, praying in dumb orat'ries,
        He passeth by; and his weak spirit fails
   To think how they may ache in icy hoods and mails.

III.   Northward he turneth through a little door,
        And scarce three steps, ere Music's golden tongue
        Flatter'd to tears this aged man and poor;
        But no—already had his deathbell rung;
        The joys of all his life were said and sung:
        His was harsh penance on St. Agnes' Eve:
        Another way he went, and soon among
        Rough ashes sat he for his soul's reprieve,
   And all night kept awake, for sinners' sake to grieve.

IV.   That ancient Beadsman heard the prelude soft;
      And so it chanc'd, for many a door was wide,
      From hurry to and fro. Soon, up aloft,
      The silver, snarling trumpets 'gan to chide:
      The level chambers, ready with their pride,
      Were glowing to receive a thousand guests:
      The carved angels, ever eager-eyed,
      Star'd, where upon their heads the cornice rests,
With hair blown back, and wings put cross-wise on their
      breasts.

V.   At length burst in the argent revelry,
      With plume, tiara, and all rich array,
      Numerous as shadows haunting faerily
      The brain, new stuff'd, in youth, with triumphs gay
      Of old romance. These let us wish away,
      And turn, sole-thoughted, to one Lady there,
      Whose heart had brooded, all that wintry day,
      On love, and wing'd St. Agnes' saintly care,
As she had heard old dames full many times declare.

VI.   They told her how, upon St. Agnes' Eve,
      Young virgins might have visions of delight,
      And soft adorings from their loves receive
      Upon the honey'd middle of the night,
      If ceremonies due they did aright;
      As, supperless to bed they must retire,
      And couch supine their beauties, lilly white;
      Nor look behind, nor sideways, but require
Of Heaven with upward eyes for all that they desire.

VII.   Full of this whim was thoughtful Madeline:
      The music, yearning like a God in pain,
      She scarcely heard: her maiden eyes divine,
      Fix'd on the floor, saw many a sweeping train
      Pass by—she heeded not at all: in vain
      Came many a tiptoe, amorous cavalier,
      And back retir'd; not cool'd by high disdain,

But she saw not: her heart was otherwhere:
She sigh'd for Agnes' dreams, the sweetest of the year

VIII.   She danc'd along with vague, regardless eyes,
         Anxious her lips, her breathing quick and short:
         The hallow'd hour was near at hand: she sighs
         Amid the timbrels, and the throng'd resort
         Of whisperers in anger, or in sport;
         'Mid looks of love, defiance, hate, and scorn,
         Hoodwink'd with faery fancy; all amort,
         Save to St. Agnes and her lambs unshorn,
And all the bliss to be before to-morrow morn.

IX.   So, purposing each moment to retire,
         She linger'd still. Meantime, across the moors
         Had come young Porphyro, with heart on fire
         For Madeline. Beside the portal doors,
         Buttress'd from moonlight, stands he, and implores
         All saints to give him sight of Madeline,
         But for one moment in the tedious hours,
         That he might gaze and worship all unseen;
    Perchance speak, kneel, touch, kiss—in sooth such things
         have been.

X.   He ventures in: let no buzz'd whisper tell:
         All eyes be muffled, or a hundred swords
         Will storm his heart, Love's fev'rous citadel:
         For him, those chambers held barbarian hordes,
         Hyena foemen, and hot-blooded lords,
         Whose very dogs would execrations howl
         Against his lineage: not one breast affords
         Him any mercy, in that mansion foul,
Save one old beldame, weak in body and in soul.

XI.   Ah, happy chance! the aged creature came,
         Shuffling along with ivory-headed wand,
         To where he stood, hid from the torch's flame,
         Behind a broad hall-pillar, far beyond

The sound of merriment and chorus bland:
He startled her; but soon she knew his face,
And grasp'd his fingers in her palsied hand,
Saying, "Mercy, Porphyro! hie thee from this place;
"They are all here to-night, the whole blood-thirsty race!

XII. "Get hence! get hence! there's dwarfish Hildebrand;
"He had a fever late, and in the fit
"He cursèd thee and thine, both house and land:
"Then there's that old Lord Maurice, not a whit
"More tame for his gray hairs—Alas me! flit!
"Flit like a ghost away."—"Ah, Gossip dear,
"We're safe enough; here in this arm-chair sit,
"And tell me how"—"Good Saints! not here, not here;
"Follow me, child, or else these stones will be thy bier."

XIII. He follow'd through a lowly arched way,
Brushing the cobwebs with his lofty plume,
And as she mutter'd "Well-a—well-a-day!"
He found him in a little moonlight room,
Pale, lattic'd, chill, and silent as a tomb.
"Now tell me where is Madeline," said he,
"O tell me, Angela, by the holy loom
"Which none but secret sisterhood may see,
"When they St. Agnes' wool are weaving piously."

XIV. "St. Agnes! Ah! it is St. Agnes' Eve—
"Yet men will murder upon holy days:
"Thou must hold water in a witch's sieve,
"And be liege-lord of all the Elves and Fays,
"To venture so: it fills me with amaze
"To see thee, Porphyro!—St. Agnes' Eve!
"God's help! my lady fair the conjuror plays
"This very night: good angels her deceive!
"But let me laugh awhile, I've mickle time to grieve."

XV. Feebly she laugheth in the languid moon,
While Porphyro upon her face doth look,

Like puzzled urchin on an aged crone
Who keepeth clos'd a wond'rous riddle-book,
As spectacled she sits in chimney nook,
But soon his eyes grew brilliant, when she told
His lady's purpose; and he scarce could brook
Tears, at the thought of those enchantments cold,
And Madeline asleep in lap of legends old.

XVI.   Sudden a thought came like a full-blown rose,
Flushing his brow, and in his pained heart
Made purple riot: then doth he propose
A stratagem, that makes the beldame start:
"A cruel man and impious thou art:
"Sweet lady, let her pray, and sleep, and dream
"Alone with her good angels, far apart
"From wicked men like thee. Go, go!—I deem
"Thou canst not surely be the same that thou didst seem."

XVII.   "I will not harm her, by all saints I swear,"
Quoth Porphyro: "O may I ne'er find grace
"When my weak voice shall whisper its last prayer,
"If one of her soft ringlets I displace,
"Or look with ruffian passion in her face:
"Good Angela, believe me by these tears;
"Or I will, even in a moment's space,
"Awake, with horrid shout, my foemen's ears,
"And beard them, though they be more fang'd than wolves
and bears."

XVIII.   "Ah! why wilt thou affright a feeble soul?
"A poor, weak, palsy-stricken, churchyard thing,
"Whose passing-bell may ere the midnight toll;
"Whose prayers for thee, each morn and evening,
"Were never miss'd."—Thus plaining, doth she bring
A gentler speech from burning Porphyro;
So woful, and of such deep sorrowing,
That Angela gives promise she will do
Whatever he shall wish, betide her weal or woe.

XIX.   Which was, to lead him, in close secrecy,
    Even to Madeline's chamber, and there hide
    Him in a closet, of such privacy
    That he might see her beauty unespied,
    And win perhaps that night a peerless bride,
    While legion'd faeries pac'd the coverlet,
    And pale enchantment held her sleepy-eyed.
    Never on such a night have lovers met,
Since Merlin paid his Demon all the monstrous debt.

XX.   "It shall be as thou wishest," said the Dame:
    "All cates and dainties shall be stored there
    "Quickly on this feast-night: by the tambour frame
    "Her own lute thou wilt see: no time to spare,
    "For I am slow and feeble, and scarce dare
    "On such a catering trust my dizzy head.
    "Wait here, my child, with patience; kneel in prayer
    "The while: Ah! thou must needs the lady wed,
"Or may I never leave my grave among the dead."

XXI.   So saying, she hobbled off with busy fear.
    The lover's endless minutes slowly pass'd;
    The dame return'd, and whisper'd in his ear
    To follow her; with aged eyes aghast
    From fright of dim espial. Safe at last,
    Through many a dusky gallery, they gain
    The maiden's chamber, silken, hush'd, and chaste;
    Where Porphyro took covert, pleas'd amain.
His poor guide hurried back with agues in her brain.

XXII.   Her falt'ring hand upon the balustrade,
    Old Angela was feeling for the stair,
    When Madeline, St. Agnes' charmed maid,
    Rose, like a mission'd spirit, unaware:
    With silver taper's light, and pious care,
    She turn'd, and down the aged gossip led
    To a safe level matting. Now prepare,
    Young Porphyro, for gazing on that bed;
She comes, she comes again, like ring-dove fray'd and fled.

XXIII.   Out went the taper as she hurried in;
        Its little smoke, in pallid moonshine, died:
        She clos'd the door, she panted, all akin
        To spirits of the air, and visions wide:
        No uttered syllable, or, woe betide!
        But to her heart, her heart was voluble,
        Paining with eloquence her balmy side;
        As though a tongueless nightingale should swell
    Her throat in vain, and die, heart-stifled, in her dell.

XXIV.   A casement high and triple-arch'd there was,
        All garlanded with carven imag'ries
        Of fruits, and flowers, and bunches of knot-grass,
        And diamonded with panes of quaint device,
        Innumerable of stains and splendid dyes,
        As are the tiger-moth's deep-damask'd wings;
        And in the midst, 'mong thousand heraldries,
        And twilight saints, and dim emblazonings,
    A shielded scutcheon blush'd with blood of queens and kings

XXV.   Full on this casement shone the wintry moon,
        And threw warm gules on Madeline's fair breast,
        As down she knelt for heaven's grace and boon;
        Rose-bloom fell on her hands, together prest,
        And on her silver cross soft amethyst,
        And on her hair a glory, like a saint:
        She seem'd a splendid angel, newly drest,
        Save wings, for heaven:—Porphyro grew faint:
    She knelt, so pure a thing, so free from mortal taint.

XXVI.   Anon his heart revives: her vespers done,
        Of all its wreathed pearls her hair she frees;
        Unclasps her warmed jewels one by one;
        Loosens her fragrant boddice; by degrees
        Her rich attire creeps rustling to her knees:
        Half-hidden, like a mermaid in sea-weed,
        Pensive awhile she dreams awake, and sees,
        In fancy, fair St. Agnes in her bed,
    But dares not look behind, or all the charm is fled.

XXVII. Soon, trembling in her soft and chilly nest,
  In sort of wakeful swoon, perplex'd she lay,
  Until the poppied warmth of sleep oppress'd
  Her soothed limbs, and soul fatigued away;
  Flown, like a thought, until the morrow-day;
  Blissfully haven'd both from joy and pain;
  Clasp'd like a missal where swart Paynims pray;
  Blinded alike from sunshine and from rain,
 As though a rose should shut, and be a bud again

XXVIII. Stol'n to this paradise, and so entranced,
  Porphyro gazed upon her empty dress,
  And listen'd to her breathing, if it chanced
  To wake into a slumberous tenderness;
  Which when he heard, that minute did he bless,
  And breath'd himself: then from the closet crept,
  Noiseless as fear in a wide wilderness,
  And over the hush'd carpet, silent, stept,
 And 'tween the curtains peep'd, where, lo!—how fast she
  slept.

XXIX. Then by the bed-side, where the faded moon
  Made a dim, silver twilight, soft he set
  A table, and, half anguish'd, threw thereon
  A cloth of woven crimson, gold, and jet:—
  O for some drowsy Morphean amulet!
  The boisterous, midnight, festive clarion,
  The kettle-drum, and far-heard clarinet,
  Affray his ears, though but in dying tone:—
 The hall door shuts again, and all the noise is gone.

XXX. And still she slept an azure-lidded sleep,
  In blanched linen, smooth, and lavender'd,
  While he from forth the closet brought a heap
  Of candied apple, quince, and plum, and gourd;
  With jellies soother than the creamy curd,

And lucent syrops, tinct with cinnamon;
Manna and dates, in argosy transferr'd
From Fez; and spiced dainties, every one,
From silken Samarcand to cedar'd Lebanon.

xxxi. These delicates he heap'd with glowing hand
On golden dishes and in baskets bright
Of wreathed silver: sumptuous they stand
In the retired quiet of the night,
Filling the chilly room with perfume light.—
"And now, my love, my seraph fair, awake!
"Thou art my heaven, and I thine eremite:
"Open thine eyes, for meek St. Agnes' sake,
"Or I shall drowse beside thee, so my soul doth ache."

xxxii. Thus whispering, his warm, unnerved arm
Sank in her pillow. Shaded was her dream
By the dusk curtains:—'twas a midnight charm
Impossible to melt as iced stream:
The lustrous salvers in the moonlight gleam;
Broad golden fringe upon the carpet lies:
It seem'd he never, never could redeem
From such a stedfast spell his lady's eyes;
So mus'd awhile, entoil'd in woofed phantasies.

xxxiii. Awakening up, he took her hollow lute,—
Tumultuous,—and, in chords that tenderest be,
He play'd an ancient ditty, long since mute,
In Provence call'd, "La belle dame sans mercy:"
Close to her ear touching the melody;—
Wherewith disturb'd, she utter'd a soft moan:
He ceased—she panted quick—and suddenly
Her blue affrayed eyes wide open shone:
Upon his knees he sank, pale as smooth-sculptured stone

xxxiv. Her eyes were open, but she still beheld,
Now wide awake, the vision of her sleep:
There was a painful change, that nigh expell'd
The blisses of her dream so pure and deep

At which fair Madeline began to weep,
And moan forth witless words with many a sigh;
While still her gaze on Porphyro would keep;
Who knelt, with joined hands and piteous eye,
Fearing to move or speak, she look'd so dreamingly.

xxxv. "Ah, Porphyro!" said she, "but even now
"Thy voice was at sweet tremble in mine ear,
"Made tuneable with every sweetest vow;
"And those sad eyes were spiritual and clear:
"How chang'd thou art! how pallid, chill, and drear!
"Give me that voice again, my Porphyro,
"Those looks immortal, those complainings dear!
"Oh leave me not in this eternal woe,
"For if thou diest, my Love, I know not where to go."

xxxvi. Beyond a mortal man impassion'd far
At these voluptuous accents, he arose,
Ethereal, flush'd, and like a throbbing star
Seen mid the sapphire heaven's deep repose;
Into her dream he melted, as the rose
Blendeth its odour with the violet,—
Solution sweet: meantime the frost-wind blows
Like Love's alarum pattering the sharp sleet
Against the window-panes; St. Agnes' moon hath set.

xxxvii. 'Tis dark; quick pattereth the flaw-blown sleet:
"This is no dream, my bride, my Madeline!"
'Tis dark: the iced gusts still rave and beat:
"No dream, alas! alas! and woe is mine!
"Porphyro will leave me here to fade and pine.—
"Cruel! what traitor could thee hither bring?
"I curse not, for my heart is lost in thine,
"Though thou forsakest a deceived thing;—
"A dove forlorn and lost with sick unpruned wing."

xxxviii. "My Madeline! sweet dreamer! lovely bride!
          "Say, may I be for aye thy vassal blest?
          "Thy beauty's shield, heart-shap'd and vermeil dyed?
          "Ah, silver shrine, here will I take my rest
          "After so many hours of toil and quest,
          "A famish'd pilgrim,—saved by miracle.
          "Though I have found, I will not rob thy nest
          "Saving of thy sweet self; if thou think'st well
       "To trust, fair Madeline, to no rude infidel.

xxxix.   "Hark! 'tis an elfin-storm from faery land,
          "Of haggard seeming, but a boon indeed:
          "Arise—arise! the morning is at hand;—
          "The bloated wassaillers will never heed:—
          "Let us away, my love, with happy speed;
          "There are no ears to hear, or eyes to see,—
          "Drown'd all in Rhenish and the sleepy mead:
          "Awake! arise! my love, and fearless be,
       "For o'er the southern moors I have a home for thee,"

xl.   She hurried at his words, beset with fears,
          For there were sleeping dragons all around,
          At glaring watch, perhaps, with ready spears—
          Down the wide stairs a darkling way they found.—
          In all the house was heard no human sound.
          A chain-droop'd lamp was flickering by each door;
          The arras, rich with horseman, hawk, and hound,
          Flutter'd in the besieging wind's uproar;
       And the long carpets rose along the gusty floor.

xli   They glide, like phantoms, into the wide hall;
          Like phantoms, to the iron porch, they glide;
          Where lay the Porter, in uneasy sprawl,
          With a huge empty flaggon by his side:
          The wakeful bloodhound rose, and shook his hide,
          But his sagacious eye an inmate owns:
          By one, and one, the bolts full easy slide:—
          The chains lie silent on the footworn stones;—
       The key turns, and the door upon its hinges groans.

XLII. And they are gone: aye, ages long ago
These lovers fled away into the storm.
That night the Baron dreamt of many a woe,
And all his warrior-guests, with shade and form
Of witch, and demon, and large coffin-worm,
Were long be-nightmar'd. Angela the old
Died palsy-twitch'd, with meagre face deform;
The Beadsman, after thousand aves told,
For aye unsought for slept among his ashes cold.

LA BELLE DAME SANS MERCI

Ah, what can ail thee, wretched wight,
Alone and palely loitering?
The sedge is wither'd from the lake,
And no birds sing.

Ah, what can ail thee, wretched wight,
So haggard and so woe-begone?
The squirrel's granary is full,
And the harvest's done.

I see a lily on thy brow,
With anguish moist and fever dew;
And on thy cheek a fading rose
Fast withereth too.

I met a Lady in the meads,
Full beautiful, a fairy's child;
Her hair was long, her foot was light,
And her eyes were wild.

I set her on my pacing steed,
And nothing else saw all day long;
For sideways would she lean, and sing
A fairy's song.

I made a garland for her head,
And bracelets too, and fragrant zone;
She look'd at me as she did love,
And made sweet moan.

She found me roots of relish sweet,
And honey wild, and manna dew;
And sure in language strange she said,
I love thee true.

She took me to her elfin grot,
And there she gaz'd and sighed deep,
And there I shut her wild sad eyes—
So kiss'd to sleep.

And there we slumber'd on the moss,
And there I dream'd, ah woe betide,
The latest dream I ever dream'd
On the cold hill side.

I saw pale Kings, and princes too,
Pale warriors, death-pale were they all;
Who cried—"La belle Dame sans merci
Hath thee in thrall."

I saw their starv'd lips in the gloam
With horrid warning gaped wide,
And I awoke, and found me here
On the cold hill side.

And this is why I sojourn here
Alone and palely loitering,
Though the sedge is wither'd from the lake,
And no birds sing.

Note:

This version is that approved by Keats for publication in Leigh Hunt's paper *The Indicator*, for May the 10th, 1820, probably about a year after the poem was first composed.

TO AUTUMN

Season of mists and mellow fruitfulness,
　Close bosom-friend of the maturing sun;
Conspiring with him how to load and bless
　With fruit the vines that round the thatch-eves run;
To bend with apples the moss'd cottage-trees,
　And fill all fruit with ripeness to the core;
　　To swell the gourd, and plump the hazel shells
With a sweet kernel; to set budding more,
And still more, later flowers for the bees,
　Until they think warm days will never cease,
　　For Summer has o'er-brimm'd their clammy cells

Who hath not seen thee oft amid thy store?
　Sometimes whoever seeks abroad may find
Thee sitting careless on a granary floor,
　Thy hair soft-lifted by the winnowing wind;
Or on a half-reap'd furrow sound asleep,
　Drows'd with the fume of poppies, while thy hook
　　Spares the next swath and all its twined flowers:
And sometimes like a gleaner thou dost keep
　Steady thy laden head across a brook;
Or by a cyder-press, with patient look,
　　Thou watchest the last oozings hours by hours.

Where are the songs of Spring? Ay, where are they?
　Think not of them, thou hast thy music too,—
While barred clouds bloom the soft-dying day,
　And touch the stubble-plains with rosy hue;
Then in a wailful choir the small gnats mourn
　Among the river sallows, borne aloft
　　Or sinking as the light wind lives or dies;
And full-grown lambs loud bleat from hilly bourn;
　Hedge-crickets sing; and now with treble soft
　The red-breast whistles from a garden-croft;
　　And gathering swallows twitter in the skies.

From *SONNET IX:*

Keen, Fitful Gusts

The stars look very cold about the sky.

From *SONNET XI:*

On First Looking into Chapman's Homer

Then felt I like some watcher of the skies
When a new planet swims into his ken;
Or like stout Cortez when with eagle eyes
He star'd at the Pacific—and all his men
Look'd at each other with a wild surmise,
Silent, upon a peak in Darien.

From *SLEEP AND POETRY*

l 371.   Thrilling liquidity of dewy piping.

From *ODE ON A GRECIAN URN*

"Beauty is truth, truth beauty,"—that is all
Ye know on earth, and all ye need to know.

Percy Bysshe Shelley

STANZAS.—APRIL, 1814 (published in 1816).

Away! the moor is dark beneath the moon,
Rapid clouds have drunk the last pale beam of even:
Away! the gathering winds will call the darkness soon,
And profoundest midnight shroud the serene lights of heaven.

Pause not. The time is past. Every voice cries, Away!
Tempt not with one last tear thy friend's ungentle mood:
Thy lover's eye, so glazed and cold, dares not entreat thy stay:
Duty and dereliction guide thee back to solitude.

Away, away, to thy sad and silent home;
Pour bitter tears on its desolated hearth;
Watch the dim shades as like ghosts they go and come,
And complicate strange webs of melancholy mirth.

The leaves of wasted autumn woods shall float around thine head:
The blooms of dewy spring shall gleam beneath thy feet:
But thy soul, or this world, must fade in the frost that binds the
dead,
Ere midnight's frown and morning's smile, ere thou and peace may
meet.

The cloud shadows of midnight possess their own repose,
For the weary winds are silent, or the moon is in the deep:
Some respite to its turbulence unresting ocean knows;
Whatever moves, or toils, or grieves, hath its appointed sleep.

Thou in the grave shalt rest—yet, till the phantoms flee
Which that house, and heath, and garden, made dear to thee
erewhile,
Thy remembrance, and repentance, and deep musings are not free
From the music of two voices and the light of one sweet smile.

From *LAON AND CYTHNA* (*The Revolt of Islam*)

CANTO I.   I.

> When the last hope of trampled France had failed
> Like a brief dream of unremaining glory,
> From visions of despair I rose, and scaled
> The peak of an aërial promontory,
> Whose caverned base with the vext surge was hoary.

CANTO III.   XII.

> Upon that rock a mighty column stood,
> Whose capital seemed sculptured in the sky,
> Which to the wanderers o'er the solitude
> Of distant seas, from ages long gone by,
> Had made a landmark; o'er its height to fly
> Scarcely the cloud, the vulture, or the blast,
> Has power—and when the shades of evening lie
> On Earth and Ocean, its carved summits cast
> The sunken day-light far thro the aërial waste.

XIII.

> They bore me to a cavern in the hill
> Beneath that column, and unbound me there;
> And one did strip me stark; and one did fill
> A vessel from the putrid pool; one bare
> A lighted torch, and four with friendless care
> Guided my steps the cavern-paths along,
> Then up a steep and dark and narrow stair
> We wound, until the torch's fiery tongue
> Amid the gushing day beamless and pallid hung.

XIV.

> They raised me to the platform of the pile,
> That column's dizzy height:—the grate of brass
> Thro' which they thrust me, open stood the while,
> As to its ponderous and suspended mass,
> With chains which ate into the flesh, alas!
> With brazen links, my naked limbs they bound:

The grate, as they departed to repass,
With horrid clangour fell, and the far sound
Of their retiring steps in the dense gloom were drowned.

xv.   The noon was calm and bright: around that column
        The overhanging sky and circling sea
        Spread forth in silentness profound and solemn
        The darkness of brief frenzy cast on me,
        So that I knew not my own misery:
        The islands and the mountains in the day
        Like clouds reposed afar: and I could see
        The town among the woods below that lay,
        And the dark rocks which bound the bright and glassy bay.

xvi.   It was so calm, that scarce the feathery weed
        Sown by some eagle on the topmost stone,
        Swayed in the air:—so bright, that noon did breed
        No shadow in the sky beside mine own—
        Mine, and the shadow of my chain alone.
        Below, the smoke of roofs involved in flame
        Rested like night, all else was clearly shewn
        In that broad glare, yet sound to me none came,
        But of the living blood that ran within my frame. . . .

xxi.   Two days thus past—I neither raved nor died—
        Thirst raged within me, like a scorpion's nest
        Built in mine entrails; I had spurned aside
        The water-vessel, while despair possest
        My thoughts, and now no drop remained: the uprest
        Of the third sun brought hunger—but the crust
        Which had been left, was to my craving breast
        Fuel, not food. I chewed the bitter dust,
        And bit my bloodless arm, and licked the brazen rust.

xxii.   My brain began to fail when the fourth morn
        Burst o'er the golden isles—a fearful sleep,
        Which through the caverns dreary and forlorn
        Of the riven soul, sent its foul dreams to sweep

With whirlwind swiftness—a fall far and deep,—
A gulf, a void, a sense of senselessness—
These things dwelt in me, even as shadows keep
Their watch in some dim charnel's loneliness,
A shoreless sea, a sky sunless and planetless. . . .

XXV.   Methought that grate was lifted, and the seven
Who brought me thither, four stiff corpses bare,
And from the frieze to the four winds of Heaven
Hung them on high by the entangled hair:
Swarthy were three—the fourth was very fair:
As they retired, the golden moon upsprung,
And eagerly, out in the giddy air,
Leaning that I might eat, I stretched and clung
Over the shapeless depth in which those corpses hung. . . .

XXVII. Then seemed it that a tameless hurricane
Arose and bore me in its dark career
Beyond the sun, beyond the stars that wane
On the verge of formless space—it languished there,
And dying, left a silence lone and drear,
More horrible than famine:—in the deep
The shape of an old man did then appear,
Stately and beautiful; that dreadful sleep
His heavenly smiles dispersed, and I could wake and
weep. . . .

XXIX. He struck my chains, and gently spake and smiled:
As they were loosened by that Hermit old,
Mine eyes were of their madness half beguiled,
To answer those kind looks—he did enfold
His giant arms around me, to uphold
My wretched frame, my scorchèd limbs he wound
In linen moist and balmy, and as cold
As dew to drooping leaves;—the chain, with sound
Like earthquake, thro' the chasm of that steep stair did
bound,

xxx.   As, lifting me, it fell. What next I heard
        Were billows leaping on the harbour-bar,
        And the shrill sea-wind, whose breath idly stirred
        My hair; I looked abroad, and saw a star
        Shining beside a sail, and distant far
        That mountain and its column . . .

xxxii. "It is a friend beside thee—take good cheer,
        Poor victim, thou art now at liberty."

Canto viii. xix.
        "Disguise it not—we have one human heart—
        All mortal thoughts confess a common home."

xxii. The past is Death's, the future is thine own.

xxiii. Wearily, wearily o'er the boundless deep.

Canto xii. i.
        The transport of a fierce and monstrous gladness
        Spread thro' the multitudinous streets, fast flying
        Upon the winds of fear; from his dull madness
        The starveling waked, and died in joy; the dying,
        Among the corpses in stark agony lying,
        Just heard the happy tidings, and in hope
        Closed their faint eyes; from house to house replying
        With loud acclaim, the living shook Heaven's cope
        And filled the startled Earth with echoes: morn did ope
        Its pale eyes, then.

xxix. Fill this dark night of things with an eternal morning.

xxxiv. A scene of joy and wonder to behold
        That river's shapes and shadows changing ever,
        Where the broad sunrise, filled with deepening gold,
        Its whirlpools, where all hues did spread and quiver,

And where melodious falls did burst and shiver
Among rocks clad with flowers, the foam and spray
Sparkled like stars upon the sunny river,
Or when the moonlight poured a holier day,
One vast and glittering lake around green islands lay.

XXXVI. Sometimes between the wide and flowering meadows,
Mile after mile we sailed, and 'twas delight
To see far off the sunbeams chase the shadows
Over the grass; sometimes beneath the night
Of wide and vaulted caves, whose roofs were bright
With starry gems, we fled, whilst from their deep
And dark-green chasms, shades beautiful and white,
Amid sweet sounds across our path would sweep ,
Like swift and lovely dreams that walk the waves of
sleep.

XXXVII. And ever as we sailed, our minds were full
Of love and wisdom . . . .

From *THE BOAT ON THE SERCHIO*

The stars burnt out in the pale blue air,
And the thin white moon lay withering there . . .

Day had kindled the dewy woods,
And the rocks above and the stream below,
And the vapours in their multitudes
And the Apennines' shroud of summer snow . .

Day had awakened all things that be. . . .

All rose to do the task He set to each,
Who shaped us to His ends and not our own;
The million rose to learn and one to teach
What none yet ever knew, or can be known.

(The lines were first detached thus from their context by
Robert Browning in his famous Essay.)

TO A SKYLARK

Hail to thee, blithe spirit,
    Bird thou never wert,
That from Heaven, oɪ near it,
    Pourest thy full heart
In profuse strains of unpremeditated art.

Higher still and higher
    From the earth thou springest;
Like a cloud of fire
    The blue deep thou wingest
And singing still dost soar, and soaring ever singest.

In the golden lightning
    Of the sunken sun,
O'er which clouds are brightning,
    Thou dost float and run,
Like an unbodied joy whose race is just begun.

The pale purple even
    Melts around thy flight;
Like a star of Heaven
    In the broad daylight,
Thou art unseen, but yet I hear thy shrill delight.

Keen as are the arrows
    Of that silver sphere,
Whose intense lamp narrows
    In the white dawn clear,
Until we hardly see, we feel that it is there.

All the earth and air
    With thy voice is loud,
As, when night is bare,
    From one lonely cloud
The moon rains out her beams and all is overflowed.

What thou art we know not:
What is most like thee?
From rainbow clouds there flow not
Drops so bright to see,
As from thy presence showers a rain of melody.

Like a poet hidden
In the light of thought,
Singing hymns unbidden,
Till the world is wrought
To sympathy with hopes and fears it heeded not:

Like a high-born maiden
In a palace tower
Soothing her love-laden
Soul in secret hour
With music sweet as love, which overflows her bower:

Like a glow-worm golden
In a dell of dew,
Scattering unbeholden
Its aërial hue
Among the flowers and grass, which screen it from the view:

Like a rose embowered
In its own green leaves,
By warm winds deflowered,
Till the scent it gives
Makes faint with too much sweet these heavy-wingèd thieves.

Sound of vernal showers
On the twinkling grass,
Rain-awakened flowers,
All that ever was
Joyous, and clear, and fresh, thy music doth surpass.

Teach us, sprite or bird,
What sweet thoughts are thine.
I have never heard
Praise of love or wine
That panted forth a flood of rapture so divine.

Chorus Hymenæal,
Or triumphal chaunt,
Matched with thine, would be all
But an empty vaunt,
A thing wherein we feel there is some hidden want.

What objects are the fountains
Of thy happy strain?
What fields, or waves, or mountains?
What shapes of sky or plain?
What love of thine own kind? what ignorance of pain.

With thy clear keen joyance
Languor cannot be:
Shadow of annoyance
Never came near thee:
Thou lovest; but ne'er knew love's sad satiety.

Waking or asleep,
Thou of Death must deem
Things more true and deep
Than we mortals dream,
Or how could thy notes flow in such a crystal stream?

We look before and after,
And pine for what is not;
Our sincerest laughter
With some pain is fraught;
Our sweetest songs are those that tell of saddest thought.

Yet, if we could scorn
Hate, and pride, and fear;
If we were things born
Not to shed a tear
I know not how thy joy we ever should come near.

Better than all measures
Of delightful sound,
Better than all treasures
That in books are found,
Thy skill to poet were, thou scorner of the ground.

Teach me half the gladness
That thy brain must know,
Such harmonious madness
From my lips would flow,
The world should listen, then, as I am listening now.

THE QUESTION

I dreamed that, as I wandered by the way,
Bare Winter suddenly was changed to Spring,
And gentle odours led my steps astray,
Mixed with a sound of waters murmuring
Along a shelving bank of turf, which lay
Under a copse, and hardly dared to fling
Its green arms round the bosom of the stream,
But kissed it and then fled, as thou mightest in dream.

There grew pied wind-flowers and violets,
Daisies, those pearled Arcturi of the earth,
The constellated flower that never sets;
Faint oxlips; tender bluebells, at whose birth
The sod scarce heaved; and that tall flower that wets—
Like a child, half in tenderness and mirth—
Its mother's face with heaven-collected tears,
When the low wind, its playmate's voice, it hears.

And in the warm hedge grew lush eglantine,
Green cowbind and the moonlight-coloured may,
And cherry-blossoms, and white cups, whose wine
Was the bright dew, yet drained not by the day;

And wild roses, and ivy serpentine,
With its dark buds and leaves, wandering astray;
And flowers azure, black, and streaked with gold
Fairer than any wakened eyes behold.

And nearer to the river's trembling edge
There grew broad flag-flowers, purple, prankt with white,
And starry river-buds among the sedge,
And floating water-lilies, broad and bright,
Which lit the oak that overhung the hedge
With moonlight beams of their own watery light;
And bulrushes, and reeds of such deep green
As soothed the dazzled eye with sober sheen.

Methought, that of these visionary flowers
I made a nosegay, bound in such a way
That the same hues, which in their natural bowers
Were mingled or opposed, the like array
Kept these imprisoned Children of the Hours
Within my hand,—and then, elate and gay,
I hastened to the spot whence I had come,
That I might there present it:—O, to whom?

CHORUS from *HELLAS*

The world's great age begins anew,
The golden years return,
The earth doth like a snake renew
Her winter weeds out-worn:
Heaven smiles, and faiths and empires gleam,
Like wrecks of a dissolving dream.

A brighter Hellas rears its mountains
From waves serener far;
A new Peneus rolls his fountains
Against the morning-star.

Where fairer Tempes bloom, there sleep
Young Cyclads on a sunnier deep.

A loftier Argo cleaves the main,
Fraught with a later prize;
Another Orpheus sings again,
And loves, and weeps, and dies.
A new Ulysses leaves once more
Calypso, for his native shore.

O, write no more the tale of Troy,
If earth Death's scroll must be:
Nor mix with Laian rage the joy
Which dawns upon the free:
Although a subtler Sphinx renew
Riddles of Death Thebes never knew.

Another Athens shall arise,
And to remoter time
Bequeath, like sunset to the skies,
The splendour of its prime;
And leave, if nought so bright may live,
All earth can take or Heaven can give.

Saturn and Love their long repose
Shall burst, more bright and good
Than all who fell, than One who rose,
Than many unsubdued;
Not gold, not blood, their altar dowers,
But votive tears and symbol flowers.

O cease! Must hate and death return?
Cease! Must men kill and die?
Cease! Drain not to its dregs the urn
Of bitter prophecy.
The world is weary of the past,
O might it die or rest at last.

From *THE WITCH OF ATLAS*

vi.   And every beast of beating heart grew bold
    Such gentleness and power even to behold.

vii.   The brinded lioness led forth her young,
    That she might teach them how they should forego
    Their inborn thirst of death; the pard unstrung
    His sinews at her feet, and sought to know
    With looks whose motions spoke without a tongue
    How he might be as gentle as the doe.
    The magic circle of her voice and eyes
    All savage natures did imparadise.

viii.   And old Silenus, shaking a green stick
    Of lilies, and the wood-gods in a crew
    Came, blithe, as in the olive copses thick
    Cicadæ are, drunk with the noonday dew:
    And Dryope and Faunus followed quick,
    Teasing the God to sing them something new;
    Till in this cave they found the lady lone,
    Sitting upon a seat of emerald stone.

ix.   And universal Pan, 'tis said, was there,
    And though none saw him,—through the adamant
    Of the deep mountains, through the trackless air,
    And through those living spirits, like a want
    He passed out of his everlasting lair
    Where the quick heart of the great world doth pant,
    And felt that wondrous lady all alone,—
    And she felt him, upon her emerald throne.

x.   And every Nymph of stream and spreading tree,
    And every shepherdess of Ocean's flocks,
    Who drives her white waves over the green sea;
    And Ocean, with the brine on his grey locks;
    And quaint Priapus with his company,

All came, much wond'ring how the enwombèd rocks
Could have brought forth so beautiful a birth:—
Her love subdued their wonder and their mirth.

XI. The herdsmen and the mountain maidens came,
And the rude Kings of pastoral Garamaunt. . . .

XII. For she was beautiful—her beauty made
The bright world dim. . . .

XXXVIII. The panther-peopled forests. . . .

LVI. And sometimes to those streams of upper air
Which whirl the Earth in its diurnal round,
She would ascend, and win the spirits there
To let her join their chorus. Mortals found
That on those days the sky was calm and fair,
And mystic snatches of harmonious sound
Wandered upon the earth where'er she passed,
And happy thoughts of hope, too sweet to last.

LVII. But her choice sport was, in the hours of sleep,
To glide adown old Nilus, where he threads
Egypt and Ethiopia, from the steep
Of utmost Axumè, until he spreads
Like a calm flock of silver-fleecèd sheep,
His waters on the plain; and crested heads
Of cities and proud temples gleam amid,
And many a vapour-belted pyramid.

LVIII. By Mœris and the Mareotid Lakes,
Strewn with faint blooms, like bridal-chamber floors,
Where naked boys, bridling tame water-snakes,
Or charioteering ghastly alligators,
Had left on the sweet waters mighty wakes
Of those huge forms—within the brazen doors
Of the great Labyrinth slept both boy and beast,
Tired with the pomp of their Osirian feast.

LIX.   And where within the surface of the river
The shadows of the massy temples lie,
And never are erased—but tremble ever
Like things which every cloud can doom to die,
Through lotus-pav'n canals, and wheresoever
The works of man pierced that serenest sky
With tombs, and towers, and fanes, 'twas her delight
To wander in the shadow of the night.

LX.   With motion like the spirit of that wind
Whose soft step deepens slumber, her light feet
Past through the peopled haunts of human kind,
Scattering sweet visions from her presence sweet,
Through fane, and palace-court, and labyrinth mined
With many a dark and subterranean street
Under the Nile, through chambers high and deep
She passed, observing mortals in their sleep.

LXI.   A pleasure sweet, doubtless it was, to see
Mortals subdued in all the shapes of sleep.
Here, lay two sister twins in infancy;
There, a lone youth, who in his dreams did weep;
Within, two lovers, linkèd innocently
In their loose locks which over both did creep,
Like ivy from one stem;—and there lay calm
Old age with snow-bright hair and folded palm.

LXII.   But other troubled forms of sleep she saw,
Not to be mirrored in a holy song—
Distortions foul of supernatural awe,
And pale imaginings of visioned wrong;
And all the code of custom's lawless law
Written upon the brows of old and young:
"This," said the Wizard Maiden, "is the strife
Which stirs the liquid surface of man's life."

LXIII. And little did the sight disturb her soul.—
  We, the weak mariners of that wide lake,
  Where'er its shores extend or billows roll,
  Our course unpiloted and starless make,
  O'er its wild surface, to an unknown goal:—
  But she, in the calm depths, her way could take,
  Where in bright bowers immortal forms abide
  Beneath the weltering of the restless tide.

LXIV. And she saw princes couched under the glow
  Of sunlike gems; and round each temple-court
  In dormitories ranged, row after row,
  She saw the priests asleep—all of one sort—
  For all were educated to be so.—
  The peasants in their huts, and in the port
  The sailors she saw cradled on the waves,
  And the dead lulled within their dreamless graves.

HYMN OF PAN

From the forests and highlands
  We come, we come;
From the river-girt islands,
Where land waves are dumb
Listening to my sweet pipings.
The wind in the reeds and the rushes,
The bees on the bells of thyme,
The birds on the myrtle bushes,
The cicale above in the lime,
And the lizards below in the grass,
Were as silent as ever old Tmolus was,
  Listening to my sweet pipings.

Liquid Peneus was flowing,
And all dark Tempe lay
In Pelion's shadow, outgrowing
The light of the dying day,
  Speeded by my sweet pipings.

The Sileni, and Sylvans, and Fauns,
And the Nymphs of the woods and waves,
To the edge of the moist river-lawns,
　　And the brink of the dewy caves,
And all that did then attend and follow
Were silent with love, as you, now, Apollo,
　　With envy of my sweet pipings.

I sang of the dancing stars,
I sang of the dædal Earth,
And of Heaven, and the Giant Wars,
And Love, and Death, and Birth;—
And then I changed my pipings:—
Singing, how down the Vale of Mænalus,
I pursued a maiden and clasped a reed:
Gods and men, we are all deluded thus!
It breaks in our bosom, and then we bleed.
All wept, as I think both ye now would
If envy or age had not frozen your blood
　　At the sorrow of my sweet pipings.

OZYMANDIAS

I met a traveller from an antique land
Who said:—Two vast and trunkless legs of stone
Stand in the desert. Near them, on the sand,
Half sunk, a shattered visage lies, whose frown,
And wrinkled lip, and sneer of cold command,
Tell that its sculptor well those passions read
Which yet survive, stamped on those lifeless things,
The hand that mocked them, and the heart that fed.

And on the pedestal, these words appear:—
"My name is Ozymandias, King of Kings,
Look on my works, ye Mighty, and despair."

Nothing beside remains. Round the decay
Of that colossal wreck, boundless and bare,
The lone and level sands stretch far away.

TO NIGHT

Swiftly walk over the western wave,
     Spirit of Night.
Out of the misty eastern cave,
Where, all the long and lone daylight,
Thou wovest dreams of joy and fear,
Which make thee terrible and dear,
     Swift be thy flight.

Wrap thy form in a mantle grey,
     Star-inwrought;
Blind with thine hair the eyes of Day;
Kiss her until she be wearied out,
Then wander o'er city, and sea, and land,
Touching all with thine opiate wand—
     Come, long-sought.

When I arose and saw the dawn,
     I sighed for thee;
When light rode high, and the dew was gone,
And noon lay heavy on flower and tree,
And the weary Day turned to his rest,
Lingering like an unloved guest,
     I sighed for thee.

Thy brother Death came, and cried,
     "Wouldst thou me?"
Thy sweet child, Sleep, the filmy-eyed,
Murmured, like a noon-tide bee,
"Shall I nestle near thy side?
Wouldst thou me?" And I replied,
     "No; not thee."

Death will come when thou art dead,
    Soon, too soon—
Sleep will come when thou art fled;
Of neither would I ask the boon
I ask of thee, belovèd Night—
Swift be thine approaching flight,
    Come soon, soon!

From *ADONAIS*

An Elegy on the Death of John Keats

LI.   Here pause: these graves are all too young as yet
To have outgrown the sorrow which consigned
Its charge to each . . . .

What Adonais is, why fear we to become?

LII.   The One remains: the many change and pass;
Heaven's light forever shines, Earth's shadows fly;
Life, like a dome of many-coloured glass,
Stains the white radiance of Eternity,
Until Death tramples it to fragments. Die,
If thou wouldst be with that which thou dost seek.
Follow where all is fled. Rome's azure sky,
Flowers, ruins, statues, music, words, are weak
The glory they transfuse with fitting truth to speak.

LIII.   Why linger? Why turn back? Why shrink, my Heart?
Thy hopes are gone before: from all things here
They have departed; thou shouldst now depart.
A light is passed from the revolving year,
And man, and woman; and what still is dear
Attracts to crush, repels to make thee wither.
The soft sky smiles; the low wind whispers near;
'Tis Adonais calls . . . O, hasten thither;
No more let Life divide what Death can join together.

LIV.   That Light, whose smile kindles the Universe,
        That Beauty, in which all things work and move,
        That Benediction, which the eclipsing Curse
        Of Birth can quench not, that sustaining Love,
        Which through the Web of Being blindly wove,
        By man and beast and earth and air and sea,
        Burns, bright or dim, as each are mirrors of
        The Fire for which all thirst, now beams on me,
        Consuming the last clouds of cold mortality.

LV.   The Breath whose might I have invoked in song
        Descends on me: my spirit's bark is driven,
        Far from the shore, far from the trembling throng
        Whose sails were never to the tempest given;
        The massy earth and spherèd skies are riven:
        I am borne darkly, fearfully, afar;
        Whilst burning through the inmost veil of Heaven,
        The Soul of Adonais, like a star,
        Beacons from the abode where the Eternal are.

From a *SONG*

Rarely, rarely, comest thou,
Spirit of Delight.

From *TO EDWARD WILLIAMS*

Happy yourself, you feel another's woe.

A FRAGMENT

The gentleness of rain was in the wind.

From *THE CLOUD*

That orbèd Maiden, with white fire laden,
Whom mortals call the moon.

From *ODE TO THE WEST WIND*

III.   Thou who didst waken from his summer dreams
The blue Mediterranean, where he lay
Lulled by the coil of his crystalline streams,

Beside a pumice isle in Baiæ's bay,
And saw, in sleep, old palaces and towers
Quivering within the wave's intenser day.

V.   Make me thy lyre, even as the forest is.

From *THE SENSITIVE PLANT*

For love, and beauty, and delight,
There is no death nor change.

Thomas Hood

I REMEMBER, I REMEMBER

I remember, I remember,
The house where I was born,
The little window where the sun
Came peeping in at morn;
He never came a wink too soon,
Nor brought too long a day,
But now, I often wish the night
Had borne my breath away.

I remember, I remember,
The roses, red and white,
The violets, and the lily-cups,
Those flowers made of light.
The lilacs where the robin built,
And where my brother set
The laburnum on his birthday,—
The tree is living yet.

I remember, I remember,
Where I was used to swing,
And thought the air must rush as fresh
To swallows on the wing:
My spirit flew in feathers then,
That is so heavy now
And summer pools could hardly cool
The fever on my brow.

I remember, I remember,
The fir-trees dark and high;
I used to think their slender tops
Were close against the sky:

It was a childish ignorance,
But now 'tis little joy
To know I'm farther off from Heav'n
Than when I was a boy.

From *THE HAUNTED HOUSE*

No human figure stirr'd, to go or come,
No face look'd forth, from shut or open casement;
No chimney smoked . . . there was no sign of Home
From parapet to basement.

O'er all there hung a shadow and a fear;
A sense of mystery the spirit daunted,
And said, as plain as whisper in the ear,
The place is Haunted.

Howbeit, the door I push'd . . . or so I dream'd . . .
Which slowly, slowly gaped . . . The hinges creaking
With such a rusty eloquence, it seem'd
That Time himself was speaking.

The wood-louse dropp'd, and roll'd into a ball,
Touched by some impulse occult or mechanic;
And nameless beetles ran along the wall
In universal panic.

There was so foul a rumour in the air,
The shadow of a Presence so atrocious;
No human creature could have feasted there
Even the most ferocious . . .

'Tis hard for human actions to account,
Whether from reason or from impulse only . . .
But some internal prompting bade me mount
The gloomy stairs and lonely.

The Death Watch tick'd behind the panell'd oak,
Inexplicable tremors shook the arras,
And echoes strange and mystical awoke,
The fancy to embarrass.

Prophetic hints that fill'd the soul with dread,
But thro' one gloomy entrance pointing mostly,
The while some secret inspiration said,
That Chamber is the Ghostly.

The spider shunn'd the interdicted room,
The moth, the beetle, and the fly were banish'd,
And where the sunbeam fell athwart the gloom
The very midge had vanish'd.

One lonely ray that glanced upon a Bed,
As if with awful aim direct and certain,
To show the BLOODY HAND in burning red
Embroider'd on the curtain.

And yet, no gory stain was on the quilt . . .
The pillow in its place had slowly rotted;
The floor alone retain'd the trace of guilt,
Those boards obscurely spotted.

Obscurely spotted to the door, and thence
With mazy doubles to the grated casement . . .
Oh what a tale they told of fear intense,
Of horror and amazement.

What human creature in the dead of night
Had coursed like hunted hare that cruel distance?
Had sought the door, the window, in his flight,
Striving for dear existence?

What shrieking Spirit in that bloody room
Its mortal frame had violently quitted?
Across the sunbeam, with a sudden gloom,
A ghostly Shadow flitted.

Across the sunbeam, and along the wall,
But painted on the air so very dimly,
It hardly veil'd the tapestry at all,
Or portrait frowning grimly.

O'er all there hung the shadow of a fear,
A sense of mystery the spirit daunted,
And said, as plain as whisper in the ear,
The place is Haunted.

Thomas Love Peacock

From *NIGHTMARE ABBEY*

Three Men of Gotham

"Seamen three, what men be ye?"
"Gotham's three wise men we be."
"Whither, in your bowl so free?"
"To rake the moon from out the sea.
The bowl goes trim. The moon doth shine
And our ballast is old wine."

From *THE MISFORTUNES OF ELPHIN*

The War Song of Dinas Vawr

The mountain sheep are sweeter,
But the valley sheep are fatter;
We therefore deemed it meeter
To carry off the latter.
We made an expedition;
We met a host and quelled it;
We forced a strong position,
And killed the men who held it.

On Dyfed's richest valley,
Where herds of kine were browsing,
We made a mighty sally,
To furnish our carousing.
Fierce warriors rushed to meet us;
We met them, and o'er-threw them:
They struggled hard to beat us;
But we conquered them, and slew them.

As we drove our prize at leisure,
The King marched forth to catch us:
His rage surpassed all measure,
But his people could not match us.
He fled to his hall-pillars,
And, ere our force we led off,
Some sacked his house and cellars
While others cut his head off.

We there, in strife bewild'ring,
Spilt blood enough to swim in;
We orphaned many children,
And widowed many women.
The eagles and the ravens
We glutted with our foemen;
The heroes and the cravens,
The spearmen and the bowmen.

We brought away from battle,
And much their land bemoaned them,
Two thousand head of cattle,
And the head of him who owned them:
Ednyfed, King of Dyfed,
His head was borne before us;
His wine and beasts supplied our feasts
And his overthrow our chorus.

From *MELINCOURT*

From the *Quintetto Upon the Christmas Pie*

MR. VAMP:

> My share of pie to win, I will dash through thick and thin
> And philosophy and liberty shall fly, fly, fly;
> And truth and taste shall know, that their everlasting foe
> Has a finger, finger, finger in the Christmas Pie.

CHORUS, with MR. FEATHERNEST, MR. KILLTHEDEAD, MR. PAPER-STAMP, and MR. ANYSIDE ANTIJACK:

> And we'll all have a finger, a finger, a finger,
> We'll all have a finger in the Christmas Pie.

MR. ANYSIDE ANTIJACK:

> My tailor is so clever, that my coat will turn for ever
> And take any colour you can dye, dye, dye,
> For my earthly wishes are among the loaves and fishes,
> And to have my little finger in the Christmas Pie.

THE FIVE:

> And we'll all have a finger, a finger, a finger,
> We'll all have a finger in the Christmas Pie.

(Said to be to the tune of *Turning, turning, turning, as the wheel goes round.*)

Joseph Blanco White

From the Sonnet *NIGHT AND DEATH*

The first lines suggest the first man's first sight of the sunset.
As the light faded:—

> Hesperus with the Host of Heaven came,
> And, lo! Creation widened in man's view.
>
> Who could have thought such darkness lay concealed
> Within thy beams, O Sun? or who could find
> Whilst flower and leaf and instinct stood revealed,
> That to such countless orbs thou mad'st us blind?
>
> If Light can thus deceive, wherefore not Life?

John Henry Newman

LEAD, KINDLY LIGHT

Lead, kindly Light, amid the encircling gloom,
    Lead Thou me on;
The night is dark, and I am far from home,
    Lead thou me on.
Keep Thou my feet; I do not ask to see
The distant scene; one step enough for me.

I was not ever thus, nor prayed that Thou
    Shouldst lead me on;
I loved to choose and see my path; but now,
    Lead Thou me on.
I loved the garish day, and, spite of fears,
Pride ruled my will: remember not past years.

So long Thy power hath blest me, sure it still
    Will lead me on
O'er moor and fen, o'er crag and torrent, till
    The night is gone;
And, with the morn, those angel faces smile,
Which I have loved long since, and lost awhile.

Walter Savage Landor

From *TO ROBERT BROWNING*

There is delight in singing, though none hear
Beside the singer; and there is delight
In praising, though the praiser sit alone
And see the praised far off him, far above.

Alfred Tennyson

MARIANA

"Mariana in the moated grange."—*Measure for Measure*.

With blackest moss the flower-plots
    Were thickly crusted, one and all:
The rusted nails fell from the knots
    That held the pear to the gable-wall.
The broken sheds look'd sad and strange:
    Unlifted was the clinking latch;
    Weeded and worn the ancient thatch
Upon the lonely moated grange.
        She only said, "My life is dreary,
           He cometh not," she said;
        She said, "I am aweary, aweary,
           I would that I were dead!"

Her tears fell with the dews at even;
    Her tears fell ere the dews were dried;
She could not look on the sweet heaven,
    Either at morn or eventide.
After the flitting of the bats,
    When thickest dark did trance the sky,
    She drew her casement-curtain by,
And glanced athwart the glooming flats.
        She only said, "The night is dreary,
           He cometh not," she said;
        She said, "I am aweary, aweary,
           I would that I were dead!"

Upon the middle of the night,
    Waking she heard the night-fowl crow:
The cock sung out an hour ere light:
    From the dark fen the oxen's low

Came to her: without hope of change,
  In sleep she seem'd to walk forlorn,
  Till cold winds woke the gray-eyed morn
About the lonely moated grange.
      She only said, "The day is dreary,
        He cometh not," she said;
      She said, "I am aweary, aweary,
        I would that I were dead!"

About a stone-cast from the wall
  A sluice with blacken'd waters slept,
And o'er it many, round and small,
  The cluster'd marish-mosses crept.
Hard by a poplar shook alway,
  All silver-green with gnarled bark:
  For leagues no other tree did mark
The level waste, the rounding gray.
      She only said, "My life is dreary,
        He cometh not," she said;
      She said, "I am aweary, aweary,
        I would that I were dead!"

And ever when the moon was low,
  And the shrill winds were up and away,
In the white curtain, to and fro,
  She saw the gusty shadow sway.
But when the moon was very low,
  And wild winds bound within their cell,
  The shadow of the poplar fell
Upon her bed, across her brow.
      She only said, "The night is dreary,
        He cometh not," she said;
      She said, "I am aweary, aweary,
        I would that I were dead!"

All day within the dreamy house,
  The doors upon their hinges creak'd;
The blue fly sung in the pane; the mouse
  Behind the mouldering wainscot shriek'd,

Or from the crevice peer'd about.
  Old faces glimmer'd thro' the doors,
  Old footsteps trod the upper floors,
Old voices called her from without.
      She only said, "My life is dreary,
        He cometh not," she said;
      She said, "I am aweary, aweary,
        I would that I were dead!"

The sparrow's chirrup on the roof,
  The slow clock ticking, and the sound
Which to the wooing wind aloof
  The poplar made, did all confound
Her sense; but most she loathed the hour
  When the thick-moted sunbeam lay
  Athwart the chambers, and the day
Was sloping toward his western bower.
      Then, said she, "I am very dreary,
        He will not come," she said;
      She wept, "I am aweary, aweary,
        Oh God, that I were dead!"

ULYSSES

It little profits that an idle king,
By this still hearth, among these barren crags,
Match'd with an aged wife, I mete and dole
Unequal laws unto a savage race,
That hoard, and sleep, and feed, and know not me.
I cannot rest from travel: I will drink
Life to the lees: all times I have enjoy'd
Greatly, have suffer'd greatly, both with those
That loved me, and alone; on shore, and when
Thro' scudding drifts the rainy Hyades
Vext the dim sea: I am become a name;
For always roaming with a hungry heart

Much have I seen and known; cities of men
And manners, climates, councils, governments,
Myself not least, but honour'd of them all;
And drunk delight of battle with my peers,
Far on the ringing plains of windy Troy.
I am a part of all that I have met;
Yet all experience is an arch wherethro'
Gleams that untravell'd world, whose margin fades
For ever and for ever when I move.
How dull it is to pause, to make an end,
To rust unburnish'd, not to shine in use!
As tho' to breathe were life. Life piled on life
Were all too little, and of one to me
Little remains: but every hour is saved
From that eternal silence, something more,
A bringer of new things; and vile it were
For some three suns to store and hoard myself,
And this gray spirit yearning in desire
To follow knowledge, like a sinking star,
Beyond the utmost bound of human thought.

This is my son, mine own Telemachus,
To whom I leave the sceptre and the isle—
Well-loved of me, discerning to fulfil
This labour, by slow prudence to make mild
A rugged people, and thro' soft degrees
Subdue them to the useful and the good.
Most blameless is he, centred in the sphere
Of common duties, decent not to fail
In offices of tenderness, and pay
Meet adoration to my household gods,
When I am gone. He works his work, I mine.

There lies the port: the vessel puffs her sail:
There gloom the dark broad seas. My mariners,
Souls that have toil'd, and wrought, and thought with me—
That ever with a frolic welcome took
The thunder and the sunshine, and opposed
Free hearts, free foreheads—you and I are old;
Old age hath yet his honour and his toil;

Death closes all: but something ere the end,
Some work of noble note, may yet be done,
Not unbecoming men that strove with Gods.
The lights begin to twinkle from the rocks:
The long day wanes: the slow moon climbs: the deep
Moans round with many voices. Come, my friends,
'Tis not too late to seek a newer world.
Push off, and sitting well in order smite
The sounding furrows; for my purpose holds
To sail beyond the sunset, and the baths
Of all the western stars, until I die.
It may be that the gulfs will wash us down:
It may be we shall touch the Happy Isles,
And see the great Achilles, whom we knew.
Tho' much is taken, much abides; and tho'
We are not now that strength which in old days
Moved earth and heaven; that which we are, we are;
One equal temper of heroic hearts,
Made weak by time and fate, but strong in will
To strive, to seek, to find, and not to yield.

THE EAGLE

Fragment

He clasps the crag with hooked hands;
Close to the sun in lonely lands,
Ring'd with the azure world, he stands.

The wrinkled sea beneath him crawls;
He watches from his mountain walls,
And like a thunderbolt he falls.

SONG: THE OWL

When cats run home and light is come,
And dew is cold upon the ground,
And the far-off stream is dumb,
And the whirring sail goes round,
And the whirring sail goes round;
Alone and warming his five wits,
The white owl in the belfry sits.

When merry milkmaids click the latch,
And rarely smells the new-mown hay,
And the cock hath sung beneath the thatch
Twice or thrice his roundelay,
Twice or thrice his roundelay;
Alone and warming his five wits,
The white owl in the belfry sits.

From *THE DYING SWAN*

The wild swan's death-hymn took the soul
Of that waste place with joy.

From *MORTE D'ARTHUR*

On one side lay the Ocean, and on one
Lay a great water, and the moon was full.

Robert Browning

From *PAULINE*

Stay we here
With the wild hawks? no, ere the hot noon come
Dive we down—safe;—see this our new retreat
Walled-in with a sloped mound of matted shrubs,
Dark, tangled, old and green—still sloping down
To a small pool whose waters lie asleep
Amid the trailing boughs turned water-plants.
And tall trees over-arch to keep us in,
Breaking the sunbeams into emerald shafts,
And in the dreamy water one small group
Of two or three strange trees are got together,
Wondering at all around—as strange beasts herd
Together far from their own land—all wildness—
No turf nor moss, for boughs and plants pave all,
And tongues of bank go shelving in the waters,
Where the pale-throated snake reclines his head,
And old grey stones lie making eddies there;
The wild mice cross them dry-shod—deeper in—
Shut thy soft eyes—now look—still deeper in:
This is the very heart of the woods—all round,
Mountain-like, heaped above us; yet even here
One pond of water gleams—far off, the river
Sweeps like a sea, barred out from land; but one—
One thin clear sheet has over-leaped and wound
Into this silent depth, which gained, it lies
Still, as but let by sufferance; the trees bend
O'er it as wild men watch a sleeping girl,
And thro' their roots long creeping plants stretch out
Their twined hair, steeped and sparkling; farther on,
Tall rushes and thick flag-knots have combined
To narrow it; so, at length, a silver thread

It winds, all noiselessly, thro' the deep wood,
Till thro' a cleft way, thro' the moss and stone,
It joins its parent-river with a shout.

From *SORDELLO*
(The page headings are from Browning's edition of 1863.)

Sordello's Birth-Place

In Mantua-territory half is slough,
Half pine-tree forest; maples, scarlet-oaks
Breed o'er the river-beds; even Mincio chokes
With sand, the summer through; but 'tis morass
In winter up to Mantua walls. There was,
Some thirty years before this evening's coil,
One spot reclaimed from the surrounding spoil,
Goito; just a castle built amid.
A few low mountains; fire and larches hid
Their main defiles, and rings of vineyard bound
The rest. Some captured creature in a pound,
Whose artless wonder quite precludes distress,
Secure beside in its own loveliness,
So peered with airy head, below, above,
The castle at its toils, the lapwings love
To glean among at grape-time.

A Vault Inside the Castle at Goito

                            Pass within
A maze of corridors contrived for sin,
Dusk winding-stairs, dim galleries got past,
You gain the inmost chambers, gain at last
A maple-panelled room: that haze which seems
Floating about the panel, if there gleams
A sunbeam over it, will turn to gold
And in light-graven characters unfold
The Arab's wisdom everywhere.

And What Sordello Would See There

                                              A vault, see; thick
Black shade about the ceiling, though fine slits
Across the buttress suffer light by fits
Upon a marvel in the midst.

                                              Nay, stoop—
A dullish grey-streaked cumbrous font, a group
Round it, each side of it, where'er one sees,
Upholds it—shrinking Caryatides
Of just-tinged marble like Eve's lilied flesh
Beneath her Maker's finger when the fresh
First pulse of life shot brightening the snow.
The font's edge burthens every shoulder, so
They muse upon the ground, eyelids half closed;
Some, with meek arms behind their backs disposed,
Some, crossed above their bosoms, some, to veil
Their eyes, some, propping chin and cheek so pale,
Some, hanging slack an utter helpless length
Dead as a buried Vestal whose whole strength
Goes when the grate above shuts heavily.
So dwell these noiseless girls, patient to see,
Like priestesses because of sin impure,
Penanced for ever, who resigned endure,
Having that once drunk sweetness to the dregs.

At Ecelin

                                              A footfall there
Suffices to upturn to the warm air
Half germinating spices; mere decay
Produces richer life; and day by day
New pollen on the lily-petal grows,
And still more labyrinthine buds the rose.

How a Poet's Soul Comes Into Play

Up and down
Runs arrowy fire, while earthly forms combine
To throb the secret forth; a touch divine—
And the scaled eyeball owns the mystic rod:
Visibly through His garden walketh God.
So fare they.

From *MEN AND WOMEN*

The Bishop orders his Tomb at St. Praxed's Church (*Rome*, 15—)

Vanity, saith the Preacher, vanity!
Draw round my bed: is Anselm keeping back?
Nephews—sons mine . . . ah God, I know not! Well—
She, men would have to be your mother once,
Old Gandolf envied me, so fair she was.
What's done is done, and she is dead beside,
Dead long ago, and I am Bishop since,
And as she died, so must we die ourselves,
And thence ye may perceive the world's a dream.

Life, how and what is it? As here I lie
In this state-chamber, dying by degrees,
Hours and long hours in the dead night, I ask
"Do I live, am I dead?" Peace, peace seems all.
St. Praxed's ever was the church for peace;
And so, about this tomb of mine. I fought
With tooth and nail to save my niche, ye know.
—Old Gandolf cozened me, despite my care;
Shrewd was that snatch from out the corner South
He graced his carrion with, God curse the same!
Yet still my niche is not so cramped but thence
One sees the pulpit o' the Epistle-side,

And somewhat of the Choir, those silent seats,
And up into the aery dome where live
The angels, and a sunbeam's sure to lurk:
And I shall fill my slab of basalt there,
And 'neath my tabernacle take my rest,
With those nine columns round me, two and two,
The odd one at my feet where Anselm stands:
Peach-blossom-marble all, the rare, the ripe
As fresh-poured red wine of a mighty pulse.
—Old Gandolf with his paltry onion-stone,
Put me where I may look at him.
                                        True peach,
Rosy and flawless: how I earned the prize!
Draw close: that conflagration of my Church
—What then? So much was saved if aught were missed.
My sons, ye would not be my death? Go dig
The white-grape vineyard where the oil-press stood,
Drop water gently till the surface sinks,
And if ye find. . . . Ah, God, I know not, I . . . .
Bedded in store of rotten fig-leaves soft,
And corded up in a tight olive-frail,
Some lump, ah God, of *lapis lazuli*,
Big as a Jew's head cut off at the nape,
Blue as a vein o'er the Madonna's breast . . .

Sons, all have I bequeathed you, villas, all,
That brave Frascati villa with its bath,
So, let the blue lump poise between my knees,
Like God the Father's globe on both His hands
Ye worship in the Jesu Church so gay,
For Gandolf shall not choose but see and burst.

Swift as a weaver's shuttle fleet our years:
Man goeth to the grave, and where is he?

Did I say basalt for my slab, sons? Black—
'Twas ever antique-black I meant. How else
Shall ye contrast my frieze to come beneath?

The bas-relief in bronze ye promised me,
Those Pans and Nymphs ye wot of, and perchance
Some tripod, thyrsus, with a vase or so,
The Saviour at His Sermon on the Mount,
St Praxed in a glory, and one Pan
Ready to twitch the Nymph's last garment off,
And Moses with the tables . . . . but I know
Ye mark me not. What do they whisper thee,
Child of my bowels, Anselm? Ah, ye hope
To revel down my villas while I gasp
Bricked o'er with beggar's mouldy travertine
Which Gandolf from his tomb-top chuckles at.
Nay, boys, ye love me—all of jasper, then.
'Tis jasper ye stand pledged to, lest I grieve.

My bath must needs be left behind, alas!
One block, pure green as a pistachio-nut.

There's plenty jasper somewhere in the world—
And have I not St Praxed's ear to pray
Horses for ye, and brown Greek manuscripts,
And mistresses with great smooth marbly limbs?
—That's if ye carve my epitaph aright,
Choice Latin, picked phrase, Tully's every word,
No gaudy ware like Gandolf's second line—
Tully, my masters? Ulpian serves his need.
And then how I shall lie through centuries,
And hear the blessed mutter of the mass,
And see God made and eaten all day long,
And feel the steady candle-flame, and taste
Good strong thick stupefying incense-smoke!

For as I lie here, hours of the dead night,
Dying in state and by such slow degrees,
I fold my arms as if they clasped a crook,
And stretch my feet forth straight as stone can point,
And let the bed-clothes for a mort-cloth drop
Into great laps and folds of sculptor's-work:

And as yon tapers dwindle, and strange thoughts
Grow, with a certain humming in my ears,
About the life before I lived this life,
And this life, too, Popes, Cardinals and Priests,
St Praxed at his sermon on the mount,
Your tall pale mother with her talking eyes,
And new-found agate urns as fresh as day,
And marble's language, Latin pure, discreet,
—Aha: ELUCESCEBAT quoth our friend?
No Tully, said I, Ulpian at the best.
Evil and brief hath been my pilgrimage,
All *lapis*, all, sons. Else I give the Pope
My villas: will ye ever eat my heart?
Ever your eyes were as a lizard's quick,
They glitter like your mother's for my soul,
Or ye would heighten my impoverished frieze,
Piece out its starved design, and fill my vase
With grapes, and add a vizor and a Term,
And to the tripod ye would tie a lynx
That in his struggle throws the thyrsus down,
To comfort me on my entablature
Whereon I am to lie till I must ask
"Do I live, am I dead?"

          There, leave me, there!
For ye have stabbed me with ingratitude
To death—ye wish it—God, ye wish it!

          Stone—
Gritstone, a-crumble, clammy squares which sweat
As if the corpse they keep were oozing through—
And no more *lapis* to delight the world.
Well; go. I bless ye. Fewer tapers there,
But in a row: and, going, turn your backs—
Ay, like departing altar ministrants,
And leave me in my church the church for peace,
That I may watch at leisure if he leers—
Old Gandolf, at me, from his onion-stone,
As still he envied me, so fair she was!

From *PARACELSUS*

Division IV. (Paracelsus Aspires)

PARACELSUS (*Sings*):
>   Heap cassia, sandal-buds, and stripes
>   Of labdanum, and aloe-balls
>   Smeared with dull nard an Indian wipes
>   From out her hair: (such balsam falls
>   Down sea-side mountain pedestals,
>   From summits where tired winds are fain,
>   Spent with the vast and howling main,
>   To treasure half their inland-gain.)
>
>   And strew faint sweetness from some old
>   Egyptian's fine worm-eaten shroud,
>   Which breaks to dust when once unrolled;
>   And shred dim perfume, like a cloud
>   From chamber long to quiet vowed,
>   With mothed and dropping arras hung,
>   Mouldering the lute and books among
>   Of Queen, long dead, who lived there young.

Matthew Arnold

From *THE STRAYED REVELLER*

A YOUTH. CIRCE.

THE YOUTH:

> Faster, faster,
> O Circe, Goddess,
> Let the wild, thronging train,
> The bright procession
> Of eddying forms,
> Sweep through my soul.
>
> Thou standest, smiling
> Down on me; thy right arm,
> Lean'd up against the column there,
> Props thy soft cheek;
> Thy left holds, hanging loosely,
> The deep cup, ivy-cinctured,
> I held but now.
>
> Is it, then, evening
> So soon? I see the night-dews,
> Cluster'd in thick beads, dim
> The agate brooch-stones
> On thy white shoulder.
> The cool night-wind, too,
> Blows through the portico,
> Stirs thy hair, Goddess,
> Waves thy white robe.

CIRCE:

> Whence art thou, sleeper?

THE YOUTH:

    When the white dawn first
    Through the rough fir-planks
    Of my hut, by the chestnuts,
    Up at the valley-head,
    Came breaking, Goddess,
    I sprang up, I threw round me
    My dappled fawn-skin;
    Passing out, from the wet turf,
    Where they lay, by the hut door,
    I snatch'd up my vine-crown, my fir-staff
    All drench'd in dew—
    Came swift down to join
    The rout early gather'd
    In the town, round the temple,
    Iacchus' white fane
    On yonder hill.

        Quick I pass'd, following
        The wood-cutters' cart-track
    Down the dark valley:—I saw
    On my left, through the beeches,
        Thy palace, Goddess,
        Smokeless, empty:
    Trembling, I enter'd; beheld
        The court all silent,
        The lions sleeping,
        On the altar, this bowl.
        I drank, Goddess—
        And sank down here, sleeping,
        On the steps of thy portico.

CIRCE:

    Foolish boy! Why tremblest thou?
    Thou lovest it, then, my wine?
    Wouldst more of it? See, how glows,
    Through the delicate, flush'd marble,
    The red, creaming liquor,
    Strown with dark seeds!

Drink, then, I chide thee not,
Deny thee not my bowl.
Come, stretch forth thy hand, then—so!
Drink, drink again

THE YOUTH:

Thanks, gracious One.
Ah, the sweet fumes again,
More soft, ah me,
More subtle-winding
Than Pan's flute-music.
Faint—faint! Ah me!
Again the sweet sleep.

*   *   *   *

The Gods are happy.
They turn on all sides
Their shining eyes:
And see, below them,
The Earth, and men.

They see Tiresias
Sitting, staff in hand
On the warm, grassy
Asopus' bank:
His robes drawn over
His old, sightless head:
Revolving inly
The doom of Thebes.

They see the Centaurs
In the upper glens
Of Pelion, in the streams,
Where red-berried ashes fringe
The clear-brown shallow pools;
With streaming flanks, and heads
Rear'd proudly, snuffing
The mountain wind.

They see the Indian
Drifting, knife in hand,
His frail boat moor'd to
A floating isle thick matted
With large-leav'd, low-creeping melon-plants,
And the dark cucumber.
He reaps, and stows them,
Drifting—drifting;—round him,
Round his green harvest-plot,
Flow the cool lake-waves:
The mountains ring them.

They see the Scythian
On the wide Stepp, unharnessing
His wheel'd house at noon.
He tethers his beast down, and makes his meal—
Mare's milk, and bread
Baked on the embers; all around
The boundless waving grass-plains stretch, thick-starr'd
With saffron and the yellow hollyhock
And flag-leav'd iris-flowers.
Sitting in his cart
He makes his meal: before him, for long miles,
Alive with bright green lizards,
And the springing bustard fowl,
The track, a straight black line,
Furrows the rich soil: here and there
Clusters of lonely mounds
Topp'd with rough-hewn
Grey, rain-blear'd statues, overpeer
The sunny waste.

They see the Ferry
On the broad, clay-laden
Lone Chorasmian stream: thereon,
With snort and strain,

Two horses, strongly swimming, tow
The ferry-boat, with woven ropes
  To either bow
Firm-harnessed by the mane:—a chief,
With shout and shaken spear
Stands at the prow, and guides them: but astern,
The cowering Merchants, in long robes,
  Sit pale beside their wealth
  Of silk bales and of balsam-drops,
  Of gold and ivory,
Of turquoise-earth and amethyst,
  Jasper and chalcedony,
And milk-barr'd onyx stones.
The loaded boat swings groaning
  In the yellow eddies;
  The Gods behold them.
They see the Heroes
  Sitting in the dark ship
On the foamless, long-heaving,
Violet sea:
At sunset nearing
  The Happy Islands.

  These things, Ulysses,
  The wise Bards also
   Behold and sing,
  But oh, what labour!
   O Prince, what pain. . .

The old Silenus
Came, lolling in the sunshine,
From the dewy forest coverts,
  This way, at noon.
Sitting by me, while his Fauns
  Down at the water side
  Sprinkled and smooth'd
  His drooping garland,
He told me these things. . . .

Faster, faster,
O Circe, Goddess,
Let the wild thronging train,
The bright procession
Of eddying forms,
Sweep through my soul.

Dante Gabriel Rossetti

MY SISTER'S SLEEP (1849)

She fell asleep on Christmas Eve:
At length the long-ungranted shade
Of weary eyelids overweigh'd
The pain nought else might yet relieve.

Our Mother, who had leaned all day
Over the bed from chime to chime,
Then raised herself for the first time,
And as she sat her down, did pray.

Her little work-table was spread
With work to finish. For the glare
Made by her candle, she had care
To work some distance from the bed

Without, there was a cold moon up,
Of winter radiance sheer and thin;
The hollow halo it was in
Was like an icy crystal cup.

Through the small room, with subtle sound
Of flame, by vents the fireshine drove
And reddened. In its dim alcove
The mirror shed a clearness round.

I had been sitting up some nights,
And my tired mind felt weak and blank;
Like a sharp strengthening wine it drank
The stillness and the broken lights.

Twelve struck. That sound, by dwindling years
Heard in each hour, crept off; and then

The ruffled silence spread again,
Like water that a pebble stirs.

Our Mother rose from where she sat:
Her needles, as she laid them down,
Met lightly, and her silken gown
Settled: no other noise than that.

"Glory unto the Newly Born",
So, as said angels, she did say:
Because we were in Christmas Day,
Though it would still be long till morn.

Just then, in the room over us,
There was a pushing back of chairs,
As some who had sat unawares
So late, now heard the hour, and rose.

With anxious, softly-stepping haste
Our Mother went where Margaret lay,
Fearing the sounds o'erhead, should they
Have broken her long watched-for rest.

She stopped an instant, calm, and turned;
But suddenly turned back again;
And all her features seemed in pain
With woe, and her eyes gazed and yearned.

For my part, I but hid my face,
And held my breath, and spoke no word:
There was none spoken; but I heard
The silence for a little space.

Our Mother bowed herself and wept:
And both my arms fell, and I said,
"God knows, I knew that she was dead."
And there, all white, my sister slept.

Then, kneeling, upon Christmas morn
A little after twelve o'clock,
We said, ere the first quarter struck,
"Christ's Blessing on the newly born."

This poem, in its earlier and somewhat longer form, was
written in 1849, and printed in January, 1850, in the first number
of *The Germ*.

THE CHOICE

I

Eat, thou, and drink; tomorrow thou shalt die.
Surely the earth, that's wise, being very old,
Needs not our help. Then loose me, love, and hold
Thy sultry hair up from my face; that I
May pour for thee this golden wine, brim-high,
Till round the glass thy fingers glow like gold.
We'll drown all hours: thy song, while hours are toll'd,
Shall leap, as fountains veil the changing sky.

Now kiss, and think that there are really those,
My own high-bosomed beauty, who increase
Vain gold, vain lore, and yet might choose our way.
Through many years they toil; then, on a day,
They die not—for their life was death—, but cease;
And round their narrow lips the mould falls close.

II

Watch, thou, and fear; tomorrow thou shalt die.
Or art thou sure thou shalt have time for death?
Is not the day which God's word promiseth
To come man knows not when? In yonder sky,
Now, while we speak, the sun speeds forth: can I
Or thou assure him of his goal? God's breath

Even at this moment haply quickeneth
The air to a flame, till spirits, always nigh
Though screened and hid, shall walk the daylight here.
And dost thou prate of all that man shall do?
Canst thou, who hast but plagues, presume to be
Glad in his gladness that comes after thee?
Will His strength slay Thy worm in Hell? Go to:
Cover thy countenance, and watch, and fear.

III

Think thou and act; tomorrow thou shalt die.
Outstretched in the sun's warmth upon the shore,
Thou sayst: "Man's measured path is all gone o'er:
Up all his years, steeply, with strain and sigh,
Man clomb until he reached the truth; and I,
Even I, am he, whom it was destined for."
How shall this be? Art thou, then, so much more
Than they who sowed, that thou shouldst reap thereby?

Nay, come up hither. From this wave-washed mound
Unto the furthest flood-brim look with me;
Then, reach on with thy thought, till it be drown'd,
Miles and miles distant though the last line be;
And though thy soul sail leagues, and leagues beyond,
Still, leagues beyond those leagues, there is more sea.

ALPHABETICAL LIST OF AUTHORS' NAMES

ARNOLD

BEAUMONT
BLAKE
BROWNING
BYRON

CHAPMAN
CHAUCER
COLERIDGE
COWPER
CRABBE

DAVIES
DENNYS
DONNE
DRYDEN

FLETCHER
FORD

GRAY

HAWES
HERRICK
HOOD
HUNT

JONSON

KEATS

LANDOR
LANGLAND
LOVELACE

MARLOWE
MARVELL
MILTON

NASH
NEWMAN

PEACOCK
POPE
PRIOR

ROSSETTI

SHAKESPEARE
SHELLEY
SIDNEY
SMART
SPENSER

TENNYSON

WEBSTER
WHITE
WORDSWORTH
WOTTON

INDEX TO AUTHORS, SOURCES, POEMS, EXCERPTS
AND SINGLE LINES.